Multiple Perspectives on the Self in SLA

SECOND LANGUAGE ACQUISITION
Series Editors: Professor David Singleton, *University of Pannonia, Hungary* and Fellow Emeritus, *Trinity College, Dublin, Ireland*

This series brings together titles dealing with a variety of aspects of language acquisition and processing in situations where a language or languages other than the native language is involved. Second language is thus interpreted in its broadest possible sense. The volumes included in the series all offer in their different ways, on the one hand, exposition and discussion of empirical findings and, on the other, some degree of theoretical reflection. In this latter connection, no particular theoretical stance is privileged in the series; nor is any relevant perspective – sociolinguistic, psycholinguistic, neurolinguistic, etc. – deemed out of place. The intended readership of the series includes final-year undergraduates working on second language acquisition projects, postgraduate students involved in second language acquisition research, and researchers and teachers in general whose interests include a second language acquisition component.

Full details of all the books in this series and of all our other publications can be found on http://www.multilingual-matters.com, or by writing to Multilingual Matters, St Nicholas House, 31–34 High Street, Bristol BS1 2AW, UK.

Multiple Perspectives on the Self in SLA

Edited by
Sarah Mercer and Marion Williams

MULTILINGUAL MATTERS
Bristol • Buffalo • Toronto

Library of Congress Cataloging in Publication Data
Multiple Perspectives on the Self in SLA/Edited by Sarah Mercer and Marion Williams.
Second Language Acquisition: 73
Includes bibliographical references and index.
1. Language acquisition—Research—Methodology. 2. Language acquisition—Study and teaching. 3. Language acquisition—Psychological aspects. 4. Language and languages—Study and teaching—Psychological aspects. 5. Psycholinguistics. I. Mercer, Sarah, editor of compilation. II. Williams, Marion, 1948- editor of compilation.
P118.15.M68 2014
401'.93–dc23 2013036366

British Library Cataloguing in Publication Data
A catalogue entry for this book is available from the British Library.

ISBN-13: 978-1-78309-135-5 (hbk)
ISBN-13: 978-1-78309-134-8 (pbk)

Multilingual Matters
UK: St Nicholas House, 31–34 High Street, Bristol BS1 2AW, UK.
USA: UTP, 2250 Military Road, Tonawanda, NY 14150, USA.
Canada: UTP, 5201 Dufferin Street, North York, Ontario M3H 5T8, Canada.

Copyright © 2014 Sarah Mercer, Marion Williams and authors of individual chapters.

Front cover: With thanks to Desmond Morris for kindly granting permission to use his painting 'The Imaginer'.

All rights reserved. No part of this work may be reproduced in any form or by any means without permission in writing from the publisher.

The policy of Multilingual Matters/Channel View Publications is to use papers that are natural, renewable and recyclable products, made from wood grown in sustainable forests. In the manufacturing process of our books, and to further support our policy, preference is given to printers that have FSC and PEFC Chain of Custody certification. The FSC and/or PEFC logos will appear on those books where full certification has been granted to the printer concerned.

Typeset by Techset Composition India (P) Ltd., Bangalore and Chennai, India.
Printed and bound in Great Britain by Short Run Press Ltd.

Contents

	Contributors	ix
1	Introduction *Marion Williams and Sarah Mercer*	1
	What This Book is About	1
	Why We Compiled This Book	1
	Who This Book is For	2
	Organisation of the Book	3
2	Self-Efficacy in Second Language Acquisition *Nicole Mills*	6
	Introduction	6
	Social Cognitive Theory	7
	Self-Efficacy and Academic Performance	9
	Self-Efficacy and Other Self Constructs	9
	Self-Efficacy and Language Learning	12
	Strategies to Guide Self-Efficacy Research	15
	Fostering Students' Self-Efficacy Beliefs	17
	Conclusion	19
3	The Dynamics of Second Language Confidence: Contact and Interaction *Sinthujaa Sampasivam and Richard Clément*	23
	Introduction	23
	Development of the Concept of L2C	23
	Definitional Issues	25
	Confidence in Different Contexts	26
	A Framework for Redefining Language Contact	31
	Conclusion	35

4	Self-Esteem and Self-Concept in Foreign Language Learning	41
	Fernando D. Rubio	
	Introduction	41
	Conceptual and Definitional Issues	42
	Theories of Self in Educational and Social Psychology	43
	The Dynamic Development of Self-Esteem and Self-Concept	46
	Relevant Research in SLA	48
	Research Approaches to Self-Concept and Self-Esteem	50
	Implications for Classroom Practice	52
	Conclusion	54
5	Identity and Poststructuralist Theory in SLA	59
	Bonny Norton	
	Introduction	59
	Central Arguments for Identity and Poststructuralist Theory in SLA	61
	Poststructuralist Theories of Language, Subjectivity and Positioning	63
	Poststructuralist Theory, SLA and Classroom Teaching	66
	Conclusion	71
6	Dual Identities Perceived by Bilinguals	75
	Chantal Hemmi	
	Introduction	75
	Different Views of Identity	75
	The Study: Identities of Six Bilingual Japanese Women	80
	Results and Discussion	83
	Conclusion and Implications	89
7	Relational Views of the Self in SLA	92
	Florentina Taylor	
	Introduction	92
	Defining the Self in Social Interaction	93
	Synchronic Relativity	94
	Diachronic Relativity	97
	Synchronic-Diachronic Perspectives in SLA	100
	Implications for Practice and Future Research	103
8	Imagined and Possible Selves: Stories We Tell Ourselves About Ourselves	109
	Stephen Ryan and Kay Irie	
	Introduction	109
	Imagining the Self	110
	Possible Selves and the Imagination in the SLA Literature	117

| | Pedagogic Applications | 120 |
| | Conclusion | 123 |

9 Motivational Perspectives on the Self in SLA:
   A Developmental View ... 127
   Ema Ushioda
   Motivation and Self-Related Cognitions: An Introductory
      Overview ... 127
   Motivation and Second Language Learning Timeline ... 128
   Motivational Factors Within and Outside the Self ... 130
   The Internalisation of Motivation Within the Self ... 133
   Concluding Remarks ... 138

10 Brain and Self: A Neurophilosophical Account ... 142
   Georg Northoff
   Introduction: Concept of Self ... 142
   Concepts of Self ... 142
   Methodological Approaches to the Experimental
      Investigation of the Self ... 148
   Neurophilosophical Reflection ... 152
   Conclusion: Self and Language ... 156

11 The Self from a Complexity Perspective ... 160
   Sarah Mercer
   Introduction ... 160
   Integrative Perspectives on the Self ... 161
   Self as a Complex Dynamic System ... 162
   Dynamic and Emergent Self ... 164
   Researching the Dynamics of the Self ... 165
   Issues for Researching the Self as a Complex Dynamic System ... 173
   Implications for Practice ... 174

12 Concluding Reflections ... 177
   Sarah Mercer and Marion Williams
   Introduction ... 177
   Defining the Self ... 177
   The Contextual Self ... 179
   The Temporal Self ... 180
   Methodological Perspectives ... 181
   Pedagogical Implications ... 182
   Future Directions ... 183

Index ... 186

Contributors

Richard Clément is Professor of Psychology as well as Director and Associate Dean of the Official Languages and Bilingualism Institute at the University of Ottawa. His current research interests include issues related to bilingualism, second language acquisition and identity change and adjustment in the acculturative process, topics on which he has published in both French and English. In 2001, he was awarded the Otto Klineberg Intercultural & International Relations Prize by the Society for the Psychological Study of Social Issues, and in 2002, he received the Robert C. Gardner Award from the International Association of Language & Social Psychology for his work on second language acquisition. He is an elected Fellow of both the Canadian and the American Psychological Associations, as well as of the Royal Society of Canada.

Chantal Hemmi, EdD TEFL, is a lecturer at the Center for Language Education and Research at Sophia University in Tokyo. Her main research interest is in the identity of bilingual people in different multicultural educational settings. She is presently teaching English for Academic Purposes (EAP) to undergraduate students employing a Content and Language Integrated Learning approach, and is conducting research in the area of critical thinking skills through students' reflective papers from a course taught at Sophia University on diversity and identity in multi-cultural Britain. She also teaches about the socio-cultural issues related to Japanese to English translation, focusing on topics on Japanese culture and language at Shirayuri College in Tokyo.

Kay Irie is an Associate Professor in the Foreign Language Center at Tokai University, Japan and an Adjunct Professor in the Graduate College of Education at Temple University Japan. Her current research interests include learner autonomy and motivation in language education.

Sarah Mercer is a lecturer at the University of Graz, Austria, where she has been working since 1996. She completed her PhD at the University of Lancaster and her 'habilitation' at the University of Graz. Her research interests include all aspects of the psychology surrounding the foreign language learning experience, in particular understandings of the self. More recently, she has begun to explore the potential of taking a complexity perspective on various aspects of language learner psychology. She is the author of *Towards an Understanding of Language Learner Self-Concept*, published by Springer and is co-editor of *Psychology for Language Learning*, published by Palgrave.

Nicole Mills is Coordinator of the Beginning French Language Program at Harvard University. She has publications in various academic journals and has edited volumes on various topics associated with self-efficacy in foreign language learning and teaching, curriculum design, social networking, motivation and engagement. She holds a PhD in Educational Studies and French and a Masters' degree in French literature from Emory University.

Georg Northoff, MD, PhD, is EJLB-CIHR Michael Smith Chair in Neurosciences and Mental Health and a Canada Research Chair in Mind, Brain Imaging and Neuroethics at the University of Ottawa Institute of Mental Health Research. He completed his initial training in medicine/psychiatry and philosophy in Germany. His main research focus is the neural basis of self and self-referential processing. Experimental work within his unit uses neuro-imaging methods to focus on the functional and biochemical mechanisms underlying self in healthy subjects as well as its psychopathology, for example, increased self-reference as commonly seen in depression. His research additionally intersects with his interests in neurophilosophy and the study of the phenomenon of consciousness.

Bonny Norton is Professor and Distinguished University Scholar in the Department of Language and Literacy Education, University of British Columbia, Canada. Her primary research interests are identity and language learning, critical literacy and international development. The second edition of *Identity and Language Learning: Extending the Conversation* has been published by Multilingual Matters (2013). In 2010, she was the inaugural recipient of the Senior Researcher Award by the Second Language Research SIG of the American Educational Research Association (AERA), and in 2012, was inducted as an AERA Fellow. Her website can be found at: http://www.educ.ubc.ca/faculty/norton/

Fernando D. Rubio is an Associate Professor at the University of Huelva (Spain) and Head of International Relations at the School of Education. His main area of research is foreign language methodology. He has published *Self-esteem and Foreign Language Learning* (2007, Cambridge Scholars Publishing) and has authored numerous scholarly texts. He has been a Visiting Professor at the University of Virginia's College at Wise (2008, 2011) and has conducted research at the University of Texas (2005). He has been a plenary speaker in many academic events in Europe, North America and South America.

Stephen Ryan is a Professor in the School of Economics at Senshu University, Tokyo. His research and publications address a range of issues relating to the psychology of second language learning, with a recent focus on mindsets and the role of the imagination in language learning. He is co-editor of *Psychology for Language Learning: Insights from Theory, Research and Practice* (2012, Palgrave Macmillan).

Sinthujaa Sampasivam is currently a graduate student at the University of Ottawa under the supervision of Professor Richard Clément. Her undergraduate honours degree was from McGill where she completed an undergraduate thesis with Professor Frances Aboud on research aiming to improve prejudice reduction programmes for children. Her senior honours thesis, under the guidance of Professor Donald Taylor, examined how survivors' guilt affected immigrants' acculturation strategies. Her current research interests include the social psychological consequences of second language acquisition and the effects of second language proficiency on acculturation.

Florentina Taylor is a lecturer in Education and MA TESOL Programme Leader at the University of York, UK. She has over 18 years' teaching experience in Higher Education, EAP and English as a foreign language (EFL) contexts. She has conducted research into self, identity and motivation in learning and teaching English as a foreign language in several European countries, as well as the perceived relevance, motivation and uptake of Modern Foreign Languages in the UK. She is author of the book *Self and Identity in Adolescent Foreign Language Learning* published by Multilingual Matters.

Ema Ushioda is an Associate Professor in ELT and Applied Linguistics at the Centre for Applied Linguistics, University of Warwick, UK, where she teaches MA courses in English Language Teaching and is Director of Graduate Studies. Her research interests are motivation for language learning and intercultural engagement, learner autonomy, sociocultural theory and teacher development. Recent publications include an edited volume on *International Perspectives on Motivation: Language Learning and Professional Challenges* (2013), *Teaching and Researching Motivation* (co-authored by Z. Dörnyei, 2011) and *Motivation, Language Identity and the L2 Self* (co-edited by Z. Dörnyei, 2009).

Marion Williams was formerly Reader in Applied Linguistics at the University of Exeter, UK, where she coordinated the postgraduate programmes in TESOL. She is interested in all aspects of psychology in language learning. Her research interests include motivation, attributions, teaching of thinking and teacher education. She is the joint author of *Psychology for Language Teachers: A Social Constructivist Approach, Thinking Through the Curriculum, Teaching Young Learners to Think,* and co-editor of *Psychology for Language Learning*. She is also a former President of IATEFL.

1 Introduction

Marion Williams and Sarah Mercer

What This Book is About

In recent years, the key role of the self in second language acquisition (SLA) has increasingly been gaining recognition from SLA writers, and there has been a dramatic increase in research on this topic. However, accompanying this growth in interest in this area, there has been an escalation in the range of theoretical conceptualisations of the self. While this is a positive indication of the vibrancy of developments in this field, there exist a number of confusions owing to the variety of definitions and overlapping terms. The aim of this book is to bring together a range of perspectives on the self, which are often seen as competing, to unite what is currently a somewhat fragmented field and to provide an overview of some of the different ways in which the self has been conceptualised. Our aim is to provide an insight into the way in which each perspective contributes to our overall understanding of the self in SLA. We hope that viewing these perspectives collectively in one volume will lead to a deeper understanding of the concept and an appreciation of the merits of the theoretical and methodological diversity in this area.

Why We Compiled This Book

For a number of years both editors have shared an interest in the insights that can be gained from the field of educational psychology in furthering our understanding of language learning processes. For example, Williams, in her book together with Burden (1997) *Psychology for Language Teachers*, examined a number of psychological areas that were receiving attention at the time and linked these to language teaching. Some 15 years later, while together compiling the book *Psychology for Language Learning* (Mercer et al., 2012), both editors were struck by the growing focus in the field on perspectives related to the self and the many different ways of conceptualising these that exist. For example, in her chapter on motivation in the 2012 book, Ushioda, referring to

Dörnyei's (2005) L2 self system of motivation, theorises the motivation construct from a self-related viewpoint, arguing that concepts of 'self' have come to dominate research on motivation in education, and that examining the self system reframes the motivation construct in enlightening ways. In addition, recent work in other areas of language learning psychology, such as goals, self-determination, attributions, mindsets and perceptions of successes and failures, all centre around notions of the self.

Similarly, in writing her book *Towards an Understanding of Language Learner Self-Concept*, Mercer (2011) found considerable overlap between various self-related terms, such as self-efficacy, self-esteem, self-concept and identity. Brinthaupt and Lipka (1992: 1) explain that there is 'wide disagreement about how to define the self, measure it, and study its development' and highlight the problems that researchers thus face in selecting constructs, differentiating between terms and comparing studies. However, we do not see this diversity as inherently problematic, but rather we choose to view it as a potential strength; if employed and integrated appropriately, epistemological and methodological diversity can give rise to a richer, more comprehensive view of the self than a single perspective alone.

As the self is a field of study that is expanding rapidly within SLA, it seems to be timely to examine the different perspectives that exist and consider the implications of the various viewpoints for the future of this growing field of research. We therefore felt a need to bring the different perspectives together to help us to see their commonalities, differences and areas of overlap to facilitate a more unified view of the self. Our intention is to see how different views might complement each other and, when combined, elaborate our understanding of the self. If we want a full picture of the self, we need to bring all the pieces of the picture together.

In working on the book, we have been delighted by the enthusiastic response of the contributors and it has been extremely rewarding and enlightening to work with such a collection of distinguished scholars, each with a different perspective on the field. While we may embrace different conceptualisations of the self, we all share a passion and conviction of the importance of the self in SLA and the need to better understand its nature and role in language learning processes.

Who This Book is For

This book is essentially aimed at those interested in the topic of the self in language learning, whether carrying out research in this field or teaching on postgraduate programmes, training teachers, studying at postgraduate level or teaching a foreign language. In order to ensure the volume remains accessible to those working at various levels of specialisation in the field, we have attempted to explain different concepts clearly as they arise. In addition, each chapter ends with guidance for further reading in the particular area, and we hope this will motivate a whole new generation of specialists in the self in SLA to keep moving the field forward.

Organisation of the Book

The book is organised into 12 chapters, with 10 of them focusing on a different perspective on the self. The introductory chapter is intended to set the scene, whereas the concluding chapter attempts to pull together the main threads and considers directions for the future. While each chapter presents a particular viewpoint, we have allowed the contributors flexibility in whether their main focus is on a theoretical perspective or an empirical research study. Indeed, we deliberately intended to encourage diversity, enabling contributors to draw out their own emphasis. The chapters have been loosely ordered sequentially from more tightly defined constructs to more holistic views of the self.

The volume begins with Mills' chapter on self-efficacy, in which she explores Bandura's social cognitive theory focusing on how self-efficacy is formed. She reports on several studies in which the subsequent implications of the theory for pedagogy are empirically investigated and concludes that it is crucial for learners to 'feel competent and capable in their ability to acquire a foreign language'. Chapter 3 by Sampasivam and Clément focuses on the construct of second language confidence (L2C) and explores the literature to consider the role of different types of contexts and situations in L2C, such as inside/outside the classroom or in computer-mediated communication. In order to create some coherence to a complex area, they propose a taxonomical framework for classifying different forms of language contact. In the next chapter, Rubio addresses the two constructs of self-concept and self-esteem and proposes a neurogenerative model to help understand how the two facets of the self might be interrelated and develop over time. As well as considering possible ways of researching these two self constructs, he also reflects on the important implications for pedagogy of a sensitivity to and understanding of the nature of self-concept and self-esteem.

Chapter 5 continues with an exploration of poststructuralist theory by Norton who considers its usefulness for helping teachers and administrators to make informed decisions about classroom practices designed to support learners in constructing and negotiating their identities through the use of language. She employs the concept of 'investment' as a way of conceptualising learners' motivation and engagement with the language practices within the classroom and argues that support is needed for teachers as well as learners working in diverse linguistic communities. She also raises important issues regarding the distribution of power and potential for social change in language teaching and learning contexts and their effects on identity positioning. The construct of identity is also addressed in Chapter 6 in which Hemmi reports on a study conducted with Japanese/English bilingual women living in Japan. She describes how the majority of the women possess multiple or at least dual identities created, in their opinion, by cultural and linguistic differences in the languages. She highlights how being bilingual can be perceived as either positive or negative; however, in the case of these women, she concluded that they hold primarily an additive view of their bilingual selves. In the next chapter, Taylor explores different types of relational selves, that is, the different sense of self one has when moving from one social interaction to another. Using three theoretical frameworks, she reports on research that has revealed the seeming contradictions and potential conflicts a learner may experience between their public and personal selves as they interact within and across different relational contexts. She draws important conclusions about the need for learners to feel accepted, and highlights the multiplicity of identities learners bring with them into the language classroom.

In Chapter 8, Ryan and Irie explore how we construct the story of ourselves and the key role played by imagination in this process. They consider how possible and imagined selves can be generated through the processes we use to create visions of ourselves beyond our actual experiences and current settings. They conclude that imagination is a powerful resource for learning and identity construction, which can also be harnessed to foster learners' sense of agency. Indeed, agency, self-regulation and motivation are key themes picked up in Chapter 9 by Ushioda. In her chapter, she explores the developmental aspects of how processes of motivation become internalised within the self. In doing so, she highlights the complex interaction of current selves, experiential factors, social-environmental influences and future-oriented dimensions of the self that affect these motivational processes. In Chapter 10, Northoff offers a less familiar perspective on the self in SLA as he explores philosophical issues about the existence of self and the role of consciousness and linguistic processing in the construction of our sense of self. He turns to neuroscience and considers findings there concerning the representation of self in terms of specific regions of the brain. He too makes the connection between self and agency, and raises important questions about the embodied self and the role of language in self representations. Finally, in Chapter 11, Mercer takes a holistic view of the self and considers how complexity perspectives can help integrate various perspectives on the self. She focuses in particular on the dynamics of the self and reports on a study examining the situational dynamics of English as a foreign Language (EFL) learners engaged in a series of speaking tasks. She concludes that a complex understanding of context is necessary in which the personal relevance of contextual factors for an individual is taken into account when exploring the interaction between self and contexts.

In the final chapter, we pull together some of the main themes that emerge across the 'multiple perspectives on the self', including definitional concerns, the interplay between self and contexts, the temporal dynamism of the self, various approaches to researching the self and a range of pedagogical implications for teachers wishing to work in self-sensitive ways. Most of all, we hope that you will enjoy reading all of the chapters. They do not need to be read sequentially, but we hope that in their entirety they will help contribute to a fuller, more comprehensive understanding of the self in SLA.

References

Brinthaupt, T.M. and Lipka, R.P. (1992) Introduction. In T.M. Brinthaupt and R.P. Lipka (eds) *The Self: Definitional and Methodological Issues* (pp. 1–11). Albany: State of University of New York Press.

Dörnyei, Z. (2005) *The Psychology of the Language Learner*. Hillsdale: Lawrence Erlbaum Associates.

Mercer, S. (2011) *Towards an Understanding of Language Learner Self-Concept*. Dordrecht: Springer.

Mercer, S., Ryan, S. and Williams, M. (eds) (2012) *Psychology for Language Learning: Insights from Research, Theory and Practice*. Basingstoke: Palgrave MacMillan.

Ushioda, E. (2012) Motivation: L2 learning as a special case? In S. Mercer, S. Ryan and M. Williams (eds) *Psychology for Language Learning: Insights from Research, Theory and Practice* (pp. 58–73). Basingstoke: Palgrave MacMillan.

Williams, M. and Burden, R.L. (1997) *Psychology for Language Teachers*. Cambridge: Cambridge University Press.

2 Self-Efficacy in Second Language Acquisition

Nicole Mills

Introduction

Ushioda and Dörnyei (2009: 1) claim that 'second language (L2) motivation is currently in the process of being radically re-conceptualized and re-theorized in the context of contemporary notions of self and identity'. This process of re-conceptualization has been associated with parallel developments in various research domains including sociolinguistics and educational psychology. Diverse theoretical foundations including social cognitive theory, socio-cultural activity theory, and self-determination theory have played key roles in re-theorizing L2 motivation and emphasizing notions of the self. The synergy between educational psychology and second language acquisition developed as L2 motivation scholars looked toward theoretical foundations in educational psychology to guide their research and transform their understanding of language development.

Influenced by the research developments associated with the relationship between the self and cognition in the field of educational psychology, foreign language (FL) motivation research transitioned from the social psychological period to the cognitive-situated period during the late 1990s. During the social psychological period, FL motivation research concentrated on integrative and instrumental aspects of motivation (Gardner, 1985). Integrative motivation refers to learners' desire to learn a FL to integrate into the FL community. Instrumental motivation refers to a desire to learn another language to attain particular career or academic goals (Shrum & Glisan, 2000). Crookes and Schmidt's (1991) influential article 'Motivation: Reopening the Research Agenda' countered the social psychological approach with their claim that although the wide-ranging research in integrative motivation was both valuable and informative, the emphasis on integrative motivation in FL research had often neglected other motivational theories from educational psychology. Reaffirming Crookes and Schmidt's (1991) concerns, Dörnyei called for:

> ...a more pragmatic, education-centred approach to motivation research, which would be consistent with the perceptions of practicing teachers and which would also be in line with the current results of mainstream educational psychological research. (Dörnyei, 1994: 273)

At this juncture, cognitive psychological influences, which had long been underplayed in FL motivation research, came to the forefront, and researchers began to heed theories of the self in educational psychology (Graham, 2006, 2007; Mills *et al.*, 2006, 2007). Attribution theory and social cognitive theory became key theoretical foundations of the cognitive-situated period in FL motivation research. By introducing the notion that one's perceptions of one's abilities and prior performances were fundamental aspects of FL motivation, social cognitive theory and the cognitively defined construct of self-efficacy received increasing attention.

Social Cognitive Theory

Social cognitive theory is a theory of human functioning that views individuals as proactive, self-reflective, and self-regulating beings. According to this theory of human behaviour, an individual's system of self-beliefs allows the person to exercise control over his/her thoughts, feelings, and actions. In other words, 'what people think, believe, and feel affects how they behave' (Bandura, 1986: 25). This notion suggests that there is interplay among personal, behavioural, and environmental influences in human functioning. This mutual interplay, or *triadic reciprocality*, suggests that human behaviour is collectively influenced by personal agency, self-beliefs, and external environmental factors. Because human functioning is embedded in social environments, individuals are regarded as both products and producers of their own environments.

Within this system of self-beliefs, individuals may show control over five specifically human capabilities: *symbolizing, forethought, vicarious learning, self-regulation,* and *self-reflection*. Individuals are therefore able to make decisions, self-assess their performance, and interpret the outcomes, develop beliefs about their competence, and, finally, mentally store this information to guide future behaviour. Of the five highlighted human capabilities, Bandura (1997) considered the practice of *self-reflection* to have the most noteworthy influence on human agency. Through reflective self-examination on the adequacy of one's thoughts and actions, people may alter their own thinking and exert influence over subsequent behaviour. Self-reflection therefore has important implications in academic settings, as the self-examined beliefs that students hold true about themselves are vital forces in their academic successes and/or failures.

Social cognitive theory and self-efficacy

Within social cognitive theory, perceptions of self-efficacy are among the most central mechanisms of self-reflection (Bandura, 1997). *Self-efficacy* refers to 'beliefs in one's capabilities to organize and execute the courses of action required to produce given attainments' (Bandura, 1997: 3). More simply, self-efficacy refers to an individual's beliefs in his/her ability to perform a designated task or complete an activity, and may be used as a predictor of future performance. Bandura (1997) suggests that self-efficacy beliefs can influence one's decisions, expended effort and perseverance, resilience to adversity, thought processes, affective states, and accomplishments. Schunk (1991) contends that self-efficacy beliefs may better forecast success than prior achievements, skills, or knowledge. For these reasons, Bandura (1997: 19) claims that self-efficacy beliefs 'affect almost everything [people] do; how they think, motivate themselves, feel, and behave'.

Self-efficacy beliefs are formed by the collective analysis of four main sources of information: *mastery experiences, vicarious experiences, verbal persuasions*, and *affective indicators* (Bandura, 1997). These various sources of information influence one's self-efficacy beliefs; either raising or lowering an individual's perceived ability to perform a designated task. Self-efficacy beliefs represent future-oriented conceptions of the self and may therefore be malleable if the aforementioned sources of self-efficacy are fostered (see Pajares & Urdan, 2006). According to Bandura (1997), *mastery experiences* are the most influential source of efficacy information. Whereas successes raise self-efficacy beliefs, failures weaken one's sense of efficacy. After repeated successful performances, it is unlikely that occasional failures will undermine beliefs in one's capabilities. Successful performances contribute, therefore, to the anticipation of future success.

Vicarious experiences, or the appraisal of abilities in relation to the accomplishments of peers, are an additional source of self-efficacy beliefs. Visualizing the successes of comparable individuals in terms of age, level, and ability can raise a person's efficacy beliefs by fostering the belief that s/he could also master comparable tasks. Conversely, observing a peer's failure can weaken an individual's belief in his/her ability to succeed. Vicarious experiences can therefore provide individuals with valuable information about their own perceived capabilities (Bandura, 1997).

Verbal persuasions, or people's judgment of another's ability to accomplish a given task, may be an additional source of self-efficacy beliefs. Verbal persuasions from mentors or teachers, such as feedback or encouragement about task performance, can provide valuable information about personal competence. Teachers, in particular, can enhance students' self-efficacy with credible feedback and guidance that encourages and motivates students. Bandura (1997: 101) claims that 'it is easier to sustain a sense of efficacy, especially when struggling with difficulties, if significant others express faith in one's capabilities than if they convey doubts'.

Finally, self-efficacy beliefs are also formed from *emotional indicators* during task completion. Whereas positive emotions may raise efficacy beliefs and contribute to the expectation of future successful performances, high levels of anxiety, stress, or fatigue can weaken one's sense of efficacy. Bandura (1997: 108) notes that 'it is not the sheer intensity of emotional and physical reactions that is important but rather how they are perceived and interpreted'.

Self-Efficacy and Academic Performance

Because of the relationship among self-efficacy beliefs, behaviour, and motivation, self-efficacy has received increasing attention in the realm of educational research over the last 30 years. Graham and Weiner's (1996) review of motivational research in the *Handbook of Educational Psychology* reveals that self-efficacy beliefs consistently predicted academic achievement in various academic domains over and above other motivational constructs and affected academic performance in various ways. Students with high self-efficacy to perform academic tasks tend to exhibit lower levels of anxiety, display increased persistence when faced with obstacles, exert greater effort, show more flexible learning strategy use, and display higher levels of intrinsic interest in academic tasks. Students with low self-efficacy, in contrast, often choose less challenging academic tasks, apply minimal effort and strategy use, and show higher signs of anxiety in the face of obstacles. Such findings revealed that confidence in one's academic capabilities is a central element to academic success (Pajares & Schunk, 2001).

Self-Efficacy and Other Self Constructs

Although emphasis has been placed on the investigation of self-efficacy beliefs in various domains of educational research in the past three decades, second language acquisition (SLA) scholars have tended to emphasise other self constructs in L2 motivation research. Research on linguistic *self-confidence*, *self-concept*, and *self-regulation* have instead been the object of much FL research. Although seemingly akin to self-efficacy, these constructs differ in their theoretical foundations and research purposes.

Linguistic self-confidence (see Sampasivam & Clément, Chapter 3, this volume)

Embedded within social psychology, Clément's theory of linguistic self-confidence defines self-confidence as 'self-perceptions of communicative competence and concomitant low levels of anxiety in using the second language' (Noels *et al.*, 1996: 248). Linguistic self-confidence is a socially defined construct based on one's ability to communicate and identify with the L2 cultural community (Dörnyei, 2005). Research from the social psychological period in the 1990s found that linguistic self-confidence was associated with target culture identification (Noels *et al.*, 1996), linguistic acculturation (Dion *et al.*, 1990), and lower levels of anxiety (MacIntyre *et al.*, 1997). By linguistic acculturation, the authors mean the process by which members of a culture acquire cultural features of another culture through language use. Whereas self-confidence measures self-perceptions from a socially defined perspective, self-efficacy assesses self-perceptions from a primarily cognitively defined perspective (Dörnyei, 2005).

Self-concept (see Rubio, Chapter 4, this volume)

Self-concept is an additional self construct that has received attention in the field of FL education research (Arnold, 2007; Mercer, 2011). Pajares and Schunk (2002: 21) describe self-concept as 'a description of one's own perceived self accompanied by a judgment of self-worth'. Generalized perceptions of self are described as global self-concept. Self-concept, however, may be divided into more specific components. Whereas non-academic self-concept can comprise self-concepts about social, emotional, or physical aspects of self, academic self-concept refers to one's perceptions of self and judgment of self-worth in academic domains (Pajares & Schunk, 2001). Academic self-concept may be further divided into specific academic-domain self-concepts, such as science self-concept or Spanish learning self-concept. Moreover, a language-specific self-concept may be separated into further domains such as Spanish reading self-concept. One's evaluation of competence and feelings of self-worth associated with Spanish would refer to an individual's Spanish learning self-concept, whereas one's Spanish reading self-concept would refer to one's perception of one's overall competence to read in Spanish. In his discussion of the *L2 motivational self system*, Dörnyei (2009) extends the traditional notion of self-concept to the notion of *possible selves*. Whereas *self-concept* refers to an individual's self-perception at the present time, *possible selves* 'represent the individual's ideas of what they might become, what they would like to become, and what they are afraid of becoming' (Dörnyei, 2009: 11) (see also Ryan & Irie, Chapter 8, this volume; Ushioda, Chapter 9, this volume).

Furthermore, self-concept is an evaluative judgment of one's perceived self, possessing both cognitive and evaluative elements. Self-efficacy, in contrast, is one's judgment of one's capability to perform a task or engage in an activity. To further assist in defining the constructs, self-efficacy survey items often include the question 'how confident are you that you can...' and ask students to evaluate their competence to do particular tasks. Responses to such self-efficacy items ask students to evaluate whether they have high or low confidence to engage in particular activities. Self-concept questions, on the other hand, often involve questions of being and feeling, such as 'how do you feel about yourself as a French student'. Answers to self-concept items reveal negative or positive feelings of self-worth associated with the subject area and how individuals feel about themselves in particular academic domains. Therefore, although self-concept beliefs may be specific to an academic domain (e.g. Spanish self-concept, German self-concept, etc.), these beliefs are not assessed at task-specific levels like self-efficacy beliefs.

Self-regulation

A large body of FL research has been conducted in autonomy and language learning strategies in FL acquisition (Chamot, 2001; Cohen & Macaro, 2007). Learning strategies have been defined as 'any thoughts, behaviors, beliefs, or emotions that facilitate the acquisition, or later transfer of new knowledge and skills' (Weinstein et al., 2000: 727). FL research suggests that learning strategies play an important role in language learning and that autonomous students tend to be successful language learners across learning contexts (Macaro, 2001). Because of an interest in shifting the focus from the product (learning strategies) to the process (self-regulation), FL research has recently begun to move its focus from language learning strategies to *self-regulation* and the degree to which individuals are active participants in their own learning (Dörnyei, 2005).

Self-regulation is defined as one's ability to use the appropriate strategies to plan, monitor, and complete a task (Zimmerman, 2000). An individual's ability to self-regulate is therefore characteristic of his/her ability to self-monitor and self-appraise his/her behaviour and to employ the appropriate strategies to achieve success. By setting personally challenging goals and using effective strategies to achieve those goals, self-regulated learners exercise control over their own behaviour. Therefore, students who believe that they are more skilful in their ability to implement appropriate learning strategies, perceive themselves as more competent in their abilities and perform better academically. In contrast, those with less self-regulatory skills use fewer learning strategies resulting in lower academic achievement (Bandura, 1997). FL researchers have found that the higher the individual's perceived self-efficacy, the higher the engagement in more effective self-regulatory strategies (Graham, 2007). Researchers conclude that self-efficacy beliefs influence students' self-regulated learning strategies and confident students tend to use more appropriate strategies to plan, monitor, and complete tasks (Mills et al., 2007). Whereas self-efficacy beliefs refer to an individual's beliefs in his/her ability to perform a designated task, self-regulation refers to one's ability to use the appropriate strategies to plan, monitor, and complete a task. Researchers have also used the construct *self-efficacy for self-regulation* in FL motivational research. This construct refers to one's *perceived* ability to use effective strategies to plan and complete a task.

Self-Efficacy and Language Learning

Self-efficacy investigations in the field of FL learning became more prominent in the 21st century as FL motivation research entered its cognitive situated period, and L2 motivation scholars looked towards theoretical foundations in educational psychology to guide their research and understanding of language development. These investigations established a relationship between self-efficacy and FL achievement, FL reading and listening proficiency, language learning strategy use, FL anxiety, and self-efficacy for self-regulation (Graham, 2006, 2007; Graham & Macaro, 2008; Hsieh & Kang, 2010; Mills *et al.*, 2006, 2007). Mills *et al.* (2007) examined the influence of self-efficacy beliefs and other motivational variables on the achievement of 303 college intermediate French students. Hierarchical multiple regression analyses revealed that French grade self-efficacy was indicative of French achievement as measured by final course grades. The findings further indicated that students with higher French grade self-efficacy reported a stronger French self-concept and perceived value of the French language. It should be noted that these analyses were correlational in nature; therefore, no causal inferences among the variables are warranted when interpreting the results.

Hsieh and Kang's (2010) investigation of 192 ninth grade English language learners in Korea reaffirmed that self-efficacy was a significant predictor of FL achievement. Multiple regression analyses revealed that those with a stronger sense of efficacy to perform English-related tasks achieved higher test scores. Findings further indicated that English language learners with high self-efficacy tended to attribute success to internal or personal factors, whereas those with lower self-efficacy attributed test results to external factors, expressing less personal control over their achievement.

Researchers also examined the relationship between self-efficacy and FL proficiency in reading and listening (Mills *et al.*, 2006). In an investigation of 95 college intermediate French students, multiple regression analyses indicated that those who reported higher French reading self-efficacy beliefs attained higher French reading proficiency scores. Furthermore, when controlling for French reading self-efficacy beliefs, reading anxiety possessed no relationship to reading proficiency. This finding supported Bandura's (1997) claim that self-efficacy beliefs predict performance over and above feelings of anxiety. Thus, individuals experience FL reading anxiety when they feel incapable of exercising control over potentially challenging texts or when they feel less efficacious in their reading abilities. These findings reveal that male and female students with higher FL reading self-efficacy experience less FL anxiety and attain higher levels of FL reading proficiency.

In the same study, French listening self-efficacy was positively associated with French listening proficiency only for the female participants. Listening anxiety, however, was positively related to the listening proficiency of both men and women. These findings could support Onwuegbuzie *et al.*'s (2001: 12) claim that a 'female-oriented foreign language culture' may exist where men feel less comfortable in the language learning context. These findings could further support motivation research reported by Williams *et al.* (2002) that male secondary-school students perceive French language learning as feminine, with girls reporting a higher level of motivation than boys. However, the researchers warned that the results associated with Mills *et al.* (2006) study may have been owing to the low inter-item reliability of the listening proficiency test, the low stakes test-taking conditions, and the limited number of male participants. Despite these limitations, the findings suggest that gender differences may also play an important role in self-efficacy beliefs in FL learning. Further research is needed to explore more fully the relationship between gender and/or gender orientation and self-efficacy beliefs in FL learning, especially given the acknowledged role of socialization processes in the formation of self beliefs (Skaalvik & Skaalvik, 2004). Future research should also continue to explore self-efficacy and its relationship to language learning outcomes, such as achievement and linguistic proficiency, particularly in speaking and writing.

Researchers have additionally found a relationship between the use of language learning strategies and FL self-efficacy (Graham, 2007; Graham & Macaro, 2008). Graham (2007) investigated the impact of listening strategy training on the listening self-efficacy of high school French language learners. The intended goal was to assess whether strategy training would positively influence students' perceived competence to perform listening tasks. Analysis of covariance (ANCOVA) test results revealed that strategy instruction accompanied by feedback that allows learners to make connections between strategy use and listening performance, strengthens language learners' listening self-efficacy beliefs. Furthermore, Graham and Macaro's (2008) study revealed that strategy instruction had the greatest impact on students' listening self-efficacy to comprehend details and opinions in French. Both studies support Graham's (2006) claims that learners with high levels of self-efficacy also display more articulated metacognition, control, and knowledge of effective learner strategies. This claim is reaffirmed in Mills *et al.*'s (2007) research, which revealed through correlation analyses that an individual's self-efficacy for self-regulation, or perceived ability to use the appropriate strategies to plan, monitor, and complete French tasks, was associated with students' confidence beliefs in their ability to attain a French grade. Therefore, those students who perceived themselves as capable of achieving a high French grade were also likely to perceive themselves as having a strong ability to self-regulate. Mills *et al.* (2007), furthermore, found that self-efficacy for self-regulation was the most significant predictor of intermediate French achievement. Results revealed that students who perceived themselves as capable of using effective metacognitive strategies to complete their French assignments were, therefore, more likely to experience academic success in French over French grade self-efficacy, French learning anxiety, and French self-concept.

Other researchers have examined the influence of curriculum and classroom practices on the development of language learners' self-efficacy beliefs. Dörnyei (2000) suggested that self-beliefs are not static, but instead fluctuating and dynamic. As such, he advocated the use of a process-oriented approach to FL motivation research to evaluate changes in self-beliefs over time. To evaluate the developmental change in self-efficacy beliefs and their relationship to classroom practices, one study evaluated the influence of a project-based learning curriculum on the development of 46 false beginner French students' self-efficacy in the five goal areas of the *Standards of Foreign Language Learning* (Mills, 2009). The *Standards of Foreign Language Learning* are national content standards developed in the United States that outline 'what students should know and be able to do in FL education' (American Council on the Teaching of Foregin Languages (ACTFL), 1996). This study aimed to evaluate what these undergraduate students' perceived themselves to be capable of knowing and doing in the goal areas of communication, cultures, connections, comparisons, and communities before and after engaging in a project-based learning curriculum. This curriculum provided students with opportunities to collaborate on sequential tasks and integrate language and content in the collective development of a final project. Attempting to cultivate the four main sources of self-efficacy beliefs outlined in 'Self-Efficacy and Academic Performance', online discussion boards and collaborative learning opportunities were established to enhance *vicarious experiences*. Consistent teacher feedback was provided through weekly journal entries, quizzes, and participation grades to offer opportunities for *verbal persuasions* and *mastery experiences*. From the beginning to the end of the project-based learning course, paired sample t-tests revealed that students perceived themselves as more competent in their ability to interact and exchange opinions, interpret both written and spoken texts, and understand the products, practices, and perspectives of French culture. They also perceived themselves as more capable to establish connections to additional bodies of knowledge, make comparisons between the French and native languages and cultures, and participate in French communities in culturally appropriate ways. Enhanced self-efficacy beliefs in the five goal areas of the Standards were attributed to the project-based learning curriculum's distinctive characteristics, such as collaborative learning and various forms of assessment and feedback, which provided students with opportunities to foster the sources of self-efficacy. Because previous self-efficacy research in language learning has revealed that strong self-efficacy beliefs are indicative of strong achievement and proficiency (Mills *et al.*, 2006, 2007), fostering self-efficacy beliefs through curricular choices may strengthen self-efficacy beliefs as well as enhance achievement and linguistic proficiency.

Similarly, Mills and Péron (2009) evaluated the influence of a global simulation course format on the writing self-efficacy beliefs of 148 intermediate French students. In this global simulation course, students created French or francophone characters that lived virtually in a building in Paris. Within this context, students collaboratively wrote a creative storyline in bi-monthly memoirs in the first person. Scholars suggest that global simulation allows students to inhabit different roles and writer identities and therefore 'validate [their] sense of self' (Levine, 2004: 27). This study therefore aimed to evaluate whether the 'validation of self' experienced in a global simulation course format influenced students' FL writing self-efficacy. After participation in this global simulation curriculum, students reported higher writing self-concept in French and a stronger sense of competence, or self-efficacy, in their writing abilities in the areas of grammar, content, expression, organization, and creativity, as measured through paired-sample t-tests. Decreased FL writing anxiety was also reported. Correlation analyses further revealed that students with higher writing self-efficacy beliefs in French generally possess lower writing anxiety and stronger writing self-concept, perceived value of writing, and self-efficacy for self-regulation. A one-way repeated measures analysis of variance (ANOVA) furthermore revealed that there was a significant difference in composition text quality from the beginning to the end of the semester.

Strategies to Guide Self-Efficacy Research

Although the last decade has been productive in studies associated with FL self-efficacy, mis-measurement of the self-efficacy construct is a problem common to self-efficacy research in various academic domains (see Zimmerman, 1996). Self-efficacy assessment in second language acquisition investigations can lack specificity, resulting in the inability to appropriately evaluate its influence (see Pajares, 1996). Bandura (1986) advises self-efficacy researchers to measure self-efficacy with a specificity that corresponds to the task and domain being assessed. According to Pajares (1996: 4), 'this caution has often gone unheeded in educational research, which has resulted in self-efficacy assessments that reflect global or generalized attitudes about capabilities bearing slight or no resemblance to the criterial task with which they are compared'. Measures of general self-confidence, self-esteem, or more generalized senses of efficacy, obscure what is being assessed and alter the beliefs of competence into more generalized personality attributes. Such assessments compel students to evaluate their perception of academic competence without a clear understanding of a specific task in mind (Pajares, 1996).

Anyadubalu (2010), for example, reported no significant relationship between self-efficacy and English language performance among middle-school students using Schwarzer and Jerusalem's (1995) *Generalized self-efficacy scale*. This measure includes generalized items such as 'if someone opposes me, I can find the means and ways to get what I want' or 'it is easy for me to stick to my aims and accomplish my goals'. Instead of measuring self-efficacy with a specificity that corresponds to English language tasks, the reported results are associated with generalized personality attributes. Other measures have evaluated self-efficacy by asking students to evaluate their academic abilities with one item (see Cheng, 2002). Although we may gain some information about students' writing *self-concept* by asking students to rate their writing ability on a scale from one to five, one broad and generalized item does not include task and domain specificity.

In other research studies, self-efficacy items were combined with items measuring other constructs (Gorsuch, 2009; Mori, 2002). Some self-efficacy scales include items measuring *anxiety*, such as 'I feel fine doing oral interview tests in the second language', or items measuring *perceived value* of learning a second language, such as 'I like interacting with my classmates in the second language' (Gorsuch, 2009). Similarly, the *Morgan–Jinks Student Efficacy Scale* (Morgan & Jinks, 1999) includes items such as 'I am a good FL student', which measures FL *self-concept*, or 'I work hard in school', which measures student *effort*. Although self-concept, anxiety, perceived value, and effort are associated with self-efficacy beliefs, the use of items measuring other constructs within self-efficacy measures confounds the variables and makes it difficult to appropriately evaluate the influence of self-efficacy on FL learning. Attention should therefore be paid to the composition of self-efficacy scales when interpreting the results of self-efficacy studies.

However, effective self-efficacy measures have been developed in FL education research (see Graham, 2007; Graham & Macaro, 2008; Mills, 2009; Mills & Péron, 2009). These scales closely align the performance measures with the self-efficacy items to increase effect sizes, or the magnitude of the relationship between the two variables. Mills and Péron (2009) developed a writing self-efficacy measure to closely match the course's composition grading rubric used to assess students' writing. The composition grading rubric included the areas of grammar, content, creativity, expression, and organization. To match this rubric, the writing self-efficacy scale included 26 items evaluating students' writing self-efficacy in the previously mentioned rubric areas (grammar, organization, etc.) One self-efficacy item within writing organization included 'how sure are you that you can accurately and effectively use transitions when writing in French?' The prompt 'how sure are you that you can...' followed by a specific FL task helps to ensure that the self-efficacy item includes appropriate task and domain specificity. Furthermore, Pajares *et al.* (2001) found that in a United States context, self-efficacy scales with response formats that ranged from 0 to 100 were psychometrically stronger because they were congruent with the manner in which students are typically graded in American schools. Therefore, Mills and Péron (2009) asked participants to report their writing self-efficacy on a 10-point Likert-type scale from 0 (not confident at all) to 100 (completely confident).

Graham (2007) further enhanced the specificity of the listening self-efficacy items in her research by playing a series of listening passages to accompany the listening self-efficacy items. After playing the passages, she asked students to report on how sure they were that they could: '(1) understand the gist; (2) understand the details; (3) work out the meaning of unknown words; and (4) understand opinions' (Graham, 2007: 84) if they were to listen to similar listening passages. Hearing the listening passages allowed the students to report their self-efficacy beliefs with a clear understanding of the specific task in mind, thus allowing for a more accurate measure of students' listening self-efficacy beliefs. The development of context-appropriate self-efficacy measures that are closely aligned with performance measures allow researchers to appropriately assess the self-efficacy of FL learners.

Fostering Students' Self-Efficacy Beliefs

Effective measures are not only useful for researchers, but may also provide instructors with valuable information about the attitudes and efficacy beliefs of FL students. By monitoring students' self-efficacy beliefs through the use of appropriately designed self-efficacy measures as described in 'Strategies to Guide Self-Efficacy Research', instructors may modify teaching practices resulting in enhanced linguistic achievement and FL proficiency among students. As explained in 'Self-Efficacy and Academic Performance', in order to form self-efficacy beliefs, individuals cognitively interpret information from four main sources. Fostering these sources of students' self-efficacy beliefs may work to enhance students' perceived capabilities in FL learning (Bandura, 1997).

First, *mastery experiences* are prior performances that may be interpreted positively or negatively. According to Bandura (1997), *mastery experiences* are the most influential source of self-efficacy. Experiences that are perceived as successful build self-efficacy, whereas experiences perceived as unsuccessful can undermine self-efficacy beliefs. To enhance students' mastery experiences in the language learning process, instructors could provide multiple opportunities for students to experience success during classroom activities. Through scaffolding and the extensive guidance and support of the language teacher, students may be given opportunities to succeed at particular FL tasks during the language learning process. Teacher-guided activities could be followed by unrehearsed FL practice in pairs or small groups. By providing students with opportunities to exchange information, discuss opinions, and present ideas with their peers in a comfortable learning environment, students may be given multiple opportunities to experience success while learning the language.

Teachers' in-class presentation and modelling of effective language learning strategies may provide further opportunities for the language students to succeed. Such strategies could include teaching strategies in vocabulary acquisition, circumlocution, process-approaches to writing, and approaches to the comprehension and analysis of reading and listening texts. Graham (2006, 2007) further suggested that self-efficacy may be enhanced through explicit language strategy training. In language strategy training as outlined by Graham (2006, 2007), learners establish language learning goals, explore and verbalize learning strategies, and observe their instructor as s/he models effective strategy use. Learners are then asked to practise using the modelled strategies and are provided accompanied feedback about the relationship between strategy use and achievement. With the integration of language learning strategy training in the classroom, learners may be given the opportunity to positively interpret their FL performance, experience success, and thereby further enhance their self-efficacy beliefs.

Furthermore, whereas students with high self-efficacy tend to attribute success to internal factors such as expended effort, preparation, and use of language learning strategies, students with low self-efficacy often attribute success to external factors and exhibit less personal control for poor outcomes. When students attribute success to internal factors, they tend to exhibit feelings of control over the learning process, place more effort in learning tasks, and show persistence in the face of obstacles (Weiner, 2000). As such, Hsieh and Kang (2010) propose *attribution retraining* to enhance students' self-efficacy beliefs in FL learning. Attribution retraining includes 'specific teacher feedback confirming learners' adequate abilities and emphasizing the effort and perseverance required to complete a given task successfully' (Hsieh & Kang, 2010: 622) (see also Ryan & Irie, Chapter 8, this volume).

Vicarious experiences, such as student observation of linguistically proficient peers, are a second source of self-efficacy. Vicarious experiences are particularly influential when students perceive a shared likeness with the observed peers and believe that the peer's performance is diagnostic of their own future capabilities. The presentation of non-native peers communicating effectively in the target language in culturally grounded contexts could inspire and enhance students' perceptions of their potential in the target language. Mills (2009) suggests that the incorporation of collaborative learning experiences in a FL curriculum may provide learners with the vicarious experiences necessary to enhance their self-efficacy beliefs. Blogs, presentations, and in-class discussions provide learners with opportunities to observe the successes of their peers at similar proficiency levels. Similarly, discussion boards that encourage collaborative reading and writing allow students to observe the capabilities of linguistically proficient peers (Mills & Péron, 2009). These peer comparisons help to establish a community of learners and create a shared sense of *collective efficacy,* or shared belief in the class community's ability to complete similar FL tasks.

A third source of efficacy is teachers' appropriate use of *verbal persuasions* and encouragement. Pajares (2002: 121) claims that 'the teacher's challenge is to ensure that their students' internal standards are rigorous without being debilitating, realistic without being self-limiting, fluid without being wishy washy, consistent without being static...'. Curricula that include various appropriate and informational forms of assessment provide students with the ability to learn from their instructor's comments and offer consistent opportunities for student mastery (Mills, 2009). In their study evaluating the writing self-efficacy beliefs of intermediate French students, Mills and Péron (2009) proposed that students' writing self-efficacy increased because of a process-oriented approach to writing that incorporated consistent teacher feedback and personalized guiding comments.

Fourth, instructors could further enhance students' efficacy beliefs by encouraging positive *emotional indicators* and establishing a low anxiety FL learning environment. Mills (2009) suggests that the positive emotional indicators experienced by students during a project-based learning course, including increased engagement, enjoyment, and motivation, may have played a key role in enhancing their self-efficacy beliefs in French. Furthermore, learner-centred curricula, which allow students to become active decision-makers and engage with a wide network of available resources both inside and outside the classroom, may also play a role in increasing students' self-efficacy (Mills, 2009). Mills and Péron (2009) suggest that freedom, choice, and experimentation may allow students to maintain control over their FL learning, leading to enhanced self-beliefs in their FL capabilities.

Conclusion

A multitude of findings from the last decade highlight the critical importance of developing the self-efficacy beliefs of language learners to ensure that learners feel competent and capable in their ability to acquire a FL. Implications from research suggest that the self-efficacy beliefs of FL learners may be fostered through: (1) appropriate instructional choices; (2) curriculum design that is attentive to the four sources of self-efficacy previously discussed; (3) strategy and attribution training; and (4) instructor monitoring of self-efficacy beliefs with appropriately designed self-efficacy measures that include task and domain specificity. If teachers explicitly and actively pay attention to fostering students' confidence in their FL abilities both inside and outside the classroom, students may enhance their self-efficacy beliefs – a central element to FL success.

> ### Recommended reading
>
> Bandura, A. (1997) *Self-Efficacy: The Exercise of Control.* New York: W.H. Freeman.
>
> This book includes a comprehensive description of social cognitive theory and the self-efficacy construct written by the originator of social cognitive theory, psychologist Albert Bandura.
>
> Pajares, F. (1996) Self-efficacy beliefs in academic settings. *Review of Educational Research* 66, 543–578.
>
> In this article, the educational psychologist, Frank Pajares, establishes the importance of social cognitive theory and the self-efficacy construct in educational research. Pajares describes relationship among self-efficacy, motivation constructs, and academic performance in various academic domains.
>
> Mills, N.A., Pajares, F. and Herron, C. (2007) Self-efficacy of college intermediate French students: Relation to achievement and motivation. *Language Learning* 57 (3), 417–442.
>
> This article makes a bridge from self-efficacy research in educational psychology to research in second language acquisition in its evaluation of the self-efficacy of college intermediate French students.

Acknowledgements

I would like to dedicate this chapter to the memory of Dr Frank Pajares. I will continue to be inspired by his wisdom, sincere dedication and willingness to go beyond the necessary to create opportunities to enhance students' confidence beliefs about their academic potential.

References

American Council on the Teaching of Foreign Languages (ACTFL) (1996) *Standards for Foreign Language Learning: Preparing for the 21st Century.* Yonkers: ACTFL.

Anyadubalu, C. (2010) Self-efficacy, anxiety, and performance in the English language among middle school students in English language program in Si Suriyothai School, Bangkok. *International Journal of Human and Social Sciences* 5 (3), 193–198.

Arnold, J. (2007) Self-concept as part of the affective domain in language learning. In F. Rubio (ed.) *Self-Esteem and Foreign Language Learning* (pp. 13–29). Newcastle: Cambridge Scholars Publishing.

Bandura, A. (1986) *Social Foundations of Thought and Action: A Social Cognitive Theory.* Englewood Cliffs: Prentice Hall.

Bandura, A. (1997) *Self-Efficacy: The Exercise of Control.* New York: W. H. Freeman.
Chamot, A.U. (2001) The role of learning strategies in second language acquisition. In M.P. Breen (ed.) *Learner Contributions to Language Learning: New Directions in Research* (pp. 25–43). London: Longman.
Cheng, Y. (2002) Factors associated with foreign language writing anxiety. *Foreign Language Annals* 35, 647–656.
Cohen, A.D. and Macaro, E. (2007) *Language Learner Strategies.* Oxford University Press: Oxford.
Crookes, G. and Schmidt, R.W. (1991) Motivation: Reopening the research agenda. *Language Learning* 41, 469–512.
Dion, K.K., Dion, K.L. and Pak, A.W. (1990) The role of self-reported language proficiencies in the cultural and psychosocial adaptation among members of Toronto Canada's Chinese community. *Journal of Asian Pacific Communication* 1, 173–189.
Dörnyei, Z. (1994) Understanding L2 motivation: On with the challenge! *The Modern Language Journal* 78, 515–523.
Dörnyei, Z. (2000) Motivation in action: Towards a process-oriented conceptualisation of student motivation. *British Journal of Educational Psychology* 70, 519–538.
Dörnyei, Z. (2005) *The Psychology of the Language Learner: Individual Differences in Second Language Acquisition.* Mahwah: Lawrence Erlbaum Associates.
Dörnyei, Z. (2009) The L2 motivational self system. In Z. Dörnyei and E. Ushioda (eds) *Motivation, Language, Identity and the L2 Self* (pp. 9–42). Bristol: Multilingual Matters.
Gardner, R.C. (1985) *Social Psychology and Second Language Learning: The Role of Attitudes and Motivation.* London: Edward Arnold.
Gorsuch, G. (2009) Investigating second language learner self-efficacy and future expectancy of second language use for high-stakes program evaluation. *Foreign Language Annals* 42, 505–540.
Graham, S. (2006) Listening comprehension: The learners' perspective. *System* 34, 165–182.
Graham, S. (2007) Learner strategies and self-efficacy: Making the connection. *Language Learning Journal* 35, 81–93.
Graham, S. and Macaro, E. (2008) Strategy instruction in listening for lower-intermediate learners of French. *Language Learning* 58 (4), 747–783.
Graham, S. and Weiner, B. (1996) Theories and principles of motivation. In D.C. Berliner and R.C. Calfee (eds) *Handbook of Educational Psychology* (pp. 63–84). New York: Simon and Schuster Macmillan.
Hsieh, P. and Kang, H. (2010) Attribution and self-efficacy and their interrelationship in the Korean EFL context. *Language Learning* 60, 606–627.
Levine, G. (2004) Global simulation: A student-centered, task-based format for intermediate foreign language courses. *Foreign Language Annals* 37 (1), 26–36.
Macaro, E. (2001) *Learning Strategies in Second and Foreign Language Classrooms.* London: Continuum.
MacIntyre, P.D., Noels, K.A. and Clément, R. (1997) Biases in self-ratings of second language proficiency: The role of language anxiety. *Language Learning* 47, 265–287.
Mercer, S. (2011) *Towards an Understanding of Language Learner Self-Concept.* Dordrecht: Springer.
Mills, N.A. (2009) A 'Guide du Routard' simulation: Enhancing the Standards through project-based learning. *Foreign Language Annals* 42 (4), 607–639.
Mills, N.A. and Péron, M. (2009) Global simulation and writing self-beliefs of college intermediate French students. *International Journal of Applied Linguistics* 156, 239–273.
Mills, N.A., Pajares, F. and Herron, C.A. (2006) A re-evaluation of the role of anxiety: Self-efficacy, anxiety, and their relation to reading and listening proficiency. *Foreign Language Annals* 39, 273–292.

Mills, N.A., Pajares, F. and Herron, C. (2007) Self-efficacy of college intermediate French students: Relation to achievement and motivation. *Language Learning* 57 (3), 417–442.

Morgan, V. and Jinks, J. (1999) Children's perceived academic self-efficacy: An inventory scale. *The Clearing House* 72 (4), 224–230.

Mori, S. (2002) Redefining motivation to read in a foreign language. *Reading in a Foreign Language* 14, 91–110.

Noels, K.A., Pon, G. and Clément, R. (1996) Language, identity, and adjustment: The role of linguistic self-confidence in the acculturation process. *Journal of Language and Social Psychology* 15, 246–264.

Onwuegbuzie, A.J., Slate, J.R. and Schwartz, R.A. (2001) The role of study skills in graduate-level educational research courses. *Journal of Educational Research* 94, 238–246.

Pajares, F. (1996) Self-efficacy beliefs in academic settings. *Review of Educational Research* 66, 543–578.

Pajares, F. (2002) Gender and perceived self-efficacy in self-regulated learning. *Theory into Practice* 41, 116–125.

Pajares, F. and Schunk, D.H. (2001) Self-beliefs and school success: Self-efficacy, self-concept, and school achievement. In R. Riding and S. Rayner (eds) *Perception* (pp. 239–266). London: Ablex Publishing.

Pajares, F. and Schunk, D.H. (2002) Self and self-belief in psychology and education: A historical perspective. In J. Aronson (ed.) *Improving Academic Achievement: Impact of Psychological Factors on Education* (pp. 3–21). Amsterdam: Academic Press.

Pajares, F. and Urdan, T. (eds) (2006) *Adolescence and Education. Vol. 5: Self-efficacy Beliefs of Adolescents*. Greenwich: Information Age Publishing.

Pajares, F., Hartley, J. and Valiante, G. (2001) Response format in writing self-efficacy assessment: Greater discrimination increases prediction. *Measurement and Evaluation in Counseling and Development* 33, 214–221.

Schunk, D.H. (1991) Self-efficacy and academic motivation. *Educational Psychologist* 26, 207–231.

Schwarzer, R. and Jerusalem, M. (1995) Generalized self-efficacy scale. In J. Weinman, S. Wright and M. Johnston (eds) *Measures in Health Psychology: A User's Portfolio. Causal and Control Beliefs* (pp. 35–37). Windsor: Nfer-Nelson.

Shrum, J. and Glisan, E. (2005) *Teacher's Handbook* (3rd edn). Boston: Heinle and Heinle.

Skaalvik, S. and Skaalvik, E.M. (2004) Gender differences in math and verbal self-concept, performance expectations and motivation. *Sex Roles* 50 (3/4), 241–252.

Ushioda, E. and Dörnyei, Z. (2009) Motivation, language identities and the L2 self: A theoretical overview. In Z. Dörnyei and E. Ushioda (eds) *Motivation, Language Identity and the L2 Self* (pp. 1–8). Bristol: Multilingual Matters.

Weiner, B. (2000) Intrapersonal and interpersonal theories of motivation from an attributional perspective. *Educational Psychology Review* 12, 1–14.

Weinstein, C.E., Husman, J. and Dierking, D.R. (2000) Self-regulation interventions with a focus on learning strategies. In M. Boekaerts, P.R. Pintrich and M. Zeidner (eds) *Handbook of Self-Regulation* (pp. 727–747). San Diego: Academic Press.

Williams, M., Burden, R. and Lanvers, U. (2002) 'French is the language of love and stuff': Student perceptions of issues related to motivation in learning a foreign language. *British Educational Research Journal* 28 (4), 503–528.

Zimmerman, B.J. (1996) Measuring and mismeasuring academic self-efficacy: *Dimensions, problems, and misconceptions*. Symposium presented at the Annual Meeting of the American Educational Research Association, New York.

Zimmerman, B.J. (2000) Attaining self-regulation: A social cognitive perspective. In M. Boekaerts, P.R. Pintrich and M. Zeidner (eds) *Handbook of Self-Regulation* (pp. 13–41). San Diego: Academic Press.

3 The Dynamics of Second Language Confidence: Contact and Interaction[1]

Sinthujaa Sampasivam and Richard Clément

Introduction

Affective variables have long been considered to play an important role in second language acquisition (SLA). Globally, they refer to 'those emotionally relevant characteristics of the individual that influence how she/he will respond to any situation' (Gardner & MacIntyre, 1993: 1). This chapter will focus specifically on second language confidence (L2C). L2C represents a key variable initially identified in the SLA context, but which is an important construct for many other aspects of language acquisition. It corresponds to a lack of anxiety when communicating in the second language (L2) coupled with positive ratings of self-proficiency (Clément, 1980).

In this chapter, we first review the history of the development of the L2C construct and then explore the different ways in which L2C can facilitate language acquisition, L2 communication, and adaptation processes. While investigating L2C, we carefully consider the role of contact with speakers (native or otherwise) of the L2, which, despite its many forms and characteristics, is consistently associated with L2C. We conclude by drawing upon Harwood's contact space framework (2010) to organize relevant types of contact and to present a novel framework exploring how they lead to the development of L2C.

Development of the Concept of L2C

Studies in SLA initially found support for language aptitude and intelligence-related variables as key predictors of L2 achievement. Gardner and

Lambert (1959) aimed to improve upon this prediction by assessing a wide variety of variables, including affective variables such as attitudes, motivations, and audience anxiety, and aptitude-related variables such as intelligence. Two factors emerged as being related to L2 achievement: language aptitude and a cluster of attitude and motivational variables, referred to as the motivation factor. It was noted that this form of motivation was associated with a willingness to be like valued members of the L2 community. In a second study, Gardner (1960) found that language aptitude and a similar cluster of attitudinal and motivational indices, which he referred to as the integrative motive, were important for successful SLA.

Gardner, Smythe and colleagues later initiated a programme of research to develop a standardized test battery that would help predict individual differences in SLA (see Gardner, 1985). Specifically, they aimed to create reliable and valid indices of students' motivations and attitudes that could be applied to language learners from different age groups, levels of L2 training, and social contexts (Gardner & Smythe, 1975). Hence, multiple factor analytical studies were conducted with students across Canada. The integrative motive and L2 achievement were consistently found to be key factors across different settings and grade levels. Findings regarding the relationship between language anxiety and L2 achievement were inconsistent; in initial studies, language anxiety appeared as a key variable across grade levels, but failed to consistently emerge during subsequent cross-validation studies. In these cross-validation studies, however, self-perception of L2 achievement was found to be influential.

These initial studies took place in Canada, in a context where Anglophone students were learning French as an L2. Subsequently, Clément, Gardner and colleagues conducted a series of factor analytic studies examining the motivational characteristics of Francophone Canadian high school students learning English (Clément et al., 1977a), how social factors affected these motivations (Clément et al., 1980), and to further establish the reliability of the French version of the *Attitudinal/Motivational Test Battery* (Clément et al., 1977b).

These studies suggested that competence in English was highly related to a factor labelled 'Self-confidence with English.' Students who were high on this factor experienced little anxiety when speaking English in class or in real-life situations, perceived themselves as being relatively competent in their English abilities, reported frequent use of English, had positive attitudes towards their English class, showed motivation and desire to learn English, had experiences with more than one language at home, and performed well on indices of achievement in English. Given that L2C develops as a consequence of prior contact with the L2 group, it is unsurprising that it would have a larger impact for Canadian Francophone samples, who, by virtue of being a North American minority, have many more opportunities for contact with the Anglophone group than the other way around (Gardner, 1985).

Following these studies that defined L2C and identified some of its core antecedents (e.g. contact with the L2/L2 users) and consequences (e.g. L2 competence), Clément (1980) put forth the social-contextual model to account for these findings. Validated by Clément and Kruidenier (1985), the socio-contextual model describes the key determinants of L2 communicative competence. According to the model, there are two motivational processes that relate to SLA, a primary attitudinal process and a secondary L2C process. The primary process concerns the antagonistic interplay between: (1) integrativeness and the desire to join the L2 group; and (2) the fear of assimilation and the fear of losing affiliation with the first language (L1) group. This interplay jointly determines the extent to which individuals make intergroup contact. In the original model, two aspects were considered: frequency of contact and quality (or pleasantness) of contact with members of the L2 group. Together, they lead to the development of L2C, affecting the motivation to learn and use the L2, and ultimately leading to increases in L2 proficiency.

Given that L2C results from contact experiences, it is considered to have a less influential role in communities with infrequent intergroup contact compared with multilingual communities. Nevertheless, the quality and quantity of contact can have different effects. Labrie and Clément (1986) found that in contexts of high quality contact, frequency of contact was not imperative for the development of L2C. In situations of low quality of contact, however, high frequency improved L2C, such that even relatively unpleasant contact increased L2C.

More recently, evidence supporting the existence of an L2C factor has also been found in a unilingual setting with Anglophone Canadians learning French (Gardner *et al.*, 1997). Findings revealed that among a number of variables associated in L2 achievement, L2C was the most important factor and was comparable with the cluster of variables described above. L2C was highly correlated with objective measures of L2 achievement and path analyses indicated that it resulted from motivation and achievement. Although L2C did not emerge as a critical factor in earlier studies with Anglophone students learning French (e.g. Gardner & Smythe, 1975), in this study conducted over 20 years later, L2C played a significant role. This may be because over time, contact with the L2 group has become more readily available and accessible through different media.

Definitional Issues

L2C has been described as a higher-order variable encompassing both a lack of anxiety and positive self-ratings of L2 proficiency. Nevertheless, as in the willingness to communicate (WTC) literature (MacIntyre *et al.*, 1998), the components of L2C are sometimes assessed independently. WTC corresponds to the psychological readiness to use the L2 when the opportunity arises. Findings in this area, for example, suggest that when the learning context emphasises and permits live communication, communication apprehension-anxiety appears to be important (Baker & MacIntyre, 2000; MacIntyre *et al.*, 2003). In other cases when the L2 is more remote or communication occurs in less challenging contexts, self-evaluation appears to be a more important determinant of WTC (Baker & MacIntyre, 2000; MacIntyre *et al.*, 2003; Yashima, 2002; Yashima *et al.*, 2004). As such, these findings support a differential perspective of the components of L2C. They suggest that it is potentially advantageous to consider L2C to be a composite variable that is dependent on the context. Indeed, researchers should be sensitive to situations where anxiety and perceived competence could diverge.

Nevertheless, a key discussion surrounding the construct of L2C is its relationship with anxiety. Language anxiety is a multifaceted construct defined as 'a feeling of tension and apprehension specifically associated with L2 contexts, including speaking, listening, and learning' (MacIntyre & Gardner, 1994: 284). Anxiety has been found to arise from past negative experiences in the L2 and has undesirable effects on L2 learners and L2 achievement (see Gardner & MacIntyre, 1993; MacIntyre & Gardner, 1991). In this sense, anxiety and L2C have been described as playing opposing roles. Nevertheless, Gardner and MacIntyre (1993) argue that the processes underlying both anxiety and L2C are comparable, given that they both develop from past experiences relating to learning and using the L2. Moreover, they suggest that in multicultural contexts, where L1 and L2 groups are in close contact, the 'social milieu enhances correlates of language anxiety and produces a more complex construct combining language anxiety, self-perceptions of proficiency and attitudinal/motivational components' (Gardner & MacIntyre, 1993: 7).

Confidence in Different Contexts

L2C has been studied in different contexts and in situations with varying levels of L2 contact. Currently, there is no framework available to organize these contexts and the types of contact they readily provide. Given the importance of contact for the development of L2C, an appropriate taxonomical approach to organizing this literature would distinguish between situations found inside and outside the classroom. This taxonomical framework provides clarity, synthesises the diverse contexts within which L2C is investigated, and offers researchers contexts within which they can situate their own research. For example, the research reviewed thus far was conducted in the classroom context and in situations where intergroup contact was relatively high. There are other classroom-bound research contexts, however, within which contact is quite low and the types of contact available vary widely. These contexts, namely foreign (as opposed to 'second') language acquisition and computer-mediated communication (CMC) will be reviewed in the subsequent sections.

In contrast to the classroom context, L2C has also been investigated outside the classroom, where its effects on sojourners, immigrants, and official language minorities' adaptation experiences have been assessed. Thus, we will also explore the consequences of contact and L2C on psychological and sociocultural adaptations.

Inside the classroom

Foreign language acquisition (FLA)

SLA studies have demonstrated how L2C develops from frequent and pleasant contact with L2 members. Considerable research has, however, also found evidence documenting its role in the FLA context, where face-to-face contact with native L2 speakers is rare. FLA (Clément & Bourhis, 1996; Clément & Gardner, 2001) refers to acquiring a language spoken in neighbouring or distant countries, and thus is not characteristic of the homeland (e.g. Americans learning French). Nevertheless, the assumed differences between both language acquisition contexts are not straightforward. For example, although Canada is a bilingual country, the opportunity to communicate in the L2 varies across different areas. As such, in areas where the L2 is not used, it may resemble a foreign language, from the point of view of acquisition.

In a clearly FLA context, Clément *et al.* (1994) conducted a study with a sample of Hungarian students learning English. In Hungary, face-to-face contact with native English speakers is rare and English is seen as an ordinary subject at school. Clément and colleagues proposed that L2C could still result from contact via media and travel. Moreover, they reasoned that feelings of anxiety are not limited to contexts of intergroup contact, but, based on Horwitz *et al.*'s (1986) research, could result from the classroom situation (e.g. a fear of evaluation). Indeed, findings supported the existence of an L2C factor, which received similar loadings as in previous research (i.e. indices of anxiety, perceived competence, contact, and motivation loaded on this factor). Clément *et al.* (1994) argued that L2C influences L2 proficiency through both a direct and indirect route. The indirect route follows the socio-contextual model, whereas the direct route suggests that contact with L2 members will provide students with skills that can be applied within the classroom context.

Findings pertaining to the importance of contact for L2C have been found in other studies (Czisér & Kormos, 2008a, 2008b; Dörnyei & Czisér, 2005). These suggest that in the FLA context, foreign media use and perceived importance of contact were better predictors of motivated learning behaviours (items concerning the different aspects of students' learning behaviour) than more direct forms of contact. Indeed, Czisér and Kormos (2008b) found that L2C predicted foreign media use, which led to positive attitudes towards the L2 community and subsequently to motivated learning behaviours. These findings suggest that L2C is a precursor to contact, whereas past research has largely found support for the reverse. Thus, it is possible that contact and L2C have a bidirectional relationship; frequent and pleasant contact could lead to the development of L2C, while feelings of L2C could also motivate learners to seek contact. It is also possible, however, that because contact in the FLA context is often through foreign media use, a certain level of L2C is needed before media can be consumed.

The reviewed studies show that L2C is generally associated with L2 motivation and proficiency even in the FLA context. The findings show that while contact remains a key variable in the FLA context, the importance placed on face-to-face contact varies. That is, although some studies suggest that even in the FLA context face-to-face contact significantly contributes to the development of L2C (Moyer, 2006; Su, 2008; Tanaka & Ellis, 2003), others suggest that indirect contact and the importance placed on contact is more influential. Further research is needed to discern which aspects of the contact situation lead to L2C, and whether these features are common to both direct and indirect forms of contact. Nevertheless, the reviewed findings suggest that regardless of the type of contact, frequent contact is key.

Computer-mediated communication (CMC)

In order to provide students with the opportunity to develop their L2 abilities, different CMC methods are increasingly being used. CMC can benefit students by not only allowing them to communicate with peers using a different medium, but also allowing them to be in contact with and have authentic conversations with native L2 speakers. CMC can take two forms: synchronous (SCMC) or asynchronous (ACMC). SCMC methods are advantageous because they include the real-time demands of communication while allowing L2 learners some leeway and self-pace during L2 production and reception (Ortega, 2009). ACMC (e.g. emails), on the other hand, does not have the real-time demands of face-to-face communication. Despite investigating the effectiveness of CMC for linguistic and some non-linguistic outcomes (see Macaro et al., 2012), only a few studies have determined its effects on L2C.

While these initial studies suggest that using CMC can help develop L2C, more research is needed to elucidate which modes are effective for which learners. Among the limited research available, findings suggest that the effectiveness of the CMC is related to the proficiency level of participants (Satar & Ozdener, 2008). That is, learning a L2 can be anxiety provoking and for beginner-level learners, methods that provide more leeway and self-pace (e.g. text chat) may be more effective. These approaches allow learners to develop a sense of L2C and alleviate anxiety (Kissau et al., 2010; Satar &

Ozdener, 2008). For more experienced learners, using CMC that resembles oral communication might be more effective (Arnold, 2007), as they might not need to rely on as many resources in order to communicate. Furthermore, using CMC to interact with native L2 speakers not only helps develop L2C and motivation, but can strengthen L2 ability and allow for the sharing of authentic cultural information (Wu et al., 2011).

Outside the classroom context
Language and acculturation
The ability to communicate in the dominant language is considered to play an active and mediating role in sojourners' and immigrants' acculturation experiences (e.g. Clément et al., 2001). Acculturation refers to the shifts in the pattern of one or both cultures that results from intergroup contact (Redfield et al., 1936), including psychological and sociocultural adjustments (Searle & Ward, 1990). Psychological adjustments refer to the person's general contentment in the society of settlement and are influenced by changes in cultural values, attitudes, and behaviours. Sociocultural adaptation encompasses the ability to successfully interact and fit into the new culture, and pertains to behavioural adjustments. Additionally, researchers have investigated academic adjustments or worry about L2 proficiency and academic performance for international students (Yu & Shen, 2010).

Short-term contact
In order to pursue higher education, students have been increasingly relocating to more industrialized countries such as Canada and Australia (Yang et al., 2006). International students are individuals who come into sustained, yet relatively short-term contact with members of their host country. For these students who seek out and immerse themselves in the L2 community, L2C is related to psychological, socio-cultural, and academic adjustment (Yang et al., 2006; Yu & Shen, 2010). Further, research has indicated that students who claimed to be well-adjusted displayed and reported the most L2C and had contacts from both the L1 and L2 groups (Swagler & Ellis, 2003). Moreover, rather than actual proficiency, a subjective sense of proficiency is associated with better adaptation. The findings from this study clearly attest to the importance of L2C for a sojourner's adaptation experience.

Long-term contact
While sojourners move for a temporary period of time, immigrants settle permanently in a new country. Their psychological adjustment and satisfaction with their lives is related to L2C. Findings also show, however, that L2C might additionally compromise L1 identity and/or ability (Noels et al., 1996; Pak et al., 1985; Young & Gardner, 1990). For example, in studies with

Chinese immigrants, L2C is generally associated with higher perceived and actual language skills in English, lower perceived and actual skills in Chinese, lower English use anxiety, and greater identification and involvement with the L2 culture (Noels *et al.*, 1996; Young & Gardner, 1990). The negative consequences of L2C on L1 abilities may result because immigrants with high perceived competence in their L2 abilities tend to not only communicate with members of the dominant group in the L2, but choose to use the L2 when communicating with the L1 group members (van Avermaet & Klatter-Folmer, 1998). Consequently, the L2 pervades private domains.

In summary, the reviewed studies demonstrate that L2C plays a powerful and positive role in adjustment and acculturation processes of international students. The studies with immigrant participants confirmed these findings, but also showed that L2C may compromise L1 identity and abilities. Finally, research conducted with immigrants has also shown how L2C can moderate the relationship between discrimination and identity incongruities and stress (Clément *et al.*, 2001). That is, only when L2C was low, did those who reported facing high levels of discrimination or had identity incongruities also report experiencing more stress. Thus, L2C can play an important buffering role and consequently relate to overall well-being.

Roles of ethnolinguistic vitality

A key construct when studying the above phenomena is ethnolinguistic vitality (Giles *et al.*, 1977). Ethnolinguistic vitality is defined as 'that which makes a group likely to behave as a distinctive and collective entity within the intergroup setting' (Giles *et al.*, 1977: 308). Three structural components are used to determine group vitality: group status, demographic representation, and institutional support. In an intergroup context, groups with high ethnolinguistic vitality are more likely to survive as a collective entity and use their language in daily activities. Although the concept is not restricted to the Canadian situation, it has been studied in that context, where French is a minority language in all of the provinces except for Québec.

The findings of these studies largely reaffirm that contact is closely associated with L2C (Clément *et al.*, 2003; Gaudet & Clément, 2005, 2009; Noels & Clément, 1996; Rubenfeld *et al.*, 2006, 2007). These studies also show a generalized impact of L2C. That is, regardless of ethnolinguistic vitality, contact with the L2 group leads to an increase in L2C, which thereafter is associated with an increase in L2 identity and various psychological benefits that resemble those found for immigrants and sojourners.

Research findings are, however, inconsistent in terms of the consequences of L2C for L1 identity (Gaudet & Clément, 2005, 2009; Noels & Clément, 1996; Rubenfeld *et al.*, 2006, 2007). Consequently, the relationship between L2C and L1 identity may not be linear. In other words, high ethnolinguistic vitality (majority) groups would evidence little effect of L2C on their L1 identity. Whereas, in contrast, relatively low vitality groups would show a strong and *negative* relationship between L2C and identity. Very low ethnolinguistic vitality groups may, however, have developed L2C to such an extent that it is no longer relevant to L1 identity. In their case, the important factors may be linked to the level of L1 community development. Home, school, and social environments that help provide sufficient contact with other L1 group members may help establish L1 communication networks (Landry *et al.*, 1991) and support systems that favour the maintenance of the L1 (Gaudet & Clément, 2009). These networks can counterbalance the consequences that result from the dominance of the L2 group (Landry *et al.*, 1991).

Overall, the findings suggest that irrespective of ethnolinguistic vitality status, the consequences of L2C for L2 identity are similar. The relationship between L2C and L1 identity, on the other hand, is much more susceptible to variations in ethnolinguistic vitality group status. Nevertheless, Clément (1986) found that despite the fact that low ethnolinguistic vitality groups tend to have better quality and more frequent contact with the L2 group, L2C and frequency of contact, rather than ethnolinguistic vitality status, were more strongly associated with L2 proficiency and acculturation. That is, only under high frequency of contact did members from the low ethnolinguistic vitality status group become more acculturated than high ethnolinguistic vitality status group members. Thus, although ethnolinguistic vitality status facilitated acculturation, contact experiences played a determining role.

A Framework for Redefining Language Contact

The research described so far points to the importance of L2C for both linguistic and non-linguistic outcomes. Regardless of the context and outcomes under investigation, contact remained the main antecedent of L2C. Contact was not, however, a homogenous variable across the literature and varied in a number of ways. Yet, in the SLA context, contact has predominately been assessed only in terms of the frequency and quality or pleasantness of contact.

Recently, Harwood (2010) described the contact space framework (see Figure 3.1) in order to organize the different forms of contact investigated in the intergroup contact literature and to clarify their consequences. This taxonomical framework uses two orthogonal dimensions to organize the different forms of contact. The first dimension, involvement of self in contact, refers to the extent to which one is involved and participating in an interaction with an outgroup (or L2) member. The second dimension, richness of self-outgroup experience, concerns both the 'multiplicity of channels and senses through which one experiences the outgroup member' (Harwood, 2010: 154) and the availability for feedback as well as the immediacy with which feedback is offered.

32 Multiple Perspectives on the Self in SLA

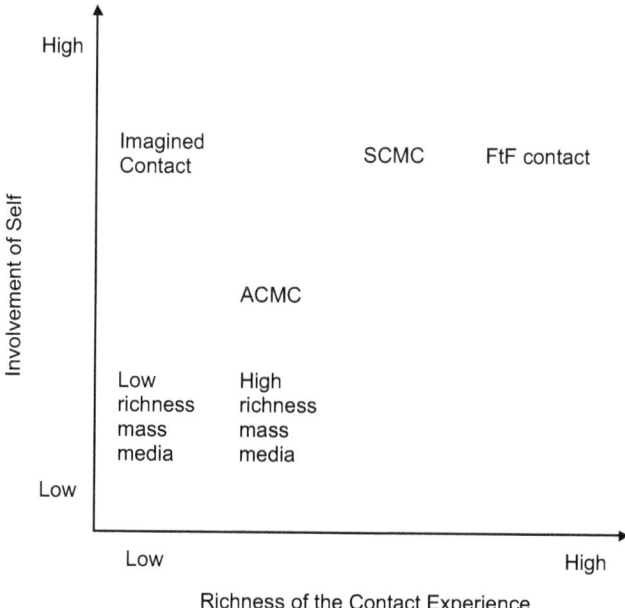

Figure 3.1 Contact space framework adapted to the SLA context. Adapted from Harwood (2010)

As can be seen, this framework includes various forms of contact, including face-to-face contact, mass-mediated contact, mediated interpersonal contact, and imagined contact. These forms of contact will be discussed here in terms of their importance for SLA-related outcomes. Subsequently, we will try to integrate the contact space framework with the contact variables traditionally studied in the SLA context (e.g. frequency and pleasantness of contact).

Contact space framework in the SLA context

Applied to the SLA situation, face-to-face contact occurs when L2 learners communicate directly with interlocutors in that language. Such contact is considered to be high on both dimensions of the contact space framework. Mass-mediated contact, on the other hand, refers to contact with the L2 group via the media (e.g. television, radio, etc.). Contact here is in terms of exposure to the L2 and its cultural artefacts. While the involvement of the self can be quite low during mass-mediated contact, richness in the L2 experience can vary depending on the type of media. Nevertheless, it is non-interactive and offers fewer cues. Mediated interpersonal contact refers to contact that occurs between individuals that does not take the form of face-to-face contact (Harwood, 2010). One such form of contact is CMC. Though

CMC methods have less immediacy and are less rich, they can vary on their placement in the contact space framework. Involvement of the self can be quite high during mediated communication, albeit the richness of the out-group experience might vary based on the communication mode (e.g. SCMC vs. ACMC). Lastly, although imagined contact/communication and its relation with L2C has not been well researched, Dörnyei (2009) recently emphasized the importance of imagined contact for L2 learners (see also Ryan & Irie, Chapter 8, this volume). Imagined contact would be low on richness, though its placement along the self-involvement dimension would depend on the degree of elaborateness and vividness of the imagined contact.

The application of this framework in the SLA literature is valuable for a number of reasons. While there is substantial support showing how frequent and pleasant contact experiences affect L2C, these variables do not capture the diverse and multifaceted ways through which contact can take place. Yet, it is not sufficient to define contact solely based on the dimensions of the contact space framework, as they lack features that are crucial to the SLA context. Consequently, our goal in the following section is to integrate this taxonomical framework with features of the contact situation typically studied in SLA literature. Here, we propose a framework describing the interrelations among these components in order to more fully capture how they relate to L2C. To this end, this framework addresses features of the contact situation that lead to L2C, but does not, at this point, focus on its consequences.

Towards an integrated framework of L2C

L2C is operationalized here according to Clément's (1980) original definition. Thus, it refers to feeling a lack of anxiety and positive self-ratings of proficiency in the L2. Richness, in this framework, refers to the multiplicity of channels through which the L2 is experienced and the immediacy with which one must provide feedback. Self-involvement, in this SLA context, refers to the extent to which one is involved in the communication part of the L2 contact.

At the centre of the model (see Figure 3.2) are richness, self-involvement, and L2C. It is expected that engaging in contact that is rich in form, or specifically contact that involves multiple channels and allows feedback, leads to an increase in L2C. That is, simply being able to comprehend or take in L2 input is expected to positively impact levels of L2C. Given that richer forms of contact require some interactivity, it is expected that such contact will also lead to greater self-involvement. Specifically, contact that is high in richness involves both the ability to comprehend and produce a response in the L2. Consequently, it requires a greater level of self-involvement. Participation in a rich contact experience with high self-involvement is likely to lead to an increase in L2C.

It is proposed that the relationship between richness and L2C is moderated by two variables: (1) frequency of contact; and (2) proficiency. That is,

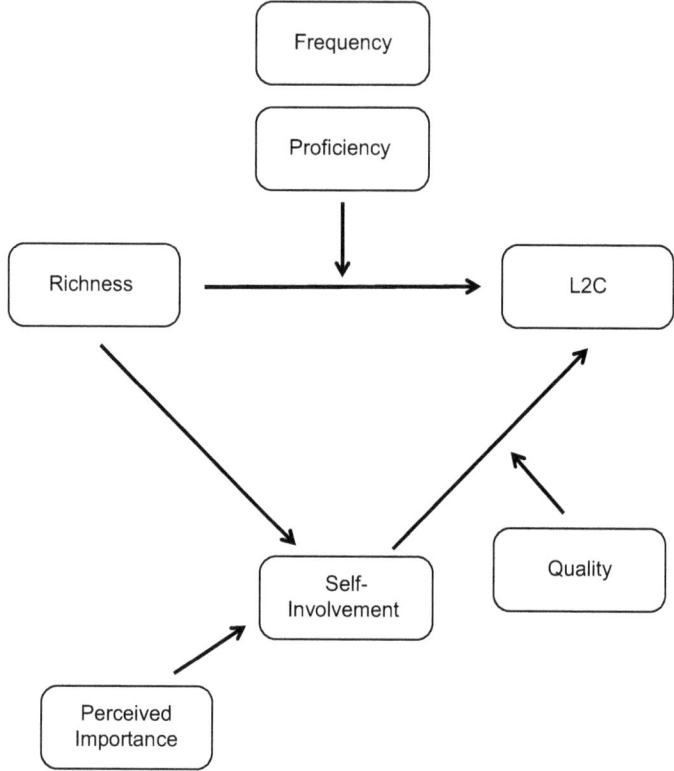

Figure 3.2 A functional model of the determinants of L2C

while richer forms of contact are expected to lead to increased L2C, even contact that is low in richness is expected to lead to increased L2C if it occurs frequently. For example, in the FLA context, only indirect forms of contact were associated with L2C (Czisér & Kormos, 2008a, 2008b). In such contexts, direct forms of contact are infrequent and might primarily be through tourism, where contact is likely to be more superficial and brief (Dörnyei & Czisér, 2005). As such, contact in forms that are more readily available and accessible (e.g. foreign media), despite being lower in richness, might lead to L2C.

Similarly, proficiency also moderates the relationship between richness and L2C. While richer forms of contact are expected to lead to increased L2C, they can be anxiety provoking for those with low L2 proficiency (Satar & Ozdener, 2008). As such, those with adequate L2 proficiency are less likely to be overwhelmed by richer forms of contact and are, therefore, more likely to experience the positive benefits of contact. For example, when considering CMC-related contact experiences, Satar and Ozdener (2008) found that for introductory-level students, only engaging in less rich forms of contact led to a decrease in anxiety and consequently to greater L2C.

In terms of self-involvement, it is expected that the perceived importance of contact or the 'value and personal significance of the contact' (van Dick *et al.*, 2004: 212) plays a determining role. In other words, contact experiences that are perceived to be important or personally relevant will, by default, involve the self to a greater extent, and thereafter be more likely to lead to L2C. For example, in the FLA context, students vary on their international posture or how much they value international communication (Yashima, 2002; Yashima *et al.*, 2004). Correspondingly, those with a strong international posture are likelier to perceive contact experiences as being important. As such, even when contact is low in richness (e.g. mass media), those who are high on international posture are expected to be more involved (e.g. be more likely to pay attention to the pronunciation of the L2 during audio contact) and are consequently expected to have higher L2C. Indeed, studies conducted by Yashima (2002) and Yashima *et al.* (2004) have demonstrated that international posture led to the motivation to learn the L2, which resulted subsequently in L2C.

Similarly, the normative pressure to use the L2 can impact on the extent to which contact experiences are perceived to be important. For groups that are frequently in contact with L2 or feel a strong normative pressure to communicate in the L2, contact experiences may be perceived to be less important, simply because they are attributed to these external factors (Clément *et al.*, 2003). For groups that do not feel a strong normative pressure to communicate in the L2, contact with the L2 group is more likely to be a purposeful, volitional act and consequently will be perceived as important.

As with the relationship between richness and L2C, that between self-involvement and L2C is moderated by a third variable, in this case, quality of contact. When contact highly involves the self, is perceived to be important and proceeds in a pleasant manner, it is likely to lead to an increase in L2C. However, when the contact highly involves the self and is perceived to be important, yet proceeds in an unpleasant fashion, it is expected to negatively impact L2C.

While these variables together determine L2C, it is expected that other contextual variables play influential roles. For example, as discussed above, ethnolinguistic vitality can help determine the extent to which contact is readily available. Ethnolinguistic vitality can also come into play in other parts of the model. For instance, learning the language of the high ethnolinguistic vitality status group might be perceived to be more important for low ethnolinguistic vitality members as they need to communicate in the L2 for key adjustment reasons (e.g. employment).

Conclusion

An extensive literature accumulated over several decades and across a number of contexts has demonstrated the importance of L2C. These findings indicate that L2C develops mainly from contact experiences and is generally associated with a variety of positive benefits relating to both linguistic and non-linguistic outcomes. By introducing a novel formulation that draws upon the contact space framework and integrates it with key contact variables typically assessed in this literature, it is possible to account for the various ways contact has been assessed in the SLA context. This new approach should provide a clearer understanding of the relationship between contact and L2C, organize the different forms of contact being studied in the SLA context, and, in applied settings, help define the type of contact necessary for positive outcomes for L2 learners at different levels.

From a more global perspective, L2C is part of a family of phenomena defining the self, which is a concept with a considerable history in psychology (Swann & Bosson, 2010). In SLA, recent theoretical formulations have increasingly emphasized self-related variables, such as the notion of possible selves as key components (Dörnyei, 2009). While this is promising, it is important to remember, however, that possible selves, while a source of motivation, have a limited impact if not accompanied by strategies for attaining desired objectives (Oyserman *et al.*, 2006). We suggest that those strategies lie in L2 interactions and that orchestrating contact situations to generate L2C is the main instrument of achieving a desired L2 self.

Recommended reading

Clément, R. (1980) Ethnicity, contact and communicative competence in a second language. In H. Giles, P. Robinson and P. Smith (eds) *Social Psychology and Language* (pp. 147–159). Oxford: Pergamon.

This article presents the original formulation of Clément's sociocontextual model of L2 acquisition.

Clément, R., Noels, K.A. and Deneault, B. (2001) Interethnic contact, identity and psychological adjustment: The mediating and moderating roles of communication. *Journal of Social Issues* 57 (3), 557–577.

An empirical paper showing the relation between discrimination, self-discrepancies in identity and well-being and how L2C may moderate the effect on the latter of the two former.

Harwood, J. (2010) The contact space: A novel framework for intergroup contact research. *Journal of Language and Social Psychology* 29 (2), 147–177.

This article provides a new, parsimonious framework that organizes different forms of contact.

Note

(1) The work described here was supported by grants from the Social Sciences and Humanities Council of Canada to the second author.

References

Arnold, N. (2007) Reducing foreign language communication apprehension with computer-mediated communication: A preliminary study. *System* 35 (4), 469–486.

Baker, S.C. and MacIntyre, P.D. (2000) The role of gender and immersion in communication and second language orientations. *Language Learning* 50 (2), 311–341.

Clément, R. (1980) Ethnicity, contact and communicative competence in a second language. In H. Giles, P. Robinson and P. Smith (eds) *Social Psychology and Language* (pp. 147–159). Oxford: Pergamon.

Clément, R. (1986) Second language proficiency and acculturation: An investigation of the effects of language status and individual characteristics. *Journal of Language and Social Psychology* 5 (4), 271–290.

Clément, R. and Bourhis, R.Y. (1996) Bilingualism and intergroup communication. *International Journal of Psycholinguistics* 12 (2), 171–191.

Clément, R. and Gardner, R.C. (2001) Second language mastery. In H. Giles and P. Robinson (eds) *The New Handbook of Language and Social Psychology* (pp. 489–504). London: Wiley.

Clément, R. and Kruidenier, B.G. (1985) Aptitude, attitude and motivation in second language proficiency: A test of Clément's model. *Journal of Language and Social Psychology* 4 (1), 21–37.

Clément, R., Baker, S.C. and MacIntyre, P.D. (2003) Willingness to communicate in a second language: The effects of context, norms, and vitality. *Journal of Language and Social Psychology* 22 (2), 190–209.

Clément, R., Dörnyei, Z. and Noels, K.A. (1994) Motivation, self-confidence, and group cohesion in the foreign language classroom. *Language Learning* 44 (3), 417–448.

Clément, R., Gardner, R.C. and Smythe, P.C. (1977a) Motivational variables in second language acquisition: A study of Francophones learning English. *Canadian Journal of Behavioural Science* 9 (2), 123–133.

Clément, R., Gardner, R.C. and Smythe, P.C. (1980) Social and individual factors in second language acquisition. *Canadian Journal of Behavioural Science* 12 (4), 293–302.

Clément, R., Major, L.J., Gardner, R.C. and Smythe, P.C. (1977b) Attitudes and motivation in second language acquisition: An investigation of Ontario Francophones. *Working Papers on Bilingualism* 12, 1–20.

Clément, R., Noels, K.A. and Deneault, B. (2001) Interethnic contact, identity and psychological adjustment: The mediating and moderating roles of communication. *Journal of Social Issues* 57 (3), 557–577.

Csizér, K. and Kormos, J. (2008a) The relationship of intercultural contact and language learning motivation among Hungarian students of English and German. *Journal of Multilingual and Multicultural Development* 29 (1), 30–48.

Csizér, K. and Kormos, J. (2008b) Modeling the role of intercultural contact in the motivation of learning English as a foreign language. *Applied Linguistics* 30 (2), 166–185.

Dörnyei, Z. (2009) The L2 motivational self system. In Z. Dörnyei and E. Ushioda (eds) *Motivation, Language Identity and the Self* (pp. 9–42). Bristol: Multilingual Matters.

Dörnyei, Z. and Csizér, K. (2005) The effects of intercultural contact and tourism on language attitudes and language learning motivation. *Journal of Language and Social Psychology* 24 (4), 327–357.

Gardner, R.C. (1960) Motivational variables in second-language acquisition. Unpublished doctoral dissertation, McGill University, Montreal.

Gardner, R.C. (1985) *Social Psychology and Second Language Learning: The Role of Attitudes and Motivation*. London: Edward Arnold Publishers.

Gardner, R.C. and Lambert, W.E. (1959) Motivational variables in second language acquisition. *Canadian Journal of Psychology* 13, 266–272.

Gardner, R.C. and MacIntyre, P.D. (1993) A student's contributions to second language learning. Part II: Affective variables. *Language Teaching* 26 (1), 1–11.

Gardner, R.C. and Smythe, P.C. (1975) Second language acquisition: a social psychological approach. *Research Bulletin No. 332*, Department of Psychology, Language Research Group.

Gardner, R.C., Tremblay, P.F. and Masgoret, A.M. (1997) Towards a full model of second language learning: An empirical investigation. *The Modern Language Journal* 81 (3), 344–362.

Gaudet, S. and Clément, R. (2005) Identity maintenance and loss: Concurrent processes among the Fransaskois. *Canadian Journal of Behavioural Science* 37 (2), 110–122.

Gaudet, S. and Clément, R. (2009) Forging an identity as a linguistic minority: Intra-and intergroup aspects of language, communication and identity. *International Journal of Intercultural Research* 33 (3), 213–227.

Giles, H., Bourhis, R.Y. and Taylor, D. (1977) Towards a theory of language in ethnic group relations. In H. Giles (ed.) *Language, Ethnicity and Intergroup Relations* (pp. 307–348). London: Academic Press.

Harwood, J. (2010) The contact space: A novel framework for intergroup contact research. *Journal of Language and Social Psychology* 29 (2), 147–177.

Horwitz, E.K., Horwitz, M.B. and Cope, J. (1986) Foreign language classroom anxiety. *The Modern language Journal* 70 (2), 125–132.

Labrie, N. and Clément, R. (1986) Ethnolinguistic vitality, self-confidence and second language proficiency: An investigation. *Journal of Multilingual and Multicultural Development* 7 (4), 269–282.

Landry, R., Allard, R. and Théberge, R. (1991) School and family French ambiance and the bilingual development of Francophone Western Canadians. *The Canadian Modern Language Review* 47 (5), 878–915.

Kissau, S., McCullough, H. and Pyke, J.G. (2010) 'Leveling the playing field': The effects of online second language instruction on student willingness to communicate in French. *CALICO Journal* 27 (2), 277–297.

Macaro, E., Handley, Z. and Walter, C. (2012) A systematic review of CALL in English as a second language: Focus on primary and secondary education. *Language Teaching* 45 (1), 1–43.

MacIntyre, P.D. and Gardner, R.C. (1991) Methods and results in the study of anxiety and language learning: A review of the literature. *Language Learning* 41 (1), 85–117.

MacIntyre, P.D. and Gardner, R.C. (1994) The subtle effects of language anxiety on cognitive processing in the second language. *Language Learning* 44 (2), 283–305.

MacIntyre, P.D., Baker, S.C., Clément, R. and Donovan, L.A. (2003) Talking in order to learn: Willingness to communicate and intensive language programs. *Canadian Modern Language Review* 59 (4), 589–607.

MacIntyre, P.D., Clément, R., Dörnyei, Z. and Noels, K.A. (1998) Conceptualizing willingness to communicate in a L2: A situational model of L2 confidence and affiliation. *The Modern Language Journal* 82 (4), 545–562.

Moyer, A. (2006) Language contact and confidence in second language listening comprehension: A pilot study of advanced learners of German. *Foreign Language Annals* 39 (2), 255–275.

Noels, K.A. and Clément, R. (1996) Communicating across cultures: Social determinants and acculturative consequences. *Canadian Journal of Behavioural Science* 28 (3), 214–228.

Noels, K.A., Pon, G. and Clément, R. (1996) Language, identity and adjustment: The role of linguistic self-confidence in the acculturation process. *Journal of Language and Social Psychology* 15 (3), 246–264.

Ortega, L. (2009) Interaction and attention to form in L2 text-based computer-mediated communication. In A. Mackey and C. Polio (eds) *Multiple Perspectives on Interaction in SLA: Research in Honor of Susan M. Gass* (pp. 226–253). New York: Routledge.

Oyserman, D., Bybee, D. and Terry, K. (2006) Possible selves and academic outcome: How and when possible selves impel action. *Journal of Personality and Social Psychology* 91 (1), 188–204.

Pak, A.W., Dion, K.L. and Dion, K.K. (1985) Correlates of self-confidence with English among Chinese students in Toronto. *Canadian Journal of Behavioural Science/Revue Canadienne des Sciences du Comportement* 17 (4), 369–378.

Redfield, R., Linton, R. and Herskovits, M.J. (1936) Memorandum for the study of acculturation. *American Anthropologist* 38 (1), 149–152.

Rubenfeld, S., Clément, R., Lussier, D. Lebrun, M. and Auger, R. (2006) Second language learning and cultural representations: Beyond competence and identity. *Language Learning* 56 (9), 609–632.

Rubenfeld, S., Clément, R., Vinograd, J., Lussier, D., Amireault, V., Auger, R. and Lebrun, M. (2007) Becoming a cultural intermediary: A further social corollary of second language mastery. *Journal of Language and Social Psychology* 26 (2), 182–203.

Satar, H.M. and Ozdener, N. (2008) The effects of synchronous CMC on speaking proficiency and anxiety: Text versus voice chat. *The Modern Language Journal* 92 (4), 595–613.

Searle, W. and Ward, C. (1990) The prediction of psychological and sociocultural adjustment during cross-cultural transitions. *International Journal of Intercultural Relations* 14 (4), 449–464.

Su, Y.C. (2008) Promoting cross-cultural awareness and understanding: Incorporating ethnographic interviews in college EFL classes in Taiwan. *Educational Studies* 34 (4), 337–398.

Swagler, M.A. and Ellis, M.V. (2003) Crossing the distance: Adjustment of Taiwanese graduate students in the United States. *Journal of Counseling Psychology* 50 (4), 420–437.

Swann, W.B. and Bosson, J.K. (2010) Self and identity. In S.T. Fiske, D.T. Gilbert and G. Lindzey (eds) *Handbook of Social Psychology Fifth Edition* (Vol 1, pp. 589–628). Hoboken: Wiley.

Tanaka, K. and Ellis, R. (2003) Study abroad, language proficiency, and learner beliefs about language learning. *JALT Journal* 25 (1), 63–85.

van Avermaet, P. and Klatter-Folmer, J. (1998) The role of L2 self-assessment in language choice behaviour: Immigrant shift to Dutch in Flanders and the Netherlands. *Te Reo (Journal of the linguistic Society of New Zealand)* 41 (1998), 137–152.

van Dick, R., Wagner, U., Pettigrew, T.F., Christ, O., Wolf, C., Petzel, T., *et al.* (2004) Role of perceived importance in intergroup contact. *Journal of Personality and Social Psychology* 87 (2), 211–227.

Wu, W.V., Yen, L.L. and Marek, M.W. (2011) Using online EFL interaction to increase confidence, motivation, and ability. *Educational Technology and Society* 14 (3), 118–129.

Yang, R.P.J., Noels, K.A. and Saumure, K.D. (2006) Multiple routes to cross-cultural adaptation for international students: mapping the paths between self-construals, English language confidence, and adjustment. *International Journal of Intercultural Relations* 30 (4), 487–506.

Yashima, T. (2002) Willingness to communicate in a second language: The Japanese EFL context. *The Modern Language Journal* 86 (1), 54–66.

Yashima, T., Zenuk-Nishide, L. and Shimizu, K. (2004) Influence of attitudes and affect on L2 communication: A study of Japanese high school students. *Language Learning* 54 (1), 119–152.

Young, M. and Gardner, R.C. (1990) Modes of acculturation and second language proficiency. *Canadian Journal of Behavioural Science* 22 (1), 59–71.
Yu, B. and Shen, H. (2010) Predicting roles of linguistic confidence, integrative motivation and second language proficiency on cross-cultural adaptation. *International Journal of Intercultural Relations* 36 (1), 72–82.

4 Self-Esteem and Self-Concept in Foreign Language Learning

Fernando D. Rubio

Introduction

Studies on the self and the affective dimension of teaching and learning a foreign language have increasingly gained recognition among scholars and practitioners in the field. However, it is surprising to note that self-concept and self-esteem have received rather less attention than some other constructs in this area. The advent of interest in the self can potentially be traced back to humanistic contributions (e.g. Rogers, 1961; Stevick, 1980, 1990). These triggered a consideration of diverse psychological phenomena of language and learning. However, the focus of attention remained largely on the two more frequently researched constructs of motivation and anxiety. While self-concept and self-esteem have been mentioned in the literature and their importance highlighted (e.g. Arnold & Brown, 1999; Cohen & Norst, 1989), empirical research has remained scarce. As a result, our picture of self-concept and self-esteem has remained incomplete and partial.

As is the case with other psychological entities (e.g. anxiety, Rubio, 2004), self-concept and self-esteem are domain-specific constructs. In the context of this book, this means that they have to be examined specifically within the framework of language learning and teaching, rather than globally or holistically. Accordingly, this chapter will offer insights into these constructs and their conceptual nature, from both a general perspective and also from one focused specifically on the field of applied linguistics. It will offer a new conception of the processes of self-concept and self-esteem formation: a neurogenerative view, in which individuals continuously generate new impressions of the self. Finally, using Reasoner's model (1982), the chapter concludes by considering possible implications for classroom practice in the domain of foreign language learning.

Conceptual and Definitional Issues

The terms self-concept, self-esteem, self-efficacy, self-worth, and other related phenomena often overlap and can be notoriously difficult to define consistently. For instance, self-esteem and self-worth are sometimes considered synonymous terms (e.g. Harter, 1999); or self-esteem and self-concept have been distinguished in terms of their relative domain-specificity, with some claiming that self-concept can be conceptualized as domain specific in contrast to self-esteem, which some claim 'does not function at the domain-specific level', such as learning a foreign language, but is conceptualized as being a more global construct (Mercer, 2008: 19). The plethora of unsuccessful attempts to define the constructs is seen throughout the literature owing to the fact that they are based on the differentiation of elements that are very difficult, if not impossible, to separate, such as feelings (emotion) and thoughts (cognition). In fact, neuroscientific research confirms that 'cognition and affect are distinct but inseparable' (Schumann, 1994: 231), and '...from a neural perspective, not only are various affective processes interrelated, but affect and cognition are also intimately intertwined' (Schumann, 1997: 238). Which comes first – the feeling or the thought? Can one go without the other? Can you do research focusing on just one of them independently of the other? We cannot offer an answer to these questions.

Ways of conceptualizing the constructs have dealt with the following levels of specificity:

- *Context*: whether it is context-dependent or not dependent.
- *Evaluation versus affect*: whether the result of the self-concept is formed by cognitive processes involving judgement, or emotional/affective perceptions affecting feelings.
- *Openness versus stability*: whether the phenomenon is open to change and can evolve or whether it is stable.

In my own understanding of the two constructs, I have come to conceptualize self-esteem as a process of evaluation and the emergent evaluation, while self-concept is the perceived entity that is evaluated. The following metaphor will hopefully clarify these conceptual dimensions. Imagine you are looking at a picture at a museum. You first take a general glance at the picture, including the frame, the canvas, or the drawing. Then, you observe colours, shapes, and figures to try to make meaning out of the picture, and study the diverse techniques the artist has employed to compose his/her work. At this point, as happens with self-esteem, you are in the process of perception and evaluation, which results in terms of liking, according to the visual image and the feelings it might provoke in you. Self-esteem would correspond to the resulting evaluation of the picture; while the picture would be the self-concept. Therefore, self-esteem is a process of evaluation and self-concept is the entity evaluated, according to the particular vision or view of that entity.

Hence, self-concept is a complex construct consisting of different dimensions or selves, namely physical, social, familiar, personal, academic, and many other situational ones. Someone's self-concept defines his/her individuality and predicts his/her behaviours, and is formed by 'the beliefs ... about oneself' (Hamlyn, 1983: 241). Self-esteem is the process and resulting evaluation of the self-concept, as Dörnyei (2005: 211) makes clear: self-esteem is 'the evaluative quality of the self-image of self-concept'. In fact, the term is conceptually self-describing: *to esteem* means to regard, to value, to appreciate, or to consider something. Thus, a person can have high or low self-esteem and not a high or low self-concept, because the self-esteem is the resulting evaluation of the perceived self-concept. The process of perception of the self-concept, as happens when looking at a picture, can vary depending on the personal maturation of the self, age, personality, situational conditions, metacognitive strategies, and many other individual or contextual factors. Finally, the two key components evaluated in the perception of one's self-concept are one's sense of competence and one's sense of worthiness; the first is related to self-efficacy (beliefs about one's abilities, aptitude, intelligence, etc.) and the second one is connected to self-worth (beliefs and feelings about being worthy of being looked at, accepted, etc.; physical image and personality would play a major role here).

To help understand the constructs better, the following sections will offer a brief overview of the literature considering first theories of self-concept and self-esteem in educational psychology, and then examining related work in the field of second language acquisition (SLA).

Theories of Self in Educational and Social Psychology

In mainstream psychology, the self has been studied from a range of perspectives, such as psychodynamic, sociocultural, behavioural, humanistic, cognitive, and phenomenological. I will briefly consider each of these in turn, highlighting the main contribution of each perspective to our understandings of self-concept and self-esteem.

A pioneer in self-studies was William James, who proposed a dynamic understanding of self-esteem, introducing values, success, and competence as its main component elements. In the mid-20th century, a psychodynamic approach developed stemming from the influence of psycho-analysis studies produced by Sigmund Freud, Alfred Adler, and other influential psychologists. White (1963), as a leading figure, described self-esteem as the result of the relationship between self and ideal self, and the drive for *effectance*, which is the need to have a sense of competence when mastering skills for adapting to the environment. Consequently, high levels of self-esteem are promoted when individuals feel competent to deal with the environment. Thus, White's theory is based on human development, and levels of self-esteem and pathologies derived from it can be explained when specific life episodes (traumas, successes, etc.) are considered. Ausubel (1968) and many other researchers have pinpointed the need that every human has to enhance their self-esteem and feel worthy and competent.

A key scholar taking a sociocultural approach to the self was Rosenberg (1965) who suggested that self-esteem is greatly influenced by social contact, which leads to certain attitudes and behaviours. He explained that 'the self is a social construction and works on the premise that self-values associated with self-esteem arise from an interplay of cultural, social, familial, and other interpersonal processes' (cited in Mruk, 1999: 123). He also considered the psychodynamic approach and stated that higher self-esteem emerged when the ideal self and the real self were close.

A behavioural perspective on the self was taken by Stanley Coopersmith, who claimed that individuals act in order to fulfil needs or achieve something (love, task success, etc.), and self-esteem is developed in respect to that relationship. Likewise, three major antecedents of self-esteem (parental warmth, clearly defined limits, and respectful treatment) result in acquired traits. He also proposed that predicted patterns of behaviours occur in relation to a person's level of self-esteem (Coopersmith, 1967); for instance, low levels of self-esteem are likely to produce defensive behaviours.

A contemporary to Rosenberg and Coopersmith was Nathaniel Branden, who was the leading figure of a humanistic vision of self-esteem. Unlike the others, Branden gave worthiness and competence equal importance in the process of self-concept evaluation, and emphasized the fact that every human has a need to maintain a balance in their self-esteem or develop a psychological homeostasis; i.e. moderate levels of self-esteem. In fact, when that balance is not established, an individual '... may evade, repress, distort his judgment'... 'feel driven to *fake* it, to create the *illusion* of self-esteem'... 'moved by the desperate sense that to face the universe without self-esteem is to stand naked, disarmed, delivered to destruction' (Branden, 1969: 110). Branden made clear that pseudo self-esteem can alleviate the psychological well-being on a short-term basis, but it is harmful over time. In another major contribution to the field, Branden (1994: 3) warned that 'self-esteem is a fundamental human need' and 'has profound consequences for every aspect of our existence' (Branden, 1994: 5).

Self-esteem has also been studied within a cognitive paradigm, in which the key processes are found when analysing how information is perceived, processed, organized, and formed in the brain after experience takes place. The result of this process creates a personal schema that influences the individual's subjective perception of reality. Seymour Epstein, as one of the main scholars within this paradigm, described self-esteem as a hierarchical structure, in which there is a basic self-esteem (most stable and influential), an intermediate self-esteem (general domains of experience), and situation-specific self-esteem (particular domains) (Epstein, 1985).

Finally, a phenomenological perspective has proposed that self-esteem is the result of the evaluation of competence and worthiness under a complex process of interaction between the world and perceived experiences within it (Mruk, 2006). The result of the interaction can be placed in a matrix that accounts for positive and negative behaviour (self-centred, narcissistic, negativistic, depressed, overachieving, antisocial, etc.). All individuals evaluate their self-concept according to their perceived worthiness and competence, and the emergent self-esteem can be conceptualized along a set of axes. An individual's self-esteem can be thought of as the result of the combination of high or low sense of worthiness and competence, and consequently four different categories can be established:

High worthiness and high competence leads to high or authentic self-esteem

A history of acceptance (being valued), of virtue (acting from one's beliefs), and success with facing challenge provides a strong sense of security, which allows taking risks and accepting challenges free of stress, since the individual's perceived abilities are good enough to solve problems. However, Mruk (1999: 159) warns that extreme senses of high worthiness and competence (+9 and +9) may also result in difficulties in understanding 'what it is like to fear rejection or worry about the possibility of failure', and anti-empathetic attitudes might develop toward other students, creating classroom conflict.

Low worthiness and low competence lead to low self-esteem, which provokes negative behaviour

Being placed in the opposite quadrant gives rise to converse attitudes and behaviours, such as passive attitudes, generated by fear of making mistakes and low expectations of success. Notwithstanding, Mruk (1999: 159) makes clear that both groups (high and low self-esteem) 'have the same feelings about the desirability of success'. Feelings of dependence and lower effect comparisons to others usually arise. In sum, insecurity prevents students from developing positive attitudes towards learning and showing their full potential. Extreme degrees of low worthiness and competence lead to depression and clinical treatment is usually needed.

Low worthiness and high competence lead to defensive behaviours in the form of overachieving performance

Self-esteem evaluation is unbalanced: on the one hand, individuals feel competent and successful in accomplishing tasks, and spend most of their time devoted to succeed in school grades, sports, social activities, etc. Neuroticism can arise when concern for success is extreme. Such individuals may also become defensive when their success is challenged. Typical behaviours appear commonly known as 'overachiever' or 'workaholic'. Goal achievement is so important to the individual that everything else is neglected, such as building good relationships with others, which gradually separates them from the group and ends up creating a low sense of belonging.

High worthiness and low competence result in self-centred behaviour

This type of behaviour is usually identified with high self-esteem, because individuals tend to act as if they had leadership skills and abilities to control the situation, and they appear to feel very good about themselves. It is really a pseudo high self-esteem, for they are actually suffering from lack of competence, even though they feel highly about themselves. When their sense of worthiness is challenged they may 'act out on others aggressively' (Mruk, 1999: 160), and bullying may appear to demonstrate leadership and power. This type of defensive self-esteem is clearly seen in the classroom when students have the need to show off in front of other peers to try to be the centre of attention. Indeed, individuals feel threatened in class, since in this environment perceptions of competence are constantly made, and they feel vulnerable. Narcissistic behaviours also develop and, for instance, body building or beauty sessions take over other types of activities where competence has to be shown.

The Dynamic Development of Self-Esteem and Self-Concept

One way in which self-esteem is dynamic is across the lifespan. It has been suggested that there are five main life stages where significant development occurs: early childhood, middle childhood, adolescence, adulthood, and old age (Harter, 1999). Most researchers in the 20th century have devoted their studies to understanding self-esteem in the early stages of life (Coopersmith, 1967; Rosenberg, 1965; White, 1963), such as childhood and adolescence. However, many researchers doubt that self-esteem is present in early childhood, since individuals are not aware of their sense of worthiness and competence at that age. A sense of worthiness emerges first when, for instance, individuals feel accepted conditionally or unconditionally, such as by parents (Rogers, 1961). Therefore, self-esteem first develops from external acceptance and later from acceptance of oneself. A sense of competence develops later in middle childhood, mainly when children need to show their abilities in educational settings, since the school functions as the primary setting for the cultivation and validation of cognitive competencies. By the end of middle childhood, individuals have made evaluations of motor and social skills, intellect, personality, and behaviour, and thus develop a global sense of self-esteem. Worthiness becomes a key concern during adolescence, as, for instance, body image supposes social acceptance and success. The following stage, adulthood, is the longest and is mainly influenced by experiences of success or failure in solving problems, and acceptance or rejection in interpersonal relationships (Epstein, 1979). Self-esteem levels peak in middle age, but decline around the time of retirement when older adults are aware of their perceived obsolete work skills and possible decline in health (Orth, 2010). However, as with all claims about typical developments in self-esteem over the lifespan, this generalization may not be true for certain cultures or individuals, such as those who have a positive perception of life and have cultivated a sense of personal growth. Considering these developmental stages highlights the importance for educators of considering the role of competence, particularly during primary school age (Bandura, 1986) and the role of worthiness during the secondary school years (Fonseca Mora, 2005).

Self-concept dynamism has also been considered within an individual, i.e. whether it is open to change or remains stable over time. This chapter offers a new perspective that describes dynamism from a neurogenerative perspective. It conceives the process of evaluating oneself as a recurring lifetime event. In other words, evaluations develop continuously throughout one's lifetime. Self-concept can be defined by a description of the different selves that the individual generates, whereas self-esteem arises from the phenomenological processes of evaluation and its intervening factors (situational circumstances, personality, etc.). Consequently, self-concept is unique for each individual and developed newly in every evaluation, and it is formed dynamically throughout life, but self-esteem processes of evaluation follow similar patterns of activation for all human beings; i.e. complex intertwined connections of affect and thought which result from self-evaluations. The resulting levels of self-esteem are changeable according to less dynamic factors, such as personality or education, and also to more dynamic ones, such as specific circumstances of context and domain. Figure 4.1 explains this process.

Advances in neuroscientific studies explain how many cognitive processes function as a network pattern that are continuously forming mental maps (not as a hierarchical or molecular structure, but a complex network); such as every time we remember a visual image we do not visualize the same one, but we make a new reconstruction of it (Damasio, 2010). I also believe such a neurogenerative process could function in respect to self-esteem formation. In other words, after a situation or thought is experienced, a person evaluates his/her self (if competence or worthiness are in play); then, s/he compares his/her actual self to his/her *ideal* or *ought to* self, resulting in a

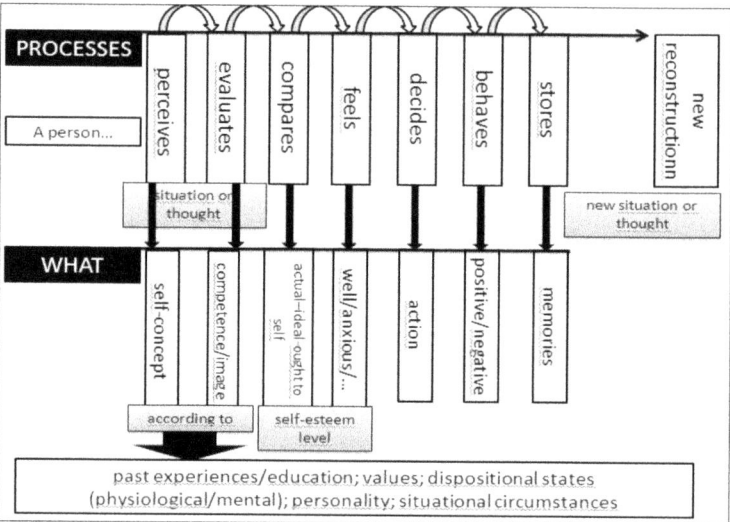

Figure 4.1 A neurogenerative conception of self-concept and self-esteem

self-esteem measure, which generates positive or negative feelings that determine behaviour (Higgins, 1987). Then, a new situation or thought or experience regenerates the process anew. Therefore, the self-concept cannot be described as stable, but past experiences/education, values, personality, and dispositional and situational states are the dynamic entities within the neurogenerative framework.

Thus, we create self-concept portraits every time competence and worthiness are in play. According to this neurogenerative view, self-esteem processes rely on tenuous self-concepts because totally new evaluations are generated repeatedly. In fact, from a phenomenological perspective, it is the perception of performance and previous experiences that mainly influence the formation of the self-concept (Mruk, 2006), and performances and thoughts are inherently unpredictable, continuously becoming part of the history of experiences. Therefore, it is difficult to argue that the self-concept is a durable entity or a stable trait (even some more stable traits, as beauty or character, can rapidly change). Obviously, it could become somewhat stable if patterns of experience follow a steady route of events. In this case, we cannot talk about a stable self-concept, but a stable pattern of events, performances, or experiences.

Relevant Research in SLA

The first studies relating language learning to self-concept and self-esteem come indirectly from research on motivation. Clément's linguistic L2 self-confidence (1986) construct was incorporated into a vast number of studies in relation to motivation (see Sampasivam & Clément, Chapter 3, this volume). For instance, Clément and Kruidenier (1985) claimed that *self-confidence* was a major factor in predicting effort and a positive attitude towards learning a foreign language. In respect to motivation, the role of the self was further developed by Dörnyei (2005), who uses Freud's ideas of the struggle between the ego and ideal ego in proposing his L2 self system of motivation. Based on Higgins' *self-discrepancy theory* (1987, 1996), Dörnyei (2009) argues that future self-guides play a major motivational function and depend on the realizations of the ideal and ought self. Thus, '... people are motivated to reach a condition where their self-concept matches their personally relevant self-guides' (Dörnyei, 2009: 18).

Self-esteem has also been researched as a variable under the umbrella of the *willingness to communicate* (WTC) phenomenon (see e.g. Fonseca Mora & Toscano Fuentes, 2007; MacIntyre *et al.*, 1998), or *communicative apprehension* (Richmond & McCroskey, 1989), which is commonly known as fear associated with communicating with another individual. McCroskey and McCroskey (1986) find a modest correlation between self-esteem and WTC ($r = 0.22$), and McCroskey and Richmond (1990: 26) explain that, 'If a person has low self-esteem it might be expected the person would be less willing to communicate because he/she feels that he/she has little of value to offer', and also 'because he/she believes others would respond negatively to what would be said'. They further point out that 'self-perceptions of competence... may have a strong influence on individuals' WTC' (McCroskey & Richmond, 1990: 27).

More recently, Rubio (2007) edited a book entitled *Self-Esteem and Foreign Language Learning*, inspired by Andres (1999). The papers introduced the construct theoretically, included reviews of the literature, reported on research on the relationship of self-esteem with other phenomena (e.g. anxiety), and offered practical suggestions for classroom practice. Self-esteem has also been studied in respect to specific language domains or skills. For example, Heyde (1979) studied the relationship of different levels of self-esteem with oral production and found a positive correlation. Likewise, a positive correlation was found with listening comprehension (Hayati & Ostadian, 2008). In contrast, a weak correlation between self-esteem and reading performance was found in other studies (Grodnick, 1996; Hassan, 1999; Soureshjani & Naseri, 2011), although Fahim and Rad (2012) found a positive correlation in their study.

Other studies from outside SLA have examined the structure of self-concept, in particular whether there is a separate language self-concept. In studies based on Marsh and Shavelson's (1985) multifaceted hierarchical model of self-concept structure, Lau *et al.* (1999) and Yeung and Wong (2004) confirmed the existence of a separate self-concept for languages and they also indicated that multilingual speakers have distinct self-concepts for each language.

In 2011, Mercer published her book *Towards an Understanding of Language Learner Self-Concept*, which offered insights into the formation and structure of self-concept based on qualitative research. Mercer found that there is a distinct self-concept for language learning and also other self-concepts across domains too (writing, reading, etc.). Extending Marsh's internal/external model (1986) of self-concept formation, Mercer (2011: 440-441) also described the internal and external factors that appeared to contribute to the development of the learner's self-concept in respect to language learning.

Internal factors:

- Internal comparisons across domains within the self-concept network
- Belief systems
- Affective reactions

External factors:

- Social comparisons with others, especially peers
- Feedback from significant others
- Perceived experiences of success/failure
- Previous language learning/use experiences in formal/informal contexts
- Critical experiences

Highlighting the complexity involved in self-concept formation, she concludes that:

> ... it is evident from these findings that learners' EFL self-concepts are part of a complicated network of self-beliefs and are formed through a myriad of interconnected factors, all of which may be processed differently depending on other psychological factors and motivations within the individual. It would therefore appear to be naïve to assume that learners' EFL self-concepts can be easily influenced in predictable ways. (cf. O'Mara *et al.*, 2006; in Mercer, 2011: 167)

Research Approaches to Self-Concept and Self-Esteem

As has been seen in this chapter so far, there is a great disparity in definitions of self-esteem and self-concept. As such, researchers have used differing definitions of the terms, leading to a confusing field with mixed results that are often difficult to compare. For novice researchers to the field, this means it is important to conduct data searches for literature using both terms (self-esteem and self-concept), and, indeed, possibly other related self-terms, in order to ensure relevant literature is not overlooked.

Essentially, the type of research conducted depends on the perspective adopted for the study. For example, a socio-cultural and a behavioural approach suggest behaviours can be observed, and content (type of belief), intensity (degree of maintenance), and stability (lasting effect) of self-beliefs can be measured. Thus, observational methods in controlled situations can be used, and interviews, surveys, and live recordings can be employed to gather data. However, as Mruk (2006) notes, no two selves are the same, and behavioural patterns are not consistent, but also, self-esteem is an evaluation of the self, which is a subjective reflexive exercise that is hard to quantify. For that reason, longitudinal case studies are perhaps more appropriate for research, using instruments that could capture specific information throughout introspection or retrospection techniques (Skaalvik & Skaalvik, 2002).

In socio-cultural approaches, an understanding of context is important and situated studies are useful, such as case studies and other types of qualitative studies. A combination of qualitative and quantitative methods has also been recommended more recently as being an effective way of drawing on the strengths of both approaches (Dörnyei, 2007). As Mercer (2008: 36) points out, 'much of the research into self-concept development tends to employ statistical methods which are perhaps less likely to reveal any unanticipated findings or individual differences, given the usual fixed-item tools employed for data collection'.

Typically, much research into self-concept and self-esteem has used self-report questionnaires. For example, Rosenberg's Self-Esteem Inventory (SEI), (Rosenberg, 1989) is probably the most widely used instrument in self-concept or self-esteem studies. Coopersmith's SEI has been another key data collection tool for self-esteem studies (Coopersmith, 1975, 1981). In respect to self-concept, a variety of questionnaires have been developed based on the ideas of hierarchical structure of the self-concept (Shavelson *et al.*, 1976), such as the ASDQ I, II (Academic Self Description Questionnaire) and SDQ I, II, III (Self Description Questionnaire) were developed (see e.g. Marsh, 1990; Online: http://www.self.ox.ac.uk/Instruments.htm).

In the field of foreign language learning, most questionnaires used have been adapted from those belonging to general academic measurements (cited above). This is important as some researchers advise: 'Researchers interested in self-concepts in particular subjects are advised to use self-concept scales specific to those subject areas in addition, perhaps, to other measures of academic self-concept' (Marsh, 1990: 623). As Mercer (2011: 22) points out, 'It is now widely accepted that research into self-concept needs to be carried out in domain-specific ways'.

Implications for Classroom Practice

Teaching approaches attending to affect and the self have been inspired by various developments in language teaching. Most notably, humanism has made a considerable contribution in drawing attention to these factors. For example, humanistic methods sought to promote a stress-free environment and to provide learners with security and learning satisfaction. Particular methods include, for example, Total Physical Response (Asher, 1969), which avoided speaking at initial stages until the learners were ready for production and included movement for body relaxation; Suggestopedia (Lozanov, 1978) used music to increase self-esteem through increased self-satisfaction (Gaston, 1968; in Richards & Rodgers, 2001: 100); and, Community Language Learning (Curran, 1972) emphasized the teacher's role as assistant and supporter of students' needs.

The next development of relevance for self-concept and self-esteem stems from diverse theories developed to highlight individual differences in the process of language learning. For instance, the theory of Multiple Intelligences (Gardner, 1982) postulates the idea that human intelligence does not arise from a single unitary quality of the mind, but that every individual is competent in at least three intelligences. This idea challenged the concept of competence, which together with worthiness form the two basic valuing dimensions of self-concept.

Also, work on learning styles is relevant to self-concept and self-esteem (see e.g. Reid, 1987). Approaches that acknowledge students' learning preferences in receiving, organizing, and producing language can help teachers understand positive or negative attitudes towards learning when students' learning styles do or do not match their teaching styles. When teachers are aware of the different styles students have, they can understand students' behaviour and can also make better decisions based on an individual basis, which may help promoting a higher sense of security.

Other approaches that can foster self-esteem include, for example, cooperative learning (Casal, 2007). It has been found that appropriate methodological procedures that generate students' feelings of satisfaction when working in groups may enhance levels of self-esteem: 'the more positive the feelings about a group (collective self-esteem), the higher one's personal self-esteem' (Luhtanen & Crocker, 1992; in Casal, 2007: 94).

In general education, the first specifically focused self-esteem school programmes appeared in the 1980s in the USA to prevent students from dropping out of classes and to avoid negative behaviours. Reasoner's model (Reasoner, 1982) was probably the most widely accepted one, which also inspired language teachers a decade later (see e.g. Andrés, 1999). Basically, the core idea consisted of introducing activities in the classroom to provide learning and personal growth at the same time. To the best of my knowledge, only two publications in the field of foreign language learning have been produced offering classroom activities for teachers aimed specifically at enhancing self-esteem in this area: Rubio (2007) and Andres and Arnold (2009). However, other relevant publications that also refer to promoting an affective atmosphere and building confidence among language learners are Davis and Rinvolucri (1991), Rinvolucri (2002), and Murphey (2006).

Reasoner's model is based on five dimensions: *security, identity, belonging, purpose,* and *competence. Security* refers to the feeling of physical and emotional safety. Security is promoted in the classroom when students have clear rules and expect consistent patterns of behaviour from the teacher. Also, students feel safe to participate when errors are considered a natural part of students' learning, and students feel valued and recognized, such as by positive feedback from the teacher (see literature on *teacher confirmation*; e.g. León, 2007).

The identity dimension of Reasoner's self-esteem model refers to the perception people have about themselves, including their physical image and personality. As has been argued throughout this chapter, a healthy sense of self requires having a realistic vision of oneself, acknowledging strengths, weaknesses, and considering points for development. This dimension has a strong link with personal values, which influence self-perceptions. According to Andres and Arnold (2009), a teacher who promotes a sense of identity honours individual uniqueness, builds positive self-images, demonstrates care and acceptance, and builds self-awareness (which reinforces more accurate self-descriptions).

A sense of belonging consists of the feeling of being accepted and forming part of a group. When students feel rejected in the classroom they may start to show disruptive behaviour in order to call for attention and gain acceptance among peers. Teachers can promote a sense of belonging by providing opportunities to be of service, encouraging peer approval and support, or developing class identity, in which every member is valued, accepted, and considered important.

A sense of purpose is related to the feeling of having objectives and direction in life. In the classroom context, a sense of purpose is achieved when students are aware of progress and acknowledge their effort as worthwhile. Teachers can encourage a sense of purpose by conveying realistic expectations and providing support to set and achieve goals, giving enough time to complete tasks, breaking objectives into sub-objectives so that they seem attainable, and showing confidence and faith in students' work progress.

Finally, *a sense of competence* in Reasoner's self-esteem model refers to the feeling of having abilities and aptitude to accomplish tasks. Teachers can help promote a sense of competence by using self-evaluation checklists to value effort and progress, adding positive comments on students' exams or activities (i.e. avoid using only negative feedback in correction), considering individual uniqueness and multiplicity of abilities (see theory on multiple intelligences), providing appropriate level of challenge and skills, having classroom celebrations when some students succeed or show improvement, and using language portfolio to collect best works, etc. (Andres & Arnold, 2009).

Conclusion

This chapter has aimed to clarify conceptual aspects of the constructs of self-concept and self-esteem, defining self-concept as the entity evaluated by an individual and referring to self-esteem as the process and result of the evaluation. This conceptual distinction may challenge other studies and definitions, but has the advantage of avoiding definitions that cannot be operationalized in which one is depicted as cognitive or the other affective, and it incorporates a sense of process into the definition. The dynamism of self-esteem has also been highlighted, both in respect to lifespan developments and openness to change, incorporating the neurogenerative view of self-concept evaluation. Thus, every self-concept evaluation means a totally new evaluation, although past evaluations continue to exert a certain degree of influence. If the neurogenerative theory were to be expanded and confirmed, it would support the development of programmes in the language classroom designed also for personal growth, since the basic tenet is that totally new evaluations are made continuously, and thus, self-esteem levels are more open to change than previous theories suggested.

In respect to pedagogy, Reasoner's model (1982) has been highlighted as one possible guide to designing language programmes or specific activities to enhance self-esteem by developing five dimensions that empower students individually and as part of a group: security, identity, belonging, purpose, and competence. Andrés and Arnold's (2009) publication asserts that language learning can be an experience related not only to language and communication, but also to personal growth.

Finally, further research is needed in both theoretical research and classroom practice in the field of foreign language learning. This would help teachers to create better learning atmospheres and learners to experience foreign language learning with optimum attitude, motivation, and willingness to learn.

> ### Recommended reading
>
> Rubio, F.D. (ed.) (2007) *Self-Esteem and Foreign Language Learning.* Newcastle: Cambridge Scholars Publishing.
>
> This book offers a theoretical background of the topic, analyses self-esteem in relation to other factors, such as an anxiety, and includes classroom activities for language teachers.

> Mercer, S. (2011) *Towards an Understanding of Language Learner Self-Concept*. Dordrecht: Springer.
>
> This book is mainly focused on research. It gives a broad picture of theoretical issues, such as conceptual entities and self-concept structure. It also adds a research project based on qualitative research.
>
> Mruk, C.J. (2006) *Self-Esteem Research, Theory and Practice. Toward a Positive Psychology of Self-Esteem* (3rd edn). New York: Springer.
>
> This book includes a comprehensive analysis and overview of the literature on self-esteem.

References

Andres, V.d. (1999) Self-esteem or the metamorphosis of butterflies. In J. Arnold (ed.) *Affect in Language Learning* (pp. 87–102). Cambridge: Cambridge University Press.

Andres, V.d. and Arnold, J. (2009) *Seeds of Confidence. Self-Esteem Activities for the EFL Classroom*. Rum: Helbling Languages.

Arnold, J. and Brown, H. (1999) A map of the terrain. In J. Arnold (ed.) *Affect in Language Learning* (pp. 19–41). Cambridge: Cambridge University Press.

Asher, J. (1969) The Total Physical Response approach to second language learning. *The Modern Language Journal* 1 (53), 3–17.

Ausubel, D. (1968) *Educational Psychology: A Cognitive View*. New York: Holt, Rinehart and Winston.

Bandura, A. (1986) *Social Foundations of Thought and Actions: A Social Cognitive Theory*. Englewood Cliffs: Prentice-Hall.

Branden, N. (1969) *The Psychology of Self-Esteem*. New York: Bantam.

Branden, N. (1994) *The Six Pillars of Self-Esteem*. New York: Bantam.

Casal, S. (2007) The social dimension of identity and self-esteem in the foreign language classroom. In F.D. Rubio (ed.) *Self-Esteem and Foreign Language Learning* (pp. 91–104). Newcastle: Cambridge Scholars Publishing.

Clément, R. (1986) Second language proficiency and acculturation: An investigation of the effects of language status and individual characteristics. *Journal of Language and Social Psychology* 5 (3), 271–290.

Clément, R. and Kruidenier, B.G. (1985) Aptitude, attitude and motivation in second language proficiency: A test on Clément's model. *Journal of Language and Social Psychology* 4 (1), 21–37.

Cohen, Y. and Norst, M.J. (1989) Fear, dependence and loss of self-esteem: Affective barriers in second language learning among adults. *RELC Journal* 20 (2), 61–77.

Coopersmith, S. (1975/1981) *Adult Form SEI Coopersmith Inventory*. Palo Alto: Consulting Psychologists Press.

Coopersmith, S. (1967) *The Antecedents of Self-Esteem*. San Francisco: Freeman.

Crooks, T. (1988) The impact of classroom evaluation practices on students. *Review of Educational Research* 58 (4), 438–481.

Curran, C.A. (1972) *Counseling-Learning: A Whole-Person Model for Education*. New York: Grune & Stratton.

Damasio, A. (2010) *Big Think*. From How memory works. See http://bigthink.com/ideas/23018 (accessed 31 March 2010).

Davis, P. and Rinvolucri, M. (1991) *The Confidence Book*. London: Longman.

Dörnyei, Z. (2005) *The Psychology of the Language Learner*. Hillsdale: Earlbaum Associates.

Dörnyei, Z. (2007) *Research Methods in Applied Linguistics*. Oxford: Oxford University Press.

Dörnyei, Z. (2009) The L2 motivational self system. In Z. Dörnyei and E. Ushioda (eds) *Motivation, Language Identity and the L2 Self* (pp. 9–42). Bristol: Multilingual Matters.

Epstein, S. (1979) The ecological study of emotions in humans. In K. Blankstein (ed.) *Advances in the Study of Communications and Affect* (pp. 47–83). New York: Plenum.

Epstein, S. (1985) The implications of cognitive-experiential self-theory for research in social psychology and personality. *Journal for the Theory of Social Behavior* 15, 283–309.

Fahim, M. and Rad, S. (2012) The relationship between self-esteem and paragraph writing of Iranian EFL learners. *Psychology* 3, 24–29.

Fonseca Mora, M.C. (2005) Individual characteristics of secondary school students. In N. McLaren, D. Madrid and A. Bueno (eds) *TEFL in Secondary Education* (pp. 79–110). Granada: Universidad de Granada.

Fonseca Mora, M.C. and Toscano Fuentes, C. (2007) Fostering teenagers' willingness to learn a foreign language. In F.D. Rubio (ed.) *Self-Esteem and Foreign Language Learning* (pp. 91–104). Newcastle: Cambridge Scholars Publishing.

Gardner, H. (1982) *Frames of Mind: The Theory of Multiple Intelligences*. New York: Basic Books.

Gaston, E.T. (1968) *Music in Therapy*. New York: Macmillan.

Grodnick, J.R. (1996) *Self-Esteem and Writing Achievement*. ERIC Document Reproduction Service, ED 395 311.

Hamlyn, D.W. (1983) *Perception, Learning and the Self: Essays in the Philosophy of Psychology*. London: Routledge.

Harter, S. (1999) *The Construction of the Self: A Developmental Perspective*. New York: Guildford Press.

Hassan, B.A. (1999) The relationship of writing apprehension and self-esteem to the writing quality and quantity of EFL university students. *Mansoura Faculty of Education Journal* 39, 1–36.

Hayati, A.M. and Ostadian, M. (2008) *The Relationship Between Self-Esteem and Listening Comprehension of EFL Students*. Shahid Chamran University of Ahvaz, Iran: Published Research, Faculty of Letters and Humanities.

Heyde, A. (1979) The relationship between self-esteem and oral production of a second language. PhD Thesis, University of Michigan.

Higgins, E.T. (1987) Self-discrepancy: A theory relating self and affect. *Psychological Review* 94 (3), 319–340.

Higgins, E.T. (1996) The 'self-digest': Self-knowledge serving self-regulatory functions. *Journal of Personality and Social Psychology* 71 (6), 1062–1083.

Lau, I.C., Yeung, A.S., Jin, J. and Low, R. (1999) Toward a hierarchical, multidimensional English self-concept. *Journal of Educational Psychology* 91 (4), 747–755.

León, I. (2007) Teacher's self-esteem: The role of confirmation. In F.D. Rubio (ed.) *Self-Esteem and Foreign Language Learning* (pp. 192–205). Newcastle: Cambridge Scholars Publishing.

Lozanov, G. (1978) *Suggestology and Outlines of Suggestopedy*. New York: Gordon and Breach.

Luhtanen, R. and Crocker, J. (1992) A collective self-esteem scale: Self-evaluation of one's identity. *Personality and Social Psychology Bulletin* 18 (3), 302–318.

MacIntyre, P.D., Clément, R., Dörnyei, Z. and Noels, K.A. (1998) Conceptualizing willingness to communicate in a L2: A situational model of L2 confidence and affiliation. *The Modern Language Journal* 84 (2), 545–562.

Marsh, H.W. (1986) Verbal and math self-concepts: An internal/external frame of reference model. *American Educational Research Journal* 23 (1), 129–149.

Marsh, H.W. (1990) The structure of academic self-concept: The Marsh/Shavelson Model. *Journal of Educational Psychology* 82 (4), 623–636.

Marsh, H.W. and Shavelson, R.J. (1985) Self-concept: Its multifaceted hierarchical structure. *Educational Psychologist* 20 (3), 107–123.

McCroskey, J.C. and McCroskey, L.L. (1986) Correlates of willingness to communicate. Paper presented at the annual convention of the Western Speech Communication Association, Tucson, AZ.

McCroskey, J.C. and Richmond, V.P. (1990) Willingness to communicate: A cognitive view. *Journal of Social Behaviour and Personality* 5 (2), 19–37.

Mercer, S. (2008) Exploring EFL learner self-concept. Unpublished PhD Thesis, University of Lancaster.

Mercer, S. (2011) *Towards an Understanding of Language Learner Self-Concept*. Dordrecht: Springer.

Mruk, C.J. (1999) *Self-Esteem. Theory, Research and Practice* (2nd edn). New York: Springer.

Mruk, C.J. (2006) *Self-Esteem Research, Theory and Practice. Toward a Positive Psychology of Self-Esteem* (3rd edn). New York: Springer.

Murphey, T. (2006) *Language Hungry! An Introduction to Language Learning, Fun and Self-Esteem*. Rum: Helbling Languages.

Orth, U. (2010) Self-esteem development from adulthood to old age: A cohort-sequential longitudinal study. *Journal of Personality and Social Psychology* 4 (98), 645.

Reasoner, R. (1982) *Building Self-Esteem: A Comprehensive Program*. Palo Alto: Consulting Psychologists Press.

Reid, J. (1987) The learning style preferences of ESL students. *TESOL Quarterly* 21 (1), 87–111.

Richards, J.C. and Rodgers, T.S. (2001) *Approaches and Methods in Language Teaching*. Cambridge: Cambridge University Press.

Richmond, V.P. and McCroskey, J.C. (1989) *Communication Apprehension, Avoidance and Effectiveness*. Scottsdale: Gorsuch Scarisbrick Publishers.

Rinvolucri, M. (2002) *Humanising your Coursebook*. London: DELTA Publishing.

Rogers, C. (1961) *On Becoming a Person*. Boston: Houghton Mifflin.

Rosenberg, M. (1965) *Society and the Adolescent Self-Image*. Princeton: Princeton University Press.

Ronseberg, M. (1989) *Society and the Adolescent Self-Image. Revised edition*. Middletown: Wesleyan University Press.

Rubio, F.D. (2004) *La Ansiedad en el Aprendizaje de Idiomas*. Huelva: Universidad de Huelva.

Rubio, F.D. (2007) Self-esteem and foreign language learning: An introduction. In F.D. Rubio (ed.) *Self-Esteem and Foreign Language Learning* (pp. 2–12). Newcastle: Cambridge Scholars Publishing.

Schumann, J.H. (1994) Where is cognition? Emotion and cognition in second language acquisition. *Studies in Second Language Acquisition* 16, 231–242.

Schumann, J.H. (1997) *The Neurobiology of Affect in Language*. Malden: Blackwell Publishers.

Shavelson, R.J., Hubner, J.J. and Stanton, G.C. (1976) Self-concept: Validation of construct interpretations. *Review of Educational Research* 46 (3), 407–441.

Skaalvik, E.M. and Skaalvik, S. (2002) Internal and external frames of reference for academic self-concept. *Educational Psychologist* 37 (4), 233–244.

Soureshjani, K.H. and Naseri, N. (2011) An investigation into the relationship between self-esteem, proficiency level, and the reading ability of Iranian EFL language learners. *Journal of Language Teaching and Research* 2 (6), 1312–1319.

Stevick, E.W. (1980) *Teaching Languages: A Way and Ways*. Rowley: Newbury House.

Stevick, E.W. (1990) *Humanism in Language Teaching*. Oxford: Oxford University Press.

White, R. (1963) Ego and reality in psychoanalytic theory: A proposal regarding independent ego energies. *Psychological Issues* 3, 125–150.

Yeung, A.S. and Wong, E.K. (2004) Domain specificity of trilingual teachers' verbal self-concepts. *Journal of Educational Psychology* 96 (2), 360–360.

5 Identity and Poststructuralist Theory in SLA

Bonny Norton

Introduction

As communities across the globe confront the challenges and possibilities of multilingualism, and look to research and theory to inform language learning and teaching, there has been an increasing interest in identity, particularly with reference to poststructuralist theory. In this chapter, I present the argument that poststructuralist theory has brought great insight into debates on identity and language learning, both inside and outside the classroom. My arguments will be made with the help of three vignettes, drawn from my published research in the international community. I will begin with a vignette of a language learner outside the classroom and draw on this vignette to outline central arguments with respect to the relevance of identity and poststructuralist theory in second language acquisition (SLA). I will then turn to the other two vignettes to illustrate how poststructuralist theory can address issues of identity in classroom practice.

The first vignette takes place in a Canadian restaurant in which Martina, a mature English language learner from the former Czechoslovakia, was struggling for recognition and respect from her Canadian co-workers, who were all younger than she was.

Martina had immigrated to Canada for a better life for her three children. Partly because she was not a proficient speaker of English, she struggled

> **Vignette #1: Martina in the workplace**
>
> In restaurant was working a lot of children but the children always thought that I am – I don't know – maybe some broom or something. They always said 'Go and clean the living room', and I was washing the dishes and they didn't do nothing. They talked to each other and they

thought that I had to do everything. And I said 'No.' The girl is only 12 years old. She is younger than my son. I said 'No, you are doing nothing. You can go and clean the tables or something'.

(Interview with Martina, Norton, 2000: 99)

to find work in her profession as a quantity surveyor, and was employed in a fast food restaurant in the greater Toronto area. Her co-workers, as well as the manager's children (who frequently visited the restaurant), were all born in Canada, and spoke English fluently. Martina communicates in this extract that engaging in social interaction with her co-workers was a struggle, primarily because she was positioned as a dehumanized and inanimate 'broom'. To resist these marginalizing practices, Martina reframed her relationship with her co-workers as a domestic one rather than a professional one, and from the identity position 'mother', rather than 'immigrant', or 'broom', she claimed the right to speak.

While this data extract has been discussed more fully in other publications (Norton, 2000; Norton Peirce, 1995), the vignette is a sobering reminder of the powerful relationship between language and identity, which is of central concern to many scholars in the field of language education and SLA. Indeed, over the past 15 years, there has been an explosion of interest in identity and language learning, and 'identity' now features in most encyclopaedias and handbooks of language learning and teaching (McKinney & Norton, 2008; Morgan & Clarke, 2011; Norton, 2010; Norton & Toohey, 2002; Ricento, 2005). In the broader field of applied linguistics, interest in identity has also gained considerable momentum. There is work, for example, on identity and pragmatics (Lo & Reyes, 2004; Spencer-Oatey & Franklin, 2009), identity and sociolinguistics (Edwards, 2009; Joseph, 2004; Omoniyi & White, 2007), identity and discourse (Benwell & Stokoe, 2006; Wodak et al., 2009; Young, 2009), and identity and foreign language learning (see e.g. Kanno, 2003, 2008; Kinginger, 2004; Kramsch, 2009; Pavlenko, 2003).

This chapter will focus on the work I have done with respect to identity and poststructuralist theory in SLA (Norton, 1997, 2000, 2001; Norton & Morgan, 2013; Norton Peirce, 1995). In reviews of the literature, many scholars have found this work helpful in reframing debates on identity (see Block, 2007a, 2007b; De Costa, 2010; Menard-Warwick, 2005; Morgan & Clarke, 2011; Ricento, 2005; Swain & Deters, 2007; Zuengler & Miller, 2006) and, as Block (2007a: 864) notes, a poststructuralist approach to identity 'has become the approach of choice among those who seek to explore links between identity and second language (L2) learning'. Poststructuralist theory has led me to define identity as multiple, changing, and a site of struggle, frequently negotiated in the context of inequitable relations of power. Identity signals the way a person understands her or his relationship to the world, how that relationship is constructed across time and space, and how the person understands possibilities for the future. It is the importance of the future that is central to the lives of many language learners, and is integral to an understanding of the sociological construct of investment that I have developed as a complement to the psychological construct of motivation in SLA.

Central Arguments for Identity and Poststructuralist Theory in SLA

In 1998, the sociolinguist, Susan Gass, made the important argument that the theoretical relevance of identity to second language learning needed to be established. The points below summarize the claims made by identity and language learning researchers, with illustrative reference to Martina's vignette above.

(i) Contemporary theories of identity offer ways to see the individual language learner situated in a larger social world. While some previous SLA research defined learners in binary terms (such as motivated or unmotivated, introverted or extroverted, inhibited or uninhibited), identity theorists see these affective descriptors as constructed in frequently inequitable relations of power, as variable over time and space, and sometimes co-existing in contradictory ways within a single individual. As illustrated in the data from Martina, identity is theorized as multiple, changing, and a site of struggle between her various identities of worker, immigrant, 'broom', and mother.

(ii) Identity theorists highlight the diverse positions from which language learners are able to participate in social life, and demonstrate how learners can, and sometimes cannot, appropriate more desirable identities with respect to the target language community. As Martina found, while some identity positions may limit and constrain opportunities for learners to listen, speak, read, or write (particularly under conditions of marginalization), other identity positions (such as 'mother') may offer enhanced sets of possibilities for social interaction and human agency, i.e. the possibility to take action in social settings.

(iii) Language learning theory and research needs to address how power in the social world affects learners' access to the target language community, and thus, to opportunities to practise listening, speaking, reading, and writing, widely acknowledged as central to the SLA process. Identity theorists are therefore concerned about the ways in which power is distributed in both formal and informal sites of language learning, as it was for Martina, and how it affects learners' opportunities to negotiate relationships with target language speakers.

(iv) Identity and the social/cultural practices we engage in (e.g. working, sharing meals, exercising, travelling) are inextricably linked to resources that are available. At the same time, these practices also serve to construct our identities. The variable practices and resources of specific settings, and an individual's access to them (as Martina found), relate powerfully to the ways in which identities of individuals are constructed. Martina was sent away to 'clean the living room'; she had to 'do everything'. Examination of practices, resources, and identities in relation to language learning offers promise for improving and enhancing learning contexts.

(v) Second language learning is not entirely determined by social conditions and contexts, partly because these conditions and contexts, themselves, are always in a process of change. In addition, language learners who struggle to speak from one identity position, as Martina did, may be able to reframe their relationship with their interlocutors, thereby changing their access to the practices and resources available within the context, and claim alternative identities from which to speak, listen, read, or write. If learners are successful in their bids for more powerful identities, their language acquisition may be enhanced.

(vi) The sociological construct of investment, explained below, complements the psychological construct of motivation in SLA. In past research (Norton, 2000; Norton, 2012, Norton Peirce, 1995) I have been concerned that most psychological theories of language learner motivation did not do justice to the complex identities of language learners, and the often inequitable relations of power they negotiate in different sites. The construct of investment seeks to make a meaningful connection between a learner's desire and commitment to learn a language, and the language practices of the classroom or community. Although Martina was a highly motivated language learner, she was not invested in the language practices of her workplace, where she experienced discriminatory practices. Such theorizing has helped to shift contemporary debates on motivation in the field of SLA (see Dörnyei & Ushioda, 2009; Ushioda, Chapter 9, this volume).

(vii) The theoretical constructs, imagined communities and imagined identities, contribute usefully to understanding SLA, because a learner's concerns for the future (or the future of the learner's children) are integral to language learner identity (see Ryan & Irie, Chapter 8, this volume). For many learners, the target language community is not only a reconstruction of past communities and historically constituted relationships, but also a community of the imagination, a desired community that offers possibilities for an enhanced range of identity options in the future. As I have argued in previous research, an imagined community assumes an imagined identity, and a learner's investment in the target language can be understood within this context.

Poststructuralist Theories of Language, Subjectivity and Positioning

Not only poststructuralist theories of language, but also of subjectivity and positioning, inform recent work on identity and language learning. These three areas will be discussed in greater detail below.

Poststructuralist theories of language

Poststructuralist theories of language have become increasingly attractive to researchers investigating identity and language learning (Norton & Morgan, 2013). Structuralist theories of language, often cited as originating with the work of the Swiss linguist, Ferdinand de Saussure (1966), emphasized the study of the linguistic knowledge (competence) that allowed idealized speakers/hearers to use and understand a language's stable patterns and structures. From this perspective, actual instances of language usage (performance), which could be affected by memory lapses, fatigue, slips, errors, and so on, were not seen as revealing of idealized patterns, and thus were of little interest in the scientific study of language. However, poststructuralist theories of language, proposed by many, but particularly by the Russian literary theorist Mikhail Bakhtin (1981, 1984, 1986), saw language not as a set of idealized forms independent of their speakers or their speaking, but rather as situated utterances in which speakers, in dialogue with others, struggle to create meanings.

For Bakhtin, language had no independent existence outside of its use, and that usage was social. He used the metaphor of speech communication being a 'chain', an ongoing conversation that new speakers (e.g. children or newcomers to speech communities) strive to join. While structural theories might see language learning as a gradual individual process of internalizing a set of rules, structures, and vocabulary of a standard language, Bakhtin saw language learning as a process of struggling to use language to participate in specific speech communities. Using language meant using a tool others had used before, and Bakhtin saw speakers as constrained by those past usages. However, he also saw speakers as able to use language to express their own meanings.

The work of the French sociologist, Pierre Bourdieu, directly addresses the poststructuralist study of the politics of language (see Albright & Luke, 2008; Bourdieu, 1977, 1991; Bourdieu & Passeron, 1977). While poststructuralists are not the only theorists interested in language and power, Bourdieu explicitly drew attention to the importance of power in structuring discourse, with interlocutors seldom sharing equal speaking 'rights'. For Bourdieu, 'legitimate' and 'illegitimate' speakers were distinguished by their differential 'rights to speech' or their 'power to impose reception' (Bourdieu,

1977: 648). In other words, a group of workers might listen more carefully to a talk given by the senior director of a company, than they would to a talk given by a junior member of the human resources department. For Bourdieu, using language was a social and political practice in which an utterance's value and meaning was determined in part by the value ascribed to the person who speaks. Recognizing that the value ascribed to a person or group can vary depending on circumstances or contexts (in Bourdieu's terms, 'fields'), he saw linguistic discourse as 'a symbolic asset which can receive different values depending on the market on which it is offered' (Bourdieu, 1977: 651). He further noted that dominant usage is associated with the dominant class. Heller (2008: 50) explicitly paralleled access to language with access to other resources. These might include friendship networks, educational activities, work opportunities, and so forth. From this perspective, the ascribed identities of both individuals and groups affect access to and opportunities for language use and learning.

Poststructuralist theories of subjectivity

Christine Weedon (1987/1997), one of the most well-known scholars working in the feminist poststructuralist tradition, argued that it is through language that the individual constructs her 'subjectivity', which she saw as 'the conscious and unconscious thoughts and emotions of the individual, her sense of herself, and her ways of understanding her relation to the world' (Weedon, 1997: 28). Her use of the term subjectivity reminds us that an individual can be simultaneously the subject *of* a set of relationships (e.g. in a position of power) or subject *to* a set of relationships (e.g. in a position of reduced power). In poststructuralist theory, subjectivity and language are seen as mutually constitutive, and are thus centrally important in how a language learner negotiates a sense of self within and across a range of sites at different points in time. It is through language that a learner gains access to, or is denied access to, powerful social networks that give learners the opportunity to speak.

Weedon used the terms subject and subjectivity to signal a break with dominant Western humanist views of the individual. While Western humanist philosophy stressed the essential, unique, fixed, and coherent *core* of an individual, Weedon's view, like that of other poststructuralists, was that the individual (i.e. the subject) was diverse, contradictory, dynamic, and changing over historical time and social space. Like Foucault (1980), Weedon argued that subjectivity is discursively constructed, and is always socially and historically embedded. Holland and Lave (2001) discuss the apparent paradox of identity being experienced as unitary and durable, while being, at the same time, variable and situated in dynamic practice. Like many other poststructuralist theorists, they emphasized that 'both the continuity and the transformation of social life are ongoing, uncertain projects' (Holland & Lave,

2001: 4) and that individuals maintain 'histories in their persons'. These theories of identity are central in my early work, and have been taken up by many identity theorists, including Kramsch (2009) whose compelling book, *The Multilingual Subject*, focuses on the subjectivity of the foreign language learner.

Language educators have found poststructural observations about subjectivity helpful in theorizing how education can lead to individual and social change. A conceptualization of subjectivity as multiple, non-unitary, and dynamic leaves room for the view that individuals need not be locked forever in particular positions. Rather, from this perspective, although some contexts and practices may limit or constrain opportunities for learners to listen, speak, read, or write, other contexts and practices may offer enhanced sets of possibilities for social interaction and human agency. Thus, pedagogical practices have the potential to be transformative in offering language learners more powerful positions than those they may occupy either inside or outside the classroom. For example, teaching students to use cameras and adopt the identity 'photographer' might offer learners enhanced possibilities for engaging with members of their community from a position of strength (Kendrick & Jones, 2008).

Postcolonial theorists, such as Stuart Hall (1992, 1997) and Homi Bhabha (1994), used poststructuralist identity theory to analyse how categories such as race and gender have been essentialized and understood in simplistic ways. In theorizing cultural identity, Hall focused on identity as changing and in process, 'becoming', and stresses that identity is 'not an essence, but a positioning' (Hall, 1997: 226) in particular historical and cultural environments. This means of theorizing difference has not been entirely satisfactory to those who would assert that their identities are homogenous and unitary, foregrounding a particular aspect of their experience such as gender, race or religious affiliation. Current worldwide expressions of nationalism and religious fundamentalism testify to this. Such unitary assertions of identity are often explained as strategic essentialism in service of political goals (see Spivak in Fuss, 1989; Yon, 1999). The terms identity politics or the politics of difference reference this particular coalescence of identity and power relations.

Poststructuralist theories of positioning

Bakhtin (1981) was particularly interested in how position or status was signalled in language in works of fiction, and in conversation in general. Many identity and language learning researchers and theorists also stress the importance of considering how contexts shape positioning among particular interlocutors. While positioning has been discussed by many poststructuralist theorists (Foucault, 1980; Hall, 1997; Henriques *et al.*, 1984; Weedon, 1987/1997), it was Davies and Harré (1990: 7) who explicitly used position as 'the central organising concept for analysing how it is that people do being a person'. They and other poststructuralist theorists have reminded us that identities are contingent, shifting, and context-dependent, and that while identities or positions are often given by social structures or ascribed by others, they can also be negotiated by agents who wish to position themselves. As Davies and Harré (1990: 7) put it, 'discursive practices constitute the speakers and hearers in certain ways and yet at the same time are a resource through which speakers and hearers can negotiate new positions'.

Recognition of the apparent paradox of positioning, reflecting the socially given and the individually struggled for, has been important in many studies of language learning. Menard-Warwick (2007), for example, identified particular positioning speech acts of both a vocational English language class teacher and her Latina students, such that learners were enabled or constrained to claim voice in the classroom. Noting that while vocational teachers often aim at empowering their students, Menard-Warwick observed that customary classroom materials and activities, as well as powerful societal discourses, often constrain students' possibilities for claiming desirable identities. She pointed out that teachers should be alert to how students position themselves in classroom discourse and to approach language instruction from a critical perspective to enable learners to name, and perhaps struggle against, some of the disempowering tendencies of the linguistic practices of their new cultures.

Poststructuralist Theory, SLA and Classroom Teaching

Poststructuralist theories of identity help us make sense of debates on what it means to be a 'good teacher' or a 'good learner' in classroom settings. By way of illustration, I now turn to two vignettes from classroom practice (vignettes #2 and 3), in South Africa and Canada, respectively, to demonstrate how poststructuralist theory has enabled me to better understand the findings of my research and their implications for pedagogy (Norton, 2000; Norton Peirce & Stein, 1995). While each of these vignettes took place at different times and in different places, what they have in common are struggles over language, identity, and power – themes of central interest to poststructuralist theory, with direct relevance to language learning and teaching (Norton & Morgan, 2013).

Vignette #2: Identity and the construction of textual meaning

This vignette, reported in the *Harvard Educational Review* (Norton Peirce & Stein, 1995), describes an incident in which African English language learners in apartheid South Africa debated the meaning of a reading text that was being piloted for use in a high-stakes English admission test developed by the University of the Witwatersrand (Wits) in Johannesburg. The passage drew on a newspaper article about monkeys that were shot by police after having taken fruit from the trees of homeowners in the coastal city of Durban. After completing the test without incident, the students had the opportunity to discuss their response to the passage. Pippa Stein, a professor from Wits, of European descent, who piloted the test, concluded her assessment of the discussion as follows:

> The atmosphere in the classroom became more and more charged as the students became increasingly interested in debating the moral issues raised in this text: Who owns the land? Why should the monkeys go hungry? Which parties have the right to the fruit? Why not seek nonviolent solutions to the problem? Most of the students entering the discussion read the monkeys passage as an example of racist discourse and appeared to identify with the plight of the dispossessed monkeys ... My assumptions about the meanings of a text were seriously challenged. Where does the meaning of a text lie? Is this text about monkeys or is it about the dispossessed? What discursive histories did each individual student bring to bear on that text in that particular place at that particular moment?

This classroom vignette raises important issues about the relationship between language, learning, and identity in the South African context. It is intriguing to observe that when the students were taking the reading test administered by Stein, they assumed the identity 'test taker', and performed as required by the dictates of the testing genre. In other words, the students were silent; they worked alone; they observed time limits; and they made little attempt to challenge the test maker's interpretation of the text. The students were relatively powerless participants who desired entry into university, but had experienced a history of apartheid, and struggled linguistically and economically. Stein, in contrast, was in a position of power relative to the students: She was from a prestigious university, a native speaker of the dominant language English, and a member of a racially and economically powerful group. She was the 'knower'. In the context of this social occasion, the contrasting identities of students and teacher, and the differentials of power, the meaning of the reading passage was stable and unitary.

Significantly, however, during the subsequent discussion, when Stein sat on the desk, inviting comment and critique, the relationship between Stein and the students changed dramatically. Stein was no longer the controller of knowledge and power, and her identity shifted from 'knower' to 'learner'. The students were no longer powerless test takers, but informed community members. While some students still took the position that the text was a simple story about monkeys that attacked people, many students positioned the text as a metaphor for inequitable social relations between blacks and whites in South Africa. Thus, while the same reading passage was read by the same students on the same day, the characteristics of the solitary test event, on the one hand, and the open communal discussion, on the other, led to contested readings of the monkeys passage. The incident demonstrates convincingly that the meaning of a text is not stable, but is re-negotiated in the context of different social occasions, shifting identities, and changing relations of power.

A structuralist conception of language, which conceives of meaning as stable and predictable, would not be able to account for the range of meanings associated with the monkeys passage in this classroom vignette. Poststructuralists such as Gunther Kress explore in persuasive terms how meanings become destabilized in the context of different social occasions. As he notes:

> Language always happens as text; and as text, it inevitably occurs in a particular generic form. That generic form arises out of the action of social subjects in particular social situations. (Kress, 1993: 27)

In theorizing language as 'text' (either spoken or written) within the context of a particular 'genre', Kress highlights the fact that language is not a neutral medium of communication, but takes on different meanings when the relationship between speakers change, together with shifts in relations of power.

> A social theory of genre will need to be closely attentive to the constantly shifting relations between the language in the spoken and in the written mode, and its relations to shifts in power. (Kress, 1993: 37)

Michel Foucault (1980), in particular, helps us to understand not only the relationship between knowledge and power, but also the subtle ways in which power operates in society. What he calls the 'capillaries of power' operate in subtle and often invisible ways. Foucault makes the case that power frequently naturalizes events and practices in ways that come to be seen as 'normal' to members of a community. As Pennycook notes:

> Foucault brings a constant scepticism towards cherished concepts and modes of thought. Taken-for-granted categories such as man, woman, class, race, ethnicity, nation, identity, awareness, emancipation, language or power must be understood as contingent, shifting and produced in the particular, rather than having some prior ontological status. (Pennycook, 2007: 39)

In the case of the monkeys passage, the newspaper reporter who wrote the story takes for granted that the rights of the powerless are secondary to the rights of the powerful, and uses language in such a way that obscures the manner in which the powerful abuse power. For example, the author positions the actions of the monkeys who were defending a trapped mother and baby as violent and extreme through words such as 'rampage', 'attacking', and 'hurled'. Later, the writer does not use the active voice to state that the police 'killed' the monkeys. Instead the writer uses the agentless passive voice to indicate that the monkeys were 'shot dead'. In the resistant reading of the text, during the class discussion, it is precisely such sets of meaning that were called into question.

The pedagogical implications of this vignette are profound. Not only does it raise questions about the construct of 'reading' that is assumed in many reading tests, but it challenges teachers to consider the conditions under which multiple readings of a text emerge, how learner identities are implicated in the construction of meaning, and how these insights might be harnessed to enhance language learning and teaching.

Vignette #3: Identity and classroom resistance

The third vignette, drawn from Norton (2000: 143), describes the experience of a young adult immigrant woman in Toronto, Canada, who grew increasingly unhappy with her English language class, and eventually withdrew from the course. As the student, pseudonymously called Mai, noted:

> I was hoping that the course would help me the same as we learnt [in the 6-month ESL course], but some night we only spend time on one man. He came from Europe. He talked about his country: what's happening and what was happening. And all the time we didn't learn at all. And tomorrow the other Indian man speak something for there. Maybe all week I didn't write any more on my book.

While the South African classroom vignette illustrates how poststructuralist theory can illuminate how unstable the construction of meaning is, the Canadian vignette illustrates how the poststructuralist construct of 'investment', which I have developed in my work (Norton, 2000; Norton, 2012; Norton Peirce, 1995) may be helpful in understanding the relationship between motivation and resistance. The construct of investment signals the complex relationship between language learner identity and language learning commitment. If learners 'invest' in learning a language, they do so with the understanding that their social and economic gains will enhance the range of identities they can claim in a particular community. Unlike more traditional notions of motivation, which often conceive of the language learner as having a unitary, fixed, and ahistorical 'personality', the construct of investment conceives of the language learner as having a complex identity, changing across time and space, and reproduced in frequently inequitable relations of power.

The construct of investment, which is beginning to have an impact on psychological constructs of language learning (see Dörnyei & Ushioda, 2009), provides for a wider range of questions for the committed language teacher. In addressing practices of resistance in the language classroom, for example, the teacher could ask not only, 'Are the students motivated to learn this language?' but also 'Are the students invested in the language practices of my classroom?' A student can be highly motivated, but if the language practices of the classroom make a learner unhappy or dissatisfied, the learner may resist participation in classroom activities, or become increasingly disruptive. Resistance can arise from practices that may, for example, be racist, sexist, or elitist. Alternatively, there could be a discrepancy between a learner's expectations of 'good teaching' and the pedagogical practices of the teacher.

At the time that Mai was taking her English class in the greater Toronto area, I met with her on a regular basis. I knew her to be highly motivated and dedicated. She worked all day in a factory, and would take public transportation to her class in the cold and dark Ontario winter evenings. Despite the challenges she faced, Mai was eager to learn English, and made many sacrifices to increase opportunities to learn the language. Over time, however, Mai grew dissatisfied with her English class. Although highly motivated, she was not invested in the language practices of the classroom.

Although limited, the data discussed provide a number of clues as to why Mai was not invested in the language practices of her English classroom. Discussed in greater detail elsewhere (Norton, 2000), I wish to focus on one important issue: the teacher's construction of student identity. Canada has often prided itself on being a multicultural country, and in this spirit, it could be argued that the teacher was attempting to validate the multicultural composition of the class by asking students to discuss events in their home countries. At the same time, however, it could be argued that the teacher had a unitary, essentialized notion of identity, focusing only on the students' cultural identities, and ignoring other identities such as gender, race, age, and class. As poststructuralists would argue, identities are complex, multiple, and changing across both time and space. Such multiplicity was not acknowledged by this possibly well-meaning teacher.

Further, while Mai was struggling with daily challenges, and was anxious about the future, the teacher focused on students' past experiences in their home countries, which bore little relationship to the complex identities the students were negotiating in their new country, and the identities they were hoping to construct in the future. An emerging body of research on language learning, imagined identities, and imagined communities (e.g.

Kanno & Norton, 2003; Norton, 2001; Pavlenko & Norton, 2007, Ryan & Irie, Chapter 8, this volume) suggests that learners' hopes and desires for the future have a significant impact on their investment in language practices in classrooms and communities. In such a context, it would be very practical for Mai's teacher to ask: 'Do the language practices of my classroom address Mai's daily challenges and her anxiety about the future?'

Promoting student investment in the language practices of classrooms does not mean that the teacher abdicates power. The teacher has an important responsibility to ensure that the activities in which students engage are meaningful to students and pedagogically rigorous. At first glance, it might appear that Mai's teacher was engaging in collaborative power sharing with her students. However, at least for Mai, the classroom activities were neither meaningful nor pedagogically sound.

Conclusion

In this chapter, I have argued that poststructuralist theory can help teachers, administrators, and policy makers make more informed decisions about classroom practice. Whether administrators are debating the importance of accent in the language classroom, whether teachers are discussing the meaning of a text, or whether students are resisting essentializing pedagogical practices, it is clear that language learning is a social practice in which experiences are organized and identities negotiated. The research discussed in this chapter suggests that language teaching is most effective when the teacher recognizes the multiple identities of students in the class, and develops pedagogical practices that enhance students' investment in the language practices of the classroom. It follows that teachers, administrators, and policy makers need to better understand the language practices of classrooms, and how learners negotiate and sometimes resist the practices made available to them. Further, administrators and policy makers need to be supportive of language teachers as they seek to be more effective in linguistically diverse classrooms. A poststructuralist understanding of identity and SLA has great relevance to educators committed to educational and social change.

Recommended reading

Kramsch, C. (2009) *The Multilingual Subject*. Oxford: Oxford University Press.

With reference to a wide variety of data from young adult foreign language learners in institutional settings, Kramsch draws on poststructuralist theory to investigate the relationship between language learning and memory, emotion, and imagination. She makes a convincing case that identity, language, and learning must be understood with reference to symbolic relations of power and possibility.

Norton, B. (2013) *Identity and Language Learning: Extending the Conversation* (2nd edn). Bristol: Multilingual Matters.

The second edition of this classic text includes a comprehensive Introduction updating the literature on identity, investment and imagined communities. The Afterword by Claire Kramsch is compelling.

Norton, B. and Toohey, K. (2011) Identity, language learning, and social change. *Language Teaching* 44 (4), 412–446.

This is a comprehensive, state-of-the-art review article on identity, language learning, and social change. Norton and Toohey draw on a wide range of contemporary research to argue that poststructuralist theories of language, identity, and power offer new and important perspectives on language learning and teaching.

Note

(1) This chapter draws extensively on Norton (2000) and articles published in *Issues in Applied Linguistics* (Norton, 2011) and *Language Teaching* (Norton & Toohey, 2011)

References

Albright, J. and Luke, A. (2008) *Pierre Bourdieu and Literacy Education*. Mahwah: Lawrence Erlbaum.
Bakhtin, M. (1981) *The Dialogic Imagination: Four Essays by M.M. Bakhtin*. Austin: University of Texas Press.
Bakhtin, M. (1984) *Problems of Dostoevsky's Poetics*. Translated by C. Emerson. Minneapolis: University of Minnesota Press.
Bakhtin, M. (1986) *Speech Genres and Other Late Essays*. Translated by V. McGee. Austin: University of Texas Press.
Benwell, B. and Stokoe, L. (2006) *Discourse and Identity*. Edinburgh: Edinburgh University Press.
Bhabha, H.K. (1994) *The Location of Culture*. London and New York: Routledge.
Block, D. (2007a) The rise of identity in SLA research, post Firth and Wagner (1997). *The Modern Language Journal* 91 (5), 863–876.
Block, D. (2007b) *Second Language Identities*. London: Continuum.
Bourdieu, P. (1977) The economics of linguistic exchanges. *Social Science Information* 16 (6), 645–668.
Bourdieu, P. (1991) *Language and Symbolic Power* (J.B. Thompson, ed.; G. Raymond & M. Adamson, trans.). Cambridge: Polity Press. (Original work published in 1982).
Bourdieu, P. and Passeron, J. (1977) *Reproduction in Education, Society, and Culture*. London/Beverly Hills: Sage Publications.
Davies, B. and Harré, R. (1990) Positioning: The discursive production of selves. *Journal for the Theory of Social Behaviour* 20 (1), 43–63.
De Costa, P. (2010) Let's collaborate: Using developments in global English research to advance socioculturally-oriented SLA identity work. *Issues in Applied Linguistics* 18 (1), 99–124.

Dörnyei, Z. and Ushioda, E. (eds) (2009) *Motivation, Language Identity and the L2 Self*. Bristol: Multilingual Matters.
Edwards, J. (2009) *Language and Identity*. Cambridge: Cambridge University Press.
Foucault, M. (1980) *Power/Knowledge: Selected Interviews and Other Writings, 1972–1977* (C. Gordon, trans.). New York: Pantheon books.
Fuss, D. (1989) *Essentially Speaking: Feminism, Nature and Difference*. New York and London: Routledge.
Gass, S. (1998) Apples and oranges: Or why apples are not orange and don't need to be. A response to Firth and Wagner. *The Modern Language Journal* 82, 83–90.
Hall, S. (1992) New ethnicities. In J. Donald and A. Rattansi (eds) *'Race', Culture and Difference* (pp. 252–259). London: Sage Publications.
Hall, S. (1997) *Representation: Cultural Representations and Signifying Practices*. London: SAGE Publications.
Heller, M. (2008) Bourdieu and 'literacy education'. In J. Albright and A. Luke (eds) *Pierre Bourdieu and Literacy Education* (pp. 50–67). New York: Routledge.
Henriques, J., Holloway, W., Urwin, C., Venn, C. and Walkerdine, V. (1984) *Changing the Subject: Psychology, Social Regulation and Subjectivity*. London: Routledge.
Holland, D. and Lave, J. (eds) (2001) *History in Person: Enduring Struggles, Contentious Practice, Intimate Identities*. Santa Fr, NM: School of American Research Press.
Joseph, J. (2004) *Language and Identity*. London: Palgrave.
Kanno, Y. (2003) *Negotiating Bilingual and Bicultural Identities: Japanese Returnees Betwixt Two Worlds*. Mahwah: Lawrence Erlbaum Associates.
Kanno, Y. (2008) *Language and Education in Japan: Unequal Access to Bilingualism*. Basingstoke: Palgrave Macmillan.
Kanno, Y. and Norton, B. (eds) (2003) Imagined communities and educational possibilities. *Journal of Language, Identity, and Education* 2 (4) (special issue).
Kendrick, M. and Jones, S. (2008) Girls' visual representations of literacy in a rural Ugandan community. *Canadian Journal of Education* 31 (3), 372–404.
Kinginger, C. (2004) Alice doesn't live here anymore: Foreign language learning and identity construction. In A. Pavlenko and A. Blackledge (eds) *Negotiation of Identities in Multilingual Contexts* (pp. 219–142). Clevedon: Multilingual Matters.
Kramsch, C. (2009) *The Multilingual Subject*. Oxford: Oxford University Press.
Kress, G. (1993) Genre as social process. In B. Cope and M. Kalantzis (eds) *The Powers of Literacy* (pp. 22–37). London: Falmer Press.
Lo, A. and Reyes, A. (eds) (2004) Language, identity and relationality in Asian Pacific America. *Pragmatics* 14 (2/3) (special issue).
McKinney, C. and Norton, B. (2008) Identity in language and literacy education. In B. Spolsky and F. Hult (eds) *The Handbook of Educational Linguistics* (pp. 192–205). Malden: Blackwell.
Menard-Warwick, J. (2005) Both a fiction and an existential fact: Theorizing identity in second language acquisition and literacy studies. *Linguistics and Education* 16 (3), 253–274.
Menard-Warwick, J. (2007) 'Because she made beds. Every day.' Social positioning, classroom discourse and language learning. *Applied Linguistics* 29 (2), 267–289.
Morgan, B. and Clarke. M. (2011) Identity in second language teaching and learning. In E. Hinkel (ed.) *Handbook of Research in Second Language Teaching and Learning* (2nd edn) (pp. 817–836). New York: Routledge.
Norton, B. (ed.) (1997) Language and identity. *TESOL Quarterly* 31 (3) (special issue).
Norton, B. (2000) *Identity and Language Learning: Gender, Ethnicity and Educational Change*. Harlow: Pearson Education/Longman.
Norton, B. (2001) Non-participation, imagined communities, and the language classroom. In M. Breen (ed.) *Learner Contributions to Language Learning: New Directions in Research* (pp. 159–171). London: Pearson Education Limited.

Norton, B. (2010) Language and identity. In N. Hornberger and S. McKay (eds) *Sociolinguistics and Language Education* (pp. 349–369). Bristol: Multilingual Matters.

Norton, B. (2011) The practice of theory in the language classroom. *Issues in Applied Linguistics* 18 (2), 171–80

Norton, B. (2012) Investment. In P. Robinson (ed.) *Routledge Encyclopaedia of Second Language Acquisition* (pp. 343–344). New York: Routledge.

Norton, B. and Morgan, B. (2013) Poststructuralism. In C. Chapelle (ed.) *Encyclopedia of Applied Linguistics*. Wiley-Blackwell.

Norton, B. and Toohey, K. (2002) Identity and language learning. In R.B. Kaplan (ed.) *The Oxford Handbook of Applied Linguistics* (pp. 115–123). New York: Oxford University Press.

Norton, B. and Toohey, K. (2011) Identity, language learning, and social change. *Language Teaching* 44 (4), 412–446.

Norton Peirce, B. (1995) Social identity, investment, and language learning. *TESOL Quarterly* 29 (1), 9–31.

Norton Peirce, B. and Stein, P. (1995) Why the 'Monkeys Passage' bombed: Tests, genres, and teaching. *Harvard Educational Review* 65 (1), 50–65.

Omoniyi, T. and White, G. (2007) *The Sociolinguistics of Identity*. London: Continuum.

Pavlenko, A. (2003) 'I never knew I was bilingual': Reimagining teacher identities in TESOL. *Journal of Language, Identity, and Education* 2 (4), 251–268.

Pavlenko, A. and Norton, B. (2007) Imagined communities, identity, and English language teaching. In J. Cummins and C. Davison (eds) *International Handbook of English Language Teaching* (pp. 669–680). New York: Springer.

Pennycook, A. (2007) *Global Englishes and Transcultural Flows*. London and New York: Routledge.

Ricento, T. (2005) Considerations of identity in L2 learning. In E. Hinkel (ed.) *Handbook of Research on Second Language Teaching and Learning* (pp. 895–911). Mahwah: Lawrence Erlbaum Associates.

Saussure, F. de (1966) *Course in General Linguistics*. (W. Baskin, trans. [1916]). New York: McGraw-Hill.

Spencer-Oatey, H. and Franklin, P. (2009) *Intercultural Interaction: A Multidisciplinary Approach to Intercultural Communication*. New York: Palgrave Macmillan

Swain, M. and Deters, P. (2007) 'New' mainstream SLA theory: Expanded and enriched. *The Modern Language Journal* 91, 820–836.

Weedon, C. (1987/1997) *Feminist Practice and Poststructuralist Theory* (2nd edn). London: Blackwell.

Wodak, R., de Cillia, R., Reisigl, M. and Liebhart, K. (2009) *The Discursive Construction of National Identity*. Edinburgh: Edinburgh University Press.

Yon, D.A. (1999) Interview with Stuart Hall, London, England August 1998. *Journal of Curriculum Theorising* 15 (4), 89–99.

Young, R. (2009) *Discursive Practice in Language Learning and Teaching*. Malden: Wiley-Blackwell.

Zuengler, J. and Miller, E. (2006) Cognitive and sociocultural perspectives: Two parallel SLA worlds? *TESOL Quarterly* 40 (1), 35–58.

6 Dual Identities Perceived by Bilinguals

Chantal Hemmi

Introduction

Recent perspectives on the notion of self have tended to view learners' selves in relation to how they interact with and position themselves within society. Such a perspective is used in this chapter in exploring the identities of bilinguals. I will first discuss what identity is and examine the concept from a number of different viewpoints. I will then consider the relevance of these perspectives in understanding the identities of bilingual people. In the second part of the chapter, I present a part of a small-scale study that consists of six case studies of bilingual Japanese women, in which I examined how these women perceived their identities and their sense of belonging in society in Japan.

Different Views of Identity

In this section, I will examine identity focusing on three different aspects: a postmodernist perspective on identity, a sociocultural perspective on identity, and finally, the role of power in shaping identities. I shall then discuss current research on the identity of bilinguals in SLA.

Postmodernist views on identity

In the last decade, the notion of identity has become important when considering issues related to education, especially in the globalised and diverse world that we live in. In attempting to define identity, it is helpful to draw on postmodernist views of reality in connection to the self. Postmodernism is largely a reaction to the assumed certainty of science to explain reality, and it requires us to 'abandon all established and preconceived values and theories' (Vidich & Lyman, 2000). In essence, it is based on the assumption that reality is not absolute but is personally constructed, as the mind tries to understand its own personal reality. Postmodernism presupposes that there is no absolute truth and the way people see the world is subjective.

A postmodernist view of identity focuses on the different identities a person has within a complex world, as people's identities cannot be defined solely by a particular role that they play in society and every individual can play more than one role in the communities that they belong to. For example, an English teacher could also be a researcher at the same time, as well as being a carer at home. Wenger (1998) argues that we all need to view ourselves in relation to each other and see ourselves as situated within different communities in order to construe who we are. Such an understanding is useful when considering bilinguals who regularly switch between two different contexts depending on which language and associated social norms are being used.

However, the self can also be viewed as an individual separate from social context. Hayes (1998) explains the historical growth of the notion of the self as an individual, which:

> ... first began to emerge with the work of the 17th-century philosophers, Decartes, Lock and Hume and became increasingly popular as European society moved out of mediaeval feudalism and into merchant based economies and ultimately capitalism. Gradually the concept of the individual rather than the community became dominant in society, and the idea of the 'self' continued to develop, until now it is regarded by people in Western societies as self-evident. (Hayes, 1998: 334)

Although it is difficult to consider the individual devoid of social context, a part of people's definitions of who they are could be perceived as something that is innate. On this issue, Wenger (1998) does not assume that there is an inherent conflict between the notions of self as an individual and the self in a social context, and rather feels this does not pose 'a dichotomy with a fundamental divergence between them' (Wenger, 1998: 147).

In attempting to unravel what is involved in identity, Wenger (1998) makes the following four points:

(1) Identity is fundamentally temporal; in other words, it is related to or limited by time.
(2) Identity is ongoing, which means that people may change, and their perceptions of who they are may change accordingly.
(3) Because identity is constructed in social contexts, the temporality of identity is more complex than a linear notion of time. In other words, identity does not change in a linear way over a certain period of time. Rather it changes through interaction and involvement with others within the different communities that people belong to.

(4) Identities are defined with respect to the interaction of multiple convergent trajectories. In other words, people change as a result of interaction with many others at a given time.

Such understandings are helpful in understanding the identities of bilinguals, who, in moving between different language contexts, reconstruct their identities over time.

To sum up, identity is the answer to the question of who we are and what we do in society relative to others and the way we associate with them through interaction. While acknowledging the individual, it is meaningful to examine people in the context of the roles they play in society, as their identities cannot be defined devoid of context. Such a contextual view provides a lens through which to examine the way in which bilinguals construe their identities. Thus, research using a postmodernist perspective will seek to understand the individual's personal and subjective construction of their identity, for example, by examining the stories that they tell.

Sociocultural perspectives on identity

Another useful perspective for understanding the nature of bilingual identities is to consider insights offered when identity is examined from a sociocultural perspective. Sociocultural theory, which stems from the work of Vygotsky (1978, 1986), is concerned with the important contributions that society makes to individual development; in other words, the ways in which cultural beliefs and interactions with others influence a person's perceptions and development.

Pavlenko and Lantolf write about second language learning as participation in a 'symbolically mediated world' (2000: 155). Vygotsky saw 'symbolic tools', such as diagrams, graphs or language, as empowering us to organise and control our mental processes. Pavlenko and Lantolf further claim that language learning is 'a struggle of concrete socially constituted and always situated beings to participate in the symbolically mediated lifeworld of another culture' (2000: 155). They see second language learning as a struggle for participation. As Holquist (1990: 37) claims, the self is 'constituted as a story, through which happenings in specific places and at specific times are made coherent'. In other words, people establish their understandings of who they are by actively negotiating their position and self-images through conversations and activities involving others.

Block (2003: 43) also describes identity construction as involving an ongoing negotiation and he argues that identities are reshaped and reconstructed in 'lifestyle sectors' (Giddens, 1991), 'communities of practice' (Lave & Wenger, 1991), 'discourse communities' (Lemke, 1995) and 'discourses' (Gee, 1996). These represent sites of struggle where conversational interactions take place and the different subjectivities or interpretations of identities are formed. The sites of struggle refer to the complex interpretations of who we are in connection to other people. These interpretations can often be fluid and sometimes even contradictory, as who the speaker is, is always connected to who the interlocutor is, and how s/he is positioned in the communities that people belong to. Weedon (1997: 32) defines these conversations as 'an enactment of different subjectivities, linking it with the notion of the conscious and unconscious thoughts and emotions of the individual, her sense of herself and her ways of understanding her relation in the world'.

In summary, sociocultural theory looks at identity as a socially situated notion and uncovers how people make sense of who they are in relation to how they are positioned in the different communities that they belong to. Research taking a sociocultural perspective helps us to understand people's identities from different angles, often through narrative accounts, capturing the voices of people taking an active role in constructing their identities through interacting with others in society. As bilinguals engage in social interactions in different cultures, they construct overlapping and often competing identities within different sites of struggle.

Power and identity

An important part of how individuals' situated identities can change, depending on who they are talking to, is related to issues of power in the different communities of practice that we engage in. Although a person may be proficient in the target language, in some cases the social positioning of the person and his/her interlocutor will affect the speakers' chances of being able to speak and thereby affect the construction of their identity in that setting.

Norton's ethnographic enquiry into immigrant women workers in Canada reveals aspects of power operating in 'the socially constructed relations among individuals, institutions and communities through which symbolic and material resources in a society are produced, distributed and validated' (Norton, 2000: 7). Norton refers to language, education, and friendship as symbolic resources, while referring to real estate and money as material resources. She claims that an individual may not have 'the right to speech' (Bourdieu, 1977), that is, the freedom to communicate their ideas when aspects of power operate between the speaker and the interlocutor. Norton refers to power at the macro level as including 'powerful institutions such as the legal system, the educational system and social welfare system' (Norton, 2000: 7). On a micro level, she refers to everyday social encounters between people with differential access to symbolic and material resources (Norton, 2000). For example, a cleaner and an office manager will have different degrees of power, the first being less important in social status than the latter (see also Norton, Chapter 5, this volume). In other cases, the lack of material resources may also restrict the cleaner from opportunities to have access to the community of people that the manager belongs to. In this way, as bilinguals construct their identities within the different communities they belong to, they may find that their participation and freedoms to express their identities are influenced by the power hierarchies and discourses in those communities.

Identity of bilinguals

The three perspectives outlined above are reflected in current writings on the identities of bilinguals within SLA. Pavlenko (2006) reminds us that in the first half of the 20th century the somewhat negative aspects of being bilingual were highlighted. Referring to Henss (1931), she says that bilinguals were seen to 'experience a pathological inner split and suffer intellectual and moral deterioration in their struggle to become one' (Pavlenko, 2006: 25). Sander (1934) refers to the 'mercenary relativism' of bilinguals who switch principles and values as they switch languages. However, as Pavlenko (2006) explains, in the second half of the 20th century, because of increased transnational migration, people started to look at the benefits of being bilingual. Despite this, Pavlenko believes that the problem of two competing identities and the notion of linguistic schizophrenia are still real, and she describes the emotions that some bilinguals experience:

(1) guilt over linguistic and ethnic disloyalties
(2) insecurity over legitimacy of a newly learnt language
(3) anxiety about the lack of wholesome oneness
(4) angst over the inability to bring together one's incommensurable worlds
(5) sadness and confusion by seeing oneself as divided
(6) a self in between
(7) a self in need of translation

(Pavlenko, 2006: 5)

These emotions could be explained by differences in the cultures connected to the languages of bilinguals. The notion of cultural identity in respect to bilinguals' identities conceptualises an individual's socialisation within two cultural worlds. Weisman (2001) uses the term 'assimilation ideology' to describe the psychological processes and social experiences of members of subordinate groups as they interact with a dominant culture. In order to accommodate the ways of the dominant culture, Weisman (2001) cites Dubois (1903) who pointed to a double consciousness that arises as a result of living with the tension of conflicting cultural values and conditions of subordination. This concept is of particular relevance to studies related to bilingualism where tension and duality in the identities of bilinguals can arise as a result of operating within two different cultures.

In Pavlenko's (2006) illuminating study on bilingual minds where she investigated the key influences that shape individuals' perceptions of the relationship between their languages and selves, she claims that bi- and multilinguals 'may perceive the world differently, and change perspectives, ways of thinking, and verbal and non-verbal behaviours when switching languages' (Pavlenko, 2006: 29). In her study conducted between 2001 and 2003 at Birkbeck College, 731 females and 308 males between the age of 16 and 70 participated in a web questionnaire designed jointly by Dewaele and Pavlenko. The participants responded to questions about different selves, which included: (1) linguistic and cultural differences; (2) distinct learning contexts; (3) different levels of language emotionality; (4) different levels of language proficiency (Pavlenko, 2006: 10).

In response to the question, 'Do you feel like a different person sometimes when you use your different languages?' one Russian–English–Hebrew–Ukranian speaker said, *'Absolutely. Speaking a different language means being a different person belonging to a different community character type emotional type'* (Pavlenko, 2006: 12). Other responses, such as *'I feel like I have a different personality in French'* and *'When I speak Dutch I feel like a more precise person'*, reveal that duality or multiplicity of identities may emerge through the use of the different languages associated with the varying cultures.

In summary, bilinguals may feel that there is more than one person inside them, depending on linguistic and/or cultural differences between the communities that they belong to. Such duality or multiplicity of identities was perhaps seen as negative in the early 20th century, but it is intriguing to observe more recently a shift in the way we view diversity in how people construe their identities.

The Study: Identities of Six Bilingual Japanese Women

The participants and context

The study was conducted in 2002 in Tokyo. The women were all known to me, and I chose the six participants, each with different careers in order to capture the different stories of bilinguals who played active roles in society. I chose to study women because I was particularly interested in finding out how they construed their identities in a male-dominated society such as Japan. Table 6.1 shows the list of participants and their professions. Pseudonyms were used to ensure confidentiality. They all used English and Japanese regularly in different ways in and outside of Japan, and they all now reside in Japan. Baker (2001: 6) cites one of the earlier definitions of bilingualism by Bloomfield (1933) who said that the speaker has native-like control of two or more languages; a strict definition that states that the person possesses the abilities of a native speaker in both of the languages. However, I employed the view of Grosjean (1982) who

Table 6.1 The background of the participants

Name	Occupation and place of employment	Years spent abroad	Countries lived in	Use of English Home = H, Work = W, Social = S	Starting age for learning English	Formal/ informal learning Formal = F Informal = I
Nanous	Designer, Japanese firm	0	Japan	H, W, S	12	F, I
Rieko	Manager, British cultural institute	5 years	Japan England	W, S	8	F, I
Mako	Dancer, Choreographer Independent	5 years	Japan USA	W, S	12	F, I
Minae	Editor Japanese publisher	12 years	Japan UK USA Vietnam	S	12	F, I
Takku	Kindergarten Teacher Trainer Independent	7 years	Japan USA	W	12	F, I
Akiko	Housewife	9 months	Japan UK	H	12	F, I

emphasises the regular use of two languages as the defining feature of bilingualism, as depending on the purpose and function of the social situations in which they use their language, one language may take dominance over the other. This implies that they may not be balanced bilinguals (Baker, 2001). Five of the participants had lived abroad and the number of years spent abroad varied between 5 and 12 years, and the countries lived in included England, USA, and Vietnam. Only one of the participants, Nanous, had not lived abroad, but was married to a Frenchman and the language used at home was English. She also used English at work as she worked for a Japanese cosmetics company that deals with other international companies using English.

Research aims and methodology

The aim of the study was to find out how the participants learnt English, how they perceived their sense of belonging in society, and how they saw their own identities in respect to their different languages.

An interpretative approach was used to investigate the women's perceptions of their identities and how they learnt their English. First, a preliminary questionnaire was used to generate data about the background of the six participants; the questions were designed to find out how they learnt English, how they use their English, and about their sense of belonging in society. One-to-one in-depth interviews were used to capture the detailed, nuanced perceptions of these women regarding their identities. I asked the participants to choose the language they wanted to use in the interview; only one of them used English, and the others chose Japanese but code-switched and used English in some parts of the interviews. I was interested in both how they saw their identities now and in understanding some of the past influences on their perceptions of who they feel they are. The first phase of interviews took place in Tokyo and each lasted approximately an hour and 30 minutes. Semi-structured and open-ended questions were used to guide the interview format; however, each interview was naturally different as I tried to respond to the uniqueness of each individual and the emerging ideas and themes of each interview. Examples of questions used to guide the interviews are:

(1) You speak both English and Japanese fluently. When do you speak English and Japanese?
(2) Tell me your story about how you learnt English.
(3) Being bilingual, do you feel different from other Japanese women who are not bilingual?
(4) You said that X was a positive/negative point about being bilingual. Can you tell me more about it?
(5) You said that you feel that you function differently/in the same way when you are using Japanese/English. Can you elaborate on that a bit more?
(6) You said that you belong to Y (country/countries). Can you tell me more about it?
(7) You said that you feel you belong to/don't belong to the majority of the people in Japan. Can you tell me in more detail about how you feel?
(8) You said that as a woman living in Japan you feel marginally different/don't feel different from other women who are not bilingual. Could you tell me in a little more detail how you feel about this?

I used a grounded theory approach to analyse the data (Glaser & Strauss, 1968), so that the findings remain close to the actual data and as far as possible retain the 'voices' of the participants. I recorded the interviews, transcribed them, and then categorised and recategorised the data using constant comparison until I felt categories emerged that best represented all of the data. Nevertheless, at the same time, I was conscious that I wished to understand the unique stories that each individual told about events that had shaped their identities. In this way, I sought to retain both an overview and individuality in reporting the findings.

Results and Discussion

The participants' backgrounds and how they learnt their English

As can be seen in Table 6.1, the preliminary questionnaire results showed that the six participants in their 30s to 40s had different occupations, and the number of years spent abroad varied from 0–12 years. Nanous had not spent any extended time abroad, but she uses English at home to communicate with her French husband. All six participants were ethnically Japanese and used English and Japanese regularly for different purposes.

All of the participants learnt English both in formal educational settings as well as in social contexts outside of school. They described the tuition they received at schools in Japan as being based on grammar translation and drills, while they learnt about aspects of language socialisation through interacting with others. Learning about English-speaking people, how to approach people, how to justify oneself, and authentic expressions used by native English speakers were mentioned as aspects of language use learnt outside the classroom. Rieko said the following about using language to approach people from a different culture:

> It's not just a matter of language. You need to learn about the personality of people, ways of thinking, the way British people think ... How you approach the people using what sort of attitude ... That is something which I learnt here, working on a daily basis.

All of the women felt that their sense of belonging was to Japan, but they felt that they belonged to a minority group of bilinguals within Japan. Minae thought that it is *'more comfortable'* to belong to the minority and Nanous simply said that she *'can enjoy'* herself and that it is *'pleasing'*. Indeed, all of the women felt happy about feeling different from the majority group. Furthermore, Nanous said:

> Because I belong to the minority group, it is appealing to my boss who belongs to the majority group.

Perceived aspects of being bilingual

Table 6.2 presents a summary of the findings regarding different aspects of being bilingual perceived by the participants. Six categories emerged from the data. The participants saw some aspects as positive and some as negative.

Table 6.2 Positive and negative aspects of being bilingual

Positive	Definitions
Ability to communicate	Able to communicate with others from abroad and be sympathetic to those who do not understand English
Enjoyment of both cultures	Able to appreciate both Japanese culture and culture surrounding English
More opportunities	Able to have more chances to work and study
Feeling free and open	Able to feel unrestricted and be open-minded
Negative	Definitions
Two faces	Having more than one persona
Not balanced	Fluency not balanced in two languages

The findings in these data correspond with Yamamoto's (2001) research on images associated with bilinguals in which the female respondents had relatively positive images of themselves as bilinguals. The category mentioned most frequently in my data was 'being able to communicate': *'I can communicate with people from all over the world. My world got bigger'* (Minae). All of the participants mentioned positive aspects belonging to this category: *'I can be sympathetic to other people who can't understand something because I know why they cannot understand something'* (Mako). *'I can communicate with people from different countries and share or exchange ideas'* (Rieko). On the whole, the women were aware of language as a social and cultural phenomenon (Fraser & Scherer, 1982) as they report using English in order to *'share or exchange ideas'* (Rieko).

Enjoyment of both cultures was mentioned by all of the participants. Examples of statements by the women are: *'I can enjoy films from both cultures'* (Takku) and *'I can understand the jokes in films that are not translated into Japanese'* (Akiko). Furthermore, interest in *'music'*, *'reading books'*, and *'drama on TV'*, and *'news'* through English were mentioned. As Baker (2001: 10) explains, 'bilinguals use their two languages for different purposes and events' and the cultural input through English is recognised by all of the participants as being valuable.

Two of the women mentioned that they had more opportunities in society owing to their two languages: *'I get more opportunities at work because I am bilingual'* (Nanous) and *'I can extend my learning opportunities even outside Japan'* (Rieko). Lastly, feeling free and open was mentioned positively by the same two women: *'I feel free and open when I speak in English'* (Rieko); *'I am more open to communicating in new languages other than English'* (Nanous).

Regarding the negative aspects of being bilingual, having two faces was mentioned by five of the participants. For example, Mako commented:

I have two faces. One for the English speaking situation and another for the Japanese. It's difficult to play both roles at the same time.

Also, Rieko said:

> I feel certain expectations from others both when speaking in Japanese and English. Sometimes I have to have *two faces* to meet those two different expectations.

Weisman (2001) stresses the positive aspect of bicultural people, demonstrating an additive model of cultural acquisition as they are able to function in and out of the two cultures. However, the above data show that while all of the respondents felt that the fact that they *'can communicate'* was a positive aspect, the duality that they experience in their verbal behaviour requires them to *'have two faces'* to meet the different expectations held by the people belonging to the cultures in the Japanese- and English-speaking communities of practice (Wenger, 1998). Thus, this duality in their identities is perceived by the participants as a factor that was *'frustrating'* (Rieko) and *'difficult'* (Mako). One possible reason for this sense of frustration is that the women perceived the Japanese language as *vague* compared with English. For example, Minae stated that:

> I find Japanese vague. Sometimes we omit the subject and it is not clear what the message is. The meaning is ambiguous.

While Rieko mentioned that:

> I write e-mail in English to my Japanese colleagues feeling I can be more honest with them. I wish I could do the same with my Japanese friends.

It is interesting that both of these comments are about language use rather than culture. Although language is often examined in connection to culture, what these findings show is that these participants are showing a preference for expressing themselves in English because of the use of the language, not the culture attached to it. The data extracts above also illustrate the difficulties in expressing ambiguity and politeness experienced by bilingual English and Japanese speakers. By saying, *'I wish I could do the same in Japanese'*, Rieko may be implying that if it were possible to omit the polite expressions of formality used in Japanese business mail, she would be able to be *'more honest'*, and become more direct in expressing herself to her correspondents.

The data also indicate that two of the participants, Nanous and Akiko, are concerned about the balance between their linguistic ability in English and Japanese. For example, Nanous explains that she feels that not being balanced in the two languages is something she sees as negative. As Nanous explained:

> As I am not fluent in a balanced way in English, I sometimes find it a bit of a burden when I am asked to be an interpreter.

On the other hand, Akiko said:

> I have stopped making an effort in developing my English more.

These two data extracts represent a negative aspect of being bilingual. It may be that the participants believe that society expects them to be a 'balanced bilingual' (Baker, 2001: 7). Nanous' statement may be more related to her identity as 'co-constructed and negotiated' (Duff & Uchida, 1997: 452) suggesting that being bilingual, others expect her to play the role of the interpreter.

To sum up, the participants commented more on the positive aspects of being bilingual than the negative aspects. *'I can communicate'* and *'enjoy both cultures'* were given by all of the women as positive aspects of their bilingual identities. However, the *'two faces'* that they perceive in the use of the two languages was felt to be a *'frustrating'* factor, even though the respondents reported being interested in using the two languages as a medium of communication.

When the participants were asked whether they see themselves to be the same person when they function in English/Japanese, four of the women mentioned that their identity is dual, one of them thought that is was multiple and one person perceived her identity as being single. Mako mentioned:

> Sometimes there is another voice in me.

Nanous also said:

> English develops another character in me.

While Rieko said that there are four people within her:

> I think there are three ... No, I think four.

Takku gave a graphic description of how her English 'exploded' upon discovering her talent in visual art when she won a prize in the New York State High School Art Competition. She explains:

> The picture was like this (drawing the picture on a piece of paper). My face was divided into two and on the right, the hair was long, sort of like sixties style. On the left, my hair was short. My eye on the right was very big and on the left was small. But my mouth on the left was big and my mouth on the right was small. On the right there was a piano and a brush for painting. I think the right represented myself in America and the left represented myself in Japan. In America I observed many things and that's why my eye was big and my mouth was small because I didn't

do much speaking. On the left my eye was small but my mouth was big 'cause I did a lot of speaking in Japanese. (Takku interview in 2002)

Even though the description of Takku's identity represents a snapshot of how she felt about herself as a teenager in New York, it offers insights into her linguistic development of English and Japanese. As an artist, Takku was able to represent visually what was happening to her when she was using the two languages, English and Japanese.

In contrast, Akiko perceives that there is only one person:

I am different from British people 'cause I was brought up here, not in England. I feel I am Japanese in the end.

Thus, five of the women perceived their identity as being dual or multiple, while Akiko seems to have a more unifying sense of self compared with the other five women. When asked about the differences between these identities and how they influence their behaviour, their responses show that there are considerable differences in their behaviour, depending on the language that they use. The most intriguing point that emerged is that the participants claim that their behaviour is partly dependent on the language used. Nanous feels that she is more outgoing when meeting new people in English: *'I can become more outgoing ... I think it's the feature of the language'*. Rieko feels *'I don't have to pretend'* when talking in English: *'I can say what I want to say and I don't have to be polite to others all the time'*. Furthermore, Minae feels that she can be more aggressive when speaking in English: *'In English I can be more aggressive'*, while acknowledging that she sometimes prefers not to be aggressive and *'remain ambiguous'* in Japanese. The one participant who felt she was the same one person in both languages was Akiko, who said, *'I am one person, and I am Japanese'*. It appears that while some individuals feel that their identities are dual or multiple, and that these different identities influence their behaviours in different language contexts, others might have a more coherent or unified sense of self.

As Terwilliger (1968: 11) explains, anthropologically oriented linguists such as Whorf, believe that 'the nature of one's language determines his entire way of life, including his thinking and all other forms of mental activity'. As our behaviour, to a great extent, is dependent on our thoughts, it is illuminating to see that the differences in the discourse of the two languages, English and Japanese, appear to affect the participants' speech and behaviour. In this respect, some of the participants discussed the need to vary their style of communication depending on the language they used. Takku comments on a paralinguistic feature of English:

I have to have more space when I speak in English because I use more gestures. I need about two metres around me when I speak in English.

This suggests that she feels that the expression of emotion is not as elaborate when speaking in Japanese as it is when using English.

Other responses are more related to the discourse features of the two languages, Minae mentioned:

In Japanese, I become more reserved. I become ambiguous.

Similarly, Mako said:

I think I am much more vague in Japanese.

The extract below from Takku highlights the differences between the discourses in the two languages:

In Japanese, there are different stages where you use polite language to suss out who these people are and it takes a longer time before you start to use language that is more relaxed. English is more direct.

Takku's comment reflects her perception that the proper use of Japanese shows that a human being is always involved in a multiplicity of social relationships (Kondo, 1990: 31). One is required to 'suss out' the social positioning of the interlocutor and find the boundaries between the self and the other (Kondo, 1990). Similarly, when Mako claims that, *'it's vague and it doesn't feel like you have reached a conclusion'*, she is perhaps describing the notion of fluidity of the self under the influence of the relationship between her and the interlocutor in the given social structure.

Nanous claims that *'English is the language of the presentation of yourself'*. She wishes that all of the meetings at work were held in English as she would be able to *'win each argument'* by being direct. She mentioned the frequent use of the passive voice when an opinion is being presented in Japanese: expressions of hedging such as 'omowaremasu' and 'kanjiraremasu' (it is felt that...) are some of her examples. In a meeting held in Japanese, Nanous said:

So when it's my turn to speak, I don't use the passive.

Rieko's data reveal interesting findings about power operating in conversations: 'Sometimes the British managers hold onto the document at the end of the meeting. Actually, I want them to hold on to the document.' This shows that she does not feel able to ask the manager who is of a higher status to hold on to the document that Rieko has produced. As Rieko is of a lower status in the hierarchy of the organisation, she felt that she did not have 'equal speaking rights' (Norton, Chapter 5, this volume). In other words, 'the power to impose reception' (Bourdieu, 1977: 648) was not existent in Reiko, given that her boss was in a position of power.

To summarise, the participants reported differences in behaviours and personas depending on which language they used, except for one participant. These differences appeared to be related to the discourse and pragmatic features of the two languages. Future research examining the link between language and identity could investigate further the ways in which the duality perceived by bilingual people is linked to the differences in the pragmatic features of the two languages.

Conclusion and Implications

In conclusion, the data from the present study show that the majority of the participants perceived a duality or multiplicity when they reflected on their identity, thinking, and behaviour. The main causes of such duality were the perceived cultural and linguistic differences between the two languages. However, one of the women did not necessarily perceive a duality in her identity and saw herself as a Japanese person and different from English people.

What is interesting is that although having more than one face was perceived as being a negative aspect of being bilingual, the participants on the whole mentioned more positive points about being bilingual, such as being able to communicate with others from abroad and appreciate both Japanese- and English-related cultures, and they felt unrestricted and open minded. In voicing more positive aspects of being bilingual, it can be concluded that these women represent an additive view of bilingual selves.

This research only focused on the identities of women, and, in the future, it would be illuminating to investigate bilingual Japanese men and their identities in order to examine whether there are any commonalities or differences between the men and women in this particular cultural context. Furthermore, other studies investigating bilingual identities across cultures and languages would be needed to add further insights into the concept of the multiple, fluid self, and the relationships between specific languages, cultures, and identities.

Recommended reading

Block, D. (2003) *The Social Turn in Second Language Acquisition*. Washington, DC: Georgetown University Press.

This book offers a clear analysis of the theories connected to the social aspect of language learning. It is helpful for understanding how the

> social side of learning can be connected to the cognitive dimensions of learning.
>
> Norton, B. (2000) *Identity and Language Learning.* Harlow: Pearson.
>
> In this book, Norton examines the lives of immigrant workers in Canada and illustrates how aspects of identity and power in society affect the right for the person to speak. It shows the reader how the participants' social identities are analysed and construed, in relation to the power hierarchies that operate in society.
>
> Pavlenko, A. (ed.) (2006) *Bilingual Minds: Emotional Experience, Expression and Representation.* Clevedon: Multilingual Matters.
>
> This volume contains 11 useful research-based accounts of bilinguals and their emotions. It is a valuable account of how bilinguals experience different emotions depending on the languages that they use.

References

Baker, C. (2001) *Foundations of Bilingual Education and Bilingualism* (3rd edn). Clevedon: Multilingual Matters.
Block, D. (2003) *The Social Turn in Second Language Acquisition.* Washington, D.C.: Georgetown University Press.
Bloomfield, L. (1933) *Language.* New York: Holt, Rinehard and Winston.
Bourdieu, P. (1977) The economics of linguistic exchanges. *Social Science Information* 16 (6), 645–668.
Dubois, W. (1903) *The Souls of Black Folk.* New York: Johnson Reprint Corporation.
Duff, P. and Uchida, Y. (1997) The negotiation of teachers' sociocultural identities and practices in postsecondary EFL classrooms. *TESOL Quarterly* 31 (3), 451–486.
Fraser, C. and Scherer, R. (1982) *Advances in the Social Psychology of Language.* Cambridge: Cambridge University Press.
Gee, J.P. (1996) *Social Linguistics and Literacies: Ideology in Discourses* (2nd edn). London: Falmer.
Giddens, A. (1991) *Modernity and Self-identity: Self and Society in the Late Modern Age.* Cambridge: Polity.
Glaser, B. and Strauss, A. (1968) *The Discovery of Grounded Theory: Strategies for Qualitative Research.* Chicago: Aldine.
Grosjean, F. (1982) *Life with Two Languages: An Introduction to Bilingualism.* Cambridge: Harvard University Press.
Hayes, N. (1998) *Foundations of Psychology.* Walton-on-Thames: Thomas Nelson & Sons Ltd.
Henss, W. (1931) Zweisprachigkeit als Pädagogisches Problem. *Ethnopolitischer Almanach* 2, 47–55.
Holquist, M. (1990) *Dialogism: Bakhtin and His World.* London: Routledge.
Kondo, D. (1990) *Crafting Selves: Power, Gender, and Discourses of Identity in a Japanese Workplace.* Chicago: University of Chicago Press.
Lave, J. and Wenger, E. (1991) *Situated Learning: Legitimate Peripheral Participation.* Cambridge: Cambridge University Press.
Lemke, J. (1995) *Textual Politics: Discourse and Social Dynamics.* London: Taylor and Francis.

Norton, B. (2000) *Identity and Language Learning*. Harlow: Pearson.
Pavlenko, A. (2006) Bilingual selves. In A. Pavlenko (ed.) *Bilingual Minds: Emotional Experience, Expression and Representation* (pp. 1–33). Clevedon: Multilingual Matters.
Pavlenko, A. and Lantolf, J. (2000) Second language learning as participation and the (re)construction of selves. In J. Lantolf (ed.) *Sociocultural Theory and Second Language Learning* (pp. 155–177). Oxford: Oxford University Press.
Sander, F. (1934) Seelische Struktur und Sprache: Strukturpsychologisches zum Zweitsprachenproblem. *Neue Psychologische Studien* 12, 59–67.
Terwilliger, R. (1968) *Meaning and Mind: A Study in the Psychology of Language*. New York: Oxford University Press.
Vidich, A. and Lyman, S. (2000) Qualitative methods – Their history in sociology and anthropology. In K. Denzin and Y. Lincoln (ed.) *Handbook of Qualitative Research* (pp. 37–84). Thousand Oaks: SAGE Publications, Inc.
Vygotsky, L. (1978) *Mind in Society*. Cambridge: Harvard University Press.
Vygotsky, L. (1986) *Thought and Language*. Cambridge: MIT Press.
Weedon, C. (1997) *Feminist Practice and Poststructuralist Theory* (2nd edn). Oxford: Blackwell.
Weisman, E. (2001) Bicultural identity and language attitudes: Perspectives of four Latina teachers. *Urban Education* 36 (2), 203–225.
Wenger, E. (1998) *Communities of Practice: Learning, Meaning, and Identity*. Cambridge: Cambridge University Press.
Yamamoto, M. (2001) Japanese attitudes towards bilingualism: A survey and its implications. In M. Goebel Noguchi and S. Fotos (eds) *Studies in Japanese Bilingualism* (pp. 1–23). Clevedon: Multilingual Matters.

7 Relational Views of the Self in SLA

Florentina Taylor

Introduction

The concept of self is now very popular in the second language acquisition (SLA) literature, with many related publications currently in press or published recently. As witnessed by this collection of papers, there are numerous theoretical, conceptual and methodological perspectives from which the self can be regarded, many of which have been borrowed from other fields, such as social or educational psychology. Comparatively less attention has been given to the multiplicity of selves that individuals may experience in their varied social interactions and the relativity of one's sense of self when moving from one social interaction to another. The purpose of this chapter is to review key studies that have explored such relational perspectives and to argue that further research is needed. Throughout the chapter, the phrase 'relational context' will be used to refer to a given social situation where the individual interacts with other persons in a particular social capacity, responding to particular social expectations. Examples of such relational contexts are teacher–pupil, peer-group or family interactions, where social roles and expectations are usually clearly defined. The term 'relativity' will be used to represent the dependence of one's sense of self on the social context with which one interacts, while the term 'relational' will emphasise the social interactional aspect that characterises this dependence.

Following a definitional introduction, this chapter reviews three main relational approaches to the study of the self that can be, and have partially been, adopted in SLA research. Owing to space limitations, this does not intend to be a comprehensive review, but will rather aim to provide examples of key approaches to exploring the relational aspects of the self, emphasising the construction of the self through social interaction within and across different relational contexts in which the individual functions.

Defining the Self in Social Interaction

Living in a society, people develop perceptions of what is and what is not desired or acceptable in a particular context, and they often do things that help them integrate into the respective group. For example, somebody who wants to become a pop star knows that being a pop star involves singing or playing an instrument, wearing a particular type of clothes, associating oneself with people who appreciate pop music and so on. As such, the person who is not yet a pop star but wants to become one will usually start by learning to sing or play an instrument, buying particular clothes and seeking the company of like-minded people. Whether or not they will achieve their goal will depend, of course, on a variety of factors – not least on their physical ability to sing or to play an instrument and how hard they work in order to achieve this. Similarly, someone who wants to be a person who travels the world and communicates in various different languages will gradually adopt the traits that they associate with this type of person (perhaps being interested in geography, seeking opportunities to travel, learning and using languages). These traits are sometimes called *self-defining goals* and represent the interface between behaviour and identity (e.g. Gollwitzer & Kirchhof, 1998). In other words, by enacting a particular behavioural trait, people may get closer to becoming the person they would like to become.

The behavioural traits, or self-defining goals, associated with a particular identity that a person displays in their social interactions are called *public selves*, and these may or may not coincide with what the person truly believes about himself/herself as an individual – the *private self* (Andersen *et al.*, 1998; Baumeister, 1986; Bennett & Sani, 2004). Moreover, a person's public selves – displayed in their varied social interactions – can sometimes be contradictory, in response to contradictory expectations resulting from different relational contexts. For example, in competitive educational environments, a student may be caught between displaying the public self of a disaffected teenager to academically disengaged peers in whose group they may wish to be accepted, while interacting with the teacher they may display the public self of an academically motivated student, as it may be in their best interest to appear so (Harter, 1999; Juvonen, 1996; Schlenker, 2003).

In social psychology, the combination of public selves that a person displays in social interaction, together with the person's private self, are defined collectively as the person's *identity* (Baumeister, 1986, 1997; Harter, 1999; Schwartz *et al.*, 2011). As Vignoles *et al.* explain:

> ... identity comprises not only 'who you think you are' (individually or collectively), but also 'who you act as being' in interpersonal and intergroup interactions – and the social recognition or otherwise that these actions receive from other individuals or groups. (Vignoles *et al.*, 2011: 2)

Although the relationship between the self and identity is sometimes conceptualised differently in SLA (e.g. Mercer, 2011), the present chapter will adopt the social psychology view of identity as an aggregate of a multitude of private and public selves associated with one individual (see also Taylor, 2013).

The relativity of the self has been represented in SLA research by three main approaches, which will serve as the organisational principle for the rest of the chapter. These three approaches can be called synchronic, diachronic and a combination of the two. These will be discussed in the following sections: synchronic relativity (discussing different ways in which an individual may be perceived across different relational contexts); diachronic relativity (exploring the relationship between an individual's sense of self at different points in time); and synchronic–diachronic perspectives, in which the two approaches are combined. Each section begins with a general discussion of the respective concepts in social/educational psychology followed by their application in the SLA literature. The chapter concludes with implications for practice and future research.

Synchronic Relativity

One of the main relational perspectives on the self can be termed *synchronic relativity*. This relativity is expressed in two different ways: first, what individuals believe about themselves sometimes differs from the way they present themselves to other people, which is typically referred to in social psychology as the difference between the private and the public self. Second, an individual may come across differently in different relational contexts, which represents the difference between a person's various public selves (Andersen *et al.*, 1998; Baumeister, 1986). The relationship between the private and the public components of one's identity is explained clearly by Baumeister:

> The public self is the self that is manifested in the presence of others, that is formed when other people attribute traits and qualities to the individual, and that is communicated to other people in the process of self-presentation. The private self is the way the person understands himself or herself and is the way the person really is . . . . (Baumeister, 1986: v)

Private self can be thought of as an alternative designation for self-concept (e.g. Hattie, 1992; Mercer, 2011; Rubio, Chapter 4, this volume) – the former being preferred in contexts where a differentiation is necessary between one's personal sense of self and its socially displayed counterparts. While the public self is delineated by one's private self (in the sense that one cannot display an image that is very evidently at odds with one's conception of oneself), the private self is also shaped by public manifestations (in the sense that a self displayed publicly may be internalised into one's private self if is accepted or approved socially).

The disclosure of a public self in social interaction is called *self-presentation*, and this can be used manipulatively (when individuals may pretend to be what they are not in order to achieve a particular goal) or as a normal feature of goal-oriented social interaction (Baumeister, 1982; Leary, 1995). As Schlenker (2003) explains, perfectly valid information about ourselves needs as much presentation skill as fabricated information in order to have the intended impact. A classic example is that of a job interview for which the candidate will wear formal clothes and use formal language as expected in a job interview situation, in order to obtain the desired job. Individuals who may not normally use formal language or clothes will still need to observe these social expectations in order to achieve their desired goal, even though the information they present about themselves in the interview may be perfectly valid in itself.

Examples like the one above are sometimes called *self-presentation sets*, and they consist of an actor, an audience and a social situation, the last two components determining the salience of a particular public self (Schlenker, 1986, 2003; Schlenker & Weigold, 1992). For example, a student (the 'actor') will behave in a certain way, displaying a particular public self, when interacting with a teacher (the 'audience') in the classroom (the 'social situation'), while the same person will display a different public self when interacting with her friends on the sports ground. A challenging situation for an individual emerges when two different audiences are present in the same social situation and the 'actor' is then in the position to decide which public self will have to take priority. As Juvonen's work (e.g. 1996) has shown, such situations require strong negotiation skills on the part of the 'actor' and there is evidence that effortful or contradictory self-presentations can drain an individual's psychological resources (e.g. Vohs *et al.*, 2005). In SLA, Taylor (e.g. 2010) has also found that students who felt they had to display a different self in their different relational contexts (i.e. with their language teacher, with their peers and with their parents) felt frustrated and confused. Crucially, when the L2 public self they displayed to their language teacher was different from what they believed privately about themselves as language learners (i.e. their L2 private selves), their learning orientation, interest in the language class, enjoyment of language learning and declared achievement were significantly affected.

Similar findings are reported by McKay and Wong (1996), in their account of four Chinese adolescent speakers of English as a second language (ESL) in California, whose development they followed for two years. The authors borrow Norton Peirce's (1995) perspective of identity as a 'site of struggle' between the different expectations of the multiple social contexts with which the individual interacts. Using ethnographic methods, such as interviews, observations, informal conversations and writing samples, McKay and Wong (1996) depict their participants as caught between contradictory social and academic expectations (e.g. peers, parents, teachers) and having to constantly resist or adopt 'established discourses' in order to forge viable social identities. Examples of such discourses are the 'colonialist/ racialised' view of immigrants, which affected the teacher–student relationship and the students' willingness to invest in language learning, or the social/academic school discourses, which pitched peer social expectations against institutional academic expectations.

Although McKay and Wong's (1996) research approach is longitudinal, their focus is not so much on identity development as on capturing the sense of struggle that these junior high-school immigrants encounter while trying to improve the language in which they communicate imperfectly, and while striving to forge an acceptable social identity at the intersection of several contradictory discourses. Heralding Ushioda's (e.g. 2009) later calls for regarding the language learner as a real person rather than a 'theoretical abstraction', McKay and Wong conclude that:

> ... contrary to the kind of ahistorical, 'stick figure' of the learner painted in much of the literature on second-language learning and many teacher training programs, learners are extremely complex social beings with a multitude of fluctuating, at times conflicting, needs and desires. (McKay & Wong, 1996: 603)

When this multitude of needs and desires is related to contradictory social expectations, such as those of a parent versus those of a classmate, as seen above, the public self that the individual chooses to display may have crucial consequences. There is evidence (including from neuro-imaging studies – e.g. Pfeifer *et al.*, 2009) that our public selves can actually change our private selves through a process called *internalisation* or its associated *carryover effect* (e.g. Leary, 1995; Schlenker *et al.*, 1994; Tice & Wallace, 2003). Schlenker (2003: 502) explains the process in simple terms: 'Act the part and it becomes incorporated into the self-concept'. Social validation given to a self-displayed publicly helps this public self to become integrated into one's core beliefs about oneself. In other words, if the people one interacts with react positively to a set of behaviours displayed by the individual, these behaviours may become part of the individual's private self if the respective people represent a group the individual wants to be accepted by and associated with. Such internationalisation processes have been discussed in the SLA literature by authors working within a self-determination theory framework (e.g. Noels, 2009; Noels *et al.*, 2003).

Internalisation can play a crucial role in the formation of an individual's private self (Baumeister, 1982; Leary, 1995), and therefore can be an important vehicle of change. When an 'audience' responds positively to a private self, the individual may be more motivated to reduce the discrepancy between their current private self and the desired self they are pursuing (Leary & Kowalski, 1990). Leary (1995) explains that, while enacting particular behaviours that are not yet part of their private self, people may learn new things about themselves; they may even come to understand that they actually *are* the way they have presented themselves.

These processes of internalisation could also make an important contribution to language education: a learner who is encouraged to display the public self of a confident L2 speaker and work towards validating this self, may eventually internalise this into their own private self if the reactions of the 'audience' reinforce this validation positively, by encouraging and appreciating the manifestation of traits typical of a confident L2 speaker. In language classrooms, however, the reality can be very different, students often preferring to keep quiet rather than speak in a foreign language and expose themselves to the potential ridicule of their peers (e.g. Bartram, 2006; Pellegrino Aveni, 2005; Williams *et al.*, 2002). This can also happen outside the classroom, where, for example, adult immigrants may feel 'stupid' and 'inferior' owing to their perceived imperfect L2 grammar or pronunciation (e.g. Norton Peirce, 1995). In such situations, maintaining one's focus on a desired self (e.g. a confident L2 speaker) and its associated set of beliefs and competences can help provide the motivational impetus to reduce the difference between what individuals feel they are in the present and what they would like to become in the future. These situations can be referred to as diachronic transitions and are discussed in the next section.

Diachronic Relativity

Two of the social psychological theories that take a diachronic relational perspective in the study of the self are *possible selves* theory and *self-discrepancy* theory, whose close relationship is reviewed briefly below (for a more comprehensive overview of possible selves in SLA, see Ryan & Irie, Chapter 8, this volume).

With the onset of adolescence, individuals begin to consider alternative routes that the future might bring. Through their self-presentation in various relational contexts, they try out possible selves that they may or may not internalise later (Dunkel, 2000; Oyserman *et al.*, 2004). Consequently, these selves are socially conditioned and contingent, as individuals usually understand whether a particular self is acceptable or unacceptable in a particular social context and react accordingly by consolidating or discarding the possible self they have tried out (Dunkel & Kerpelman, 2006; Wurf & Markus, 1991). For this reason, possible selves can be thought of as being closely related to public selves.

Desirable and undesirable self-images have been shown to mediate long-term motivation by channelling the actions necessary for the achievement of a self-relevant goal (Cross & Markus, 1991; Markus & Nurius, 1987; Markus & Ruvolo, 1989; Ruvolo & Markus, 1992). This motivational process is explained clearly by Dunkel *et al.* (2006), who split the pursuit and integration of a possible self into four distinct stages: (a) as individuals contemplate change, they generate possible selves; (b) as they decide to pursue change, they try to validate their chosen possible selves; (c) as they pursue some possible selves, they eliminate others; and (d) when possible selves are achieved, they are integrated into their current self. The constant reiteration of this process takes the individual further along a desired path. Similar to self-presentations or public selves, possible selves have been considered to enter a mutually influential relationship to one's private self (Erikson, 2007; Markus & Nurius, 1987; Strahan & Wilson, 2006; Wurf & Markus, 1991).

The role of significant others in generating possible selves is important, and people one has never met (such as celebrities, famous gangsters or fictional characters) can be equally powerful inspirations in selecting a desired self, especially for younger adolescents (Harter, 1999; Oyserman & Fryberg, 2006; Zentner & Renaud, 2007). Similar to the display of divergent public selves, different relational contexts can inspire the adoption of contradictory possible selves. In other words, a particular self can be desired in one context and feared in another, such as in the case of a diligent student who works hard in order to attain a particular desired self, only to be labelled a 'nerd' and excluded from peer groups for being 'too keen' (Dweck, 1999; Taylor, 2013).

A complementary theory to the possible selves model is self-discrepancy theory (e.g. Higgins, 1987; Higgins *et al.*, 1994; see also Ushioda, Chapter 9, this volume). Based on the earlier actual/ideal dichotomy conceptualised by Carl Rogers in the 1950s (Rogers, 1951; Rogers & Dymond, 1954), this theory proposes the existence of three 'domains of the self' (the *actual self*, the *ideal self* and the *ought self*) and two 'standpoints on the self' (own versus significant other). The actual self is defined as a person's beliefs of what s/he is as an individual in the present, the ideal self represents what they would like to become in the future and the ought self is defined as what individuals feel they should become. Higgins and his associates maintain that discrepancies between one's actual self and the relevant self guides (ideal self and ought self) can produce discomfort, which, in turn, can activate the behaviour necessary to eliminate the associated negative emotions by resolving the discrepancy.

Sometimes, a person will have several conflicting ought selves. Van Hook and Higgins (1988: 625) maintain that such discrepancies can induce a 'chronic double approach–avoidance conflict (feeling muddled, indecisive, distractible, unsure of self or goals, rebellious, confused about identity)'. Being caught between two different expectations, the person will be in a no-win situation: approaching the first ought-self guide entails avoiding the second, and approaching the second means avoiding the first – hence, a double approach–avoidance conflict (also, Higgins, 1996, 2006). This is the reason why McKay and Wong's (1996) and Taylor's (2010) adolescents felt confused and frustrated when confronted with conflicting social expectations. For example, presenting oneself as academically engaged is likely to attract negative reactions from one's peers, while giving in to the pressure of some peers not to do well academically so as not to appear better than them (Dweck, 1999; Seifert & O'Keefe, 2001), for instance, will very likely upset the teachers and parents. As can be seen, there are clear parallels with possible selves and self-presentation theories, as these all emphasise that when a person has to accommodate contradictory social expectations (whether for the future or in the present), the individual's relationship with the respective relational contexts is likely to be strained and frustrating.

In SLA, a persuasive account of the constant struggle to reach one's ideal self through the day-to-day self-presentation in social interaction is reported by Pellegrino Aveni (2005), who conducted a grounded-theory exploration of American undergraduates studying in post-Soviet Russia. Having analysed narratives, interviews and classroom observations, she concludes that 'language learners can be severely hindered in their ability to create or approximate their ideal image of the self they wish to project in the second language' (Pellegrino Aveni, 2005: 35) because of their imperfect L2 grammar, vocabulary and pronunciation. Because of their limited L2 communicative competence, they may feel that their cognitive sophistication goes unnoticed by others, leaving them feeling vulnerable and socially disadvantaged. As the author convincingly demonstrates, the easiest way for her study-abroad participants to cope with this threat to their social self-presentation is, unfortunately, to refuse to use the foreign language thereby depriving themselves of the very practice that would ensure improved proficiency and decrease the perceived discrepancy between their ideal and actual L2 self.

Potential differences between the actual and the ideal self have also featured in discussions of Dörnyei's (2005) *L2 Motivational Self System*, which is built around the ideal/ought self dichotomy (Higgins, 1987) reviewed briefly above. The declared main component of the model is the ideal L2 self, which Dörnyei (2009: 29) characterises as 'a powerful motivator to learn the L2 because of the desire to reduce the discrepancy between our actual and ideal selves'. Nevertheless, the model does not explicitly include an actual self, which would be a crucial component, as the motivational value of the ideal self can only be understood in relation to one's actual self. In practical educational terms, for example, a teacher can only help a student reduce the discrepancy between their actual self and their ideal self if they understand the starting point of this motivational process – the actual or current self. As such, the core value of the L2 Motivational Self System stands in reinforcing the motivational potential of the ideal self confirmed repeatedly in the literature, without, however, relating it to the initial point of an actual self and without exploring the relational aspects of the self system.

Synchronic-Diachronic Perspectives in SLA

The final relational perspective on the self concerns research strands that combine the two previously discussed angles (synchronic and diachronic), emphasising both the multitude of selves manifested by an individual in society and the developmental journey from what an individual is to what they are aiming to become. One of the most prolific areas of SLA that have combined the two perspectives is perhaps the literature associated with poststructuralist approaches to the study of negotiated identities, its main focus being immigrant speakers of English as a second language in countries such as the USA or Canada (see Norton, Chapter 5, this volume, and Hemmi, Chapter 6, this volume). Volumes edited by Aneta Pavlenko and her colleagues (e.g. Pavlenko & Blackledge, 2004b; Pavlenko & Lantolf, 2000; Pavlenko *et al.*, 2001), or the work of authors such as Goldstein (1997), Miller (2003), Norton (1997, 2000), Norton Peirce (1995) and Toohey (2000) have all focused on depicting the individual's struggle to find a place for oneself in society by balancing and negotiating different, often contradictory, identities (see also Hemmi, Chapter 6, this volume). Such studies often adopt ethnographic methods, in particular narratives, and regard identities as emergent from the interaction of multiple factors, such as age, race, class, ethnicity, gender, sexual orientation, institutional affiliation, geopolitical locale and so on (see Pavlenko & Blackledge, 2004a).

A strong accent on the relationship between the individual's identity construction and their multiple relational contexts is particularly visible, for example, in Norton's work (e.g. Norton, 2000; Norton Peirce, 1995) with immigrant women in Canada. Her theory of social identity emphasises the power relations and social inequities that language learners face in their daily lives. She explains:

> Subjectivity is produced in a variety of social sites, all of which are structured by relations of power in which the person takes up different subject positions – teacher, mother, manager, critic – some positions of which may be in conflict with others. (Norton Peirce, 1995: 15)

Like Pavlenko (2004), Norton regards the individual's identity as a complex combination and synergy of the roles they enact in their multiple sociorelational contexts. Although SLA poststructuralists have traditionally not drawn on social psychological theories such as self-presentation, there are clear parallels between this view of identity and theories of the self in social interaction developed, for example, by Leary (Leary, 1995; Leary & Allen, 2011). (For an overview of poststructuralist views on identity, see Norton, Chapter 5, this volume.)

A closer link to the social-psychological view of the self from a relational perspective characterises my own work (e.g. Taylor, 2010, 2013) with adolescent learners of English as a foreign language in Romania. A novel perspective of this research, which used self-reported questionnaires and in-depth one-to-one interviews, is the comparison between the public selves displayed by language learners in four relational contexts: with their English teacher, with their classmates, with their best friends and with their families, as well as how these public selves relate to the learner's private self and their interest and achievement in language learning. This approach brings together self-discrepancy and self-presentation theories, applying them to language learning by considering identity as an aggregate of four main self components placed along two actual/possible and private/public axes (*private* = what the individual thinks s/he is; *public* = what the individual wants other people to think s/he is; *ideal* = what the individual would like to become; *imposed* = what other people would like the individual to become) (see Table 7.1).

This research (Taylor, 2010, 2013) explored the L2 facet of the Quadripolar Model of Identity, but comparisons are also being made with other subjects (see e.g. Taylor *et al.*, 2013, for L2 versus Mathematics in four European countries). One of the crucial findings of the L2-focused research was that the participants displayed public selves that they felt were imposed on them socially in each relational context, and these public selves bore little resemblance to what these teenagers believed about themselves as language learners (see Figure 7.1).

Figure 7.1 is a graphical representation of two types of correlations: between the participants' L2 private self and their L2 public self (light grey), and the correlation between their L2 public selves and L2 imposed selves (dark grey) in each relational context. The light bars indicate a tendency for participants to hide their private self in social interaction, or to give impressions that they personally think are not part of their private self. This difference is less pronounced in interaction with the teacher ($r = 0.24$, $p < 0.001$), where students would not be able to pretend they are what they are not, as language learners, but more pronounced in interaction with classmates ($r = 0.10$, $p < 0.001$), where participants are perhaps likely to pretend they are not interested in language learning, in contrast to their private feelings. In stark opposition to the private/public correlations, the relationship between the public selves that these students display and the perceived imposed self in each relational context is very strong, in particular for classmates and friends ($r = 0.69$, 0.72, respectively, $p < 0.001$). This echoes the findings of,

Table 7.1 A quadripolar model of identity

Self dimension	Internal	External
Possible	Ideal	Imposed
Actual	Private	Public

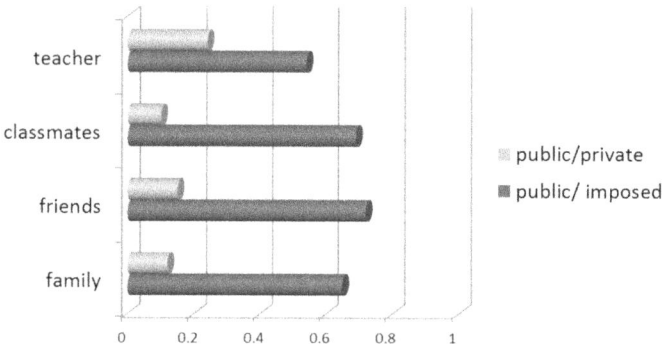

Figure 7.1 Public/private self and public/imposed self correlations in four relational contexts

for example, Williams *et al.* (2002), who reported that several of their participants considered it was not 'cool' for boys to like languages, and, even if they did, they felt it was not appropriate to show it to their classmates.

The fact that there seems to be little connection between what these teenagers think of themselves as language learners and what they choose to show other people about themselves indicates they may have a strong need for social approval, which encourages them to display a self that may not necessarily correspond to their private self in order to acquire a particular social status (Covington, 1992; Leary, 1995), such as that of a diligent learner when interacting with the English teacher, or a disengaged teenager when interacting with their peers. This is an important finding, demonstrating the existence of context-dependent public self display similar to the self-presentation strategies discussed, for example, by Juvonen (1996) with reference to peers and teachers, but hardly ever mentioned in the language learning literature before. This also relates well to the self-presentation and impression management literature (Leary, 1995; Schlenker, 2003), which shows how the audience determines the salience of a particular public self in a particular social context.

The in-depth interviews also showed that the participants were reportedly striving to negotiate a strategic position in their interactions with various relational contexts, and to display a public self that they felt would serve their momentary purposes better. A clear example can be seen in this 17-year-old girl's words:

> Parents are busy with their jobs and with housework. They don't know you as you really are and can often be wrong about you. My mum and dad want different things to what I want – we've all got different opinions in my family. For example, my dad wants me to become a teacher because I loved playing teacher with the teddy bears and dolls when I was little. My mum wants me to do Medicine, but the problem is I hate

blood and I'm not strong enough to do Medicine. (...) I give my mum the impression that I'm gathering stuff about Medicine, and my dad knows I'm considering getting into teaching, but it's hard to work with children – I can see it in my own class how hard it is for the teacher to keep everyone afloat. (Taylor, 2010: 205)

This is a student who confessed she was secretly preparing to get a degree in Journalism, which was the career she wanted, but was torn between her father's and mother's expectations, described above, and those of her English teacher, who wanted her to do an English-related degree – as the student stated in the same interview.

Similar strategic self-presentation needs were invoked by other 17-year-olds, such as this female student:

I've noticed it's best to agree with the teacher, although sometimes I've got a different opinion. Because she often clings on to her view and I can't convince her that this is my opinion and my choice. Career options, for example. Maybe that's what I like, but she doesn't like it and is against it. It's a subjective thing. I've tried, but I've realised it's not worth it. (Taylor, 2010: 202)

Or this male student, who expresses his frustration with this need for strategic self-presentation in unambiguous terms:

I'll normally tell you straight all I've got to say, and it's a compromise for me having to hide the truth and to take roundabout routes. I hate this. But I've got to do it to avoid conflicts, especially with the teachers but also with my parents.

While such strategic self-presentation is, to a certain extent, necessary in all our daily interactions (e.g. Schlenker, 2003), these findings indicate not only that there is little relationship between what these students believe about themselves as language learners and the public selves they display in various relational contexts, but also – crucially – that students who feel they need to display a public self that is different from their private self have lower interest in the English class, lower feelings of being appreciated as individuals by the teacher, lower affective affiliations with the language, lower inclinations to see English as part of their future and lower declared achievement (Taylor, 2010, 2013).

Implications for Practice and Future Research

A leitmotif that appears to traverse all the literature reviewed above is the need for individuals to feel accepted for what they believe they are, and supported in their pursuit of what they would like to become through self-presentations that need the validation of a supportive 'audience'. In language education, this would mean, for example, allowing learners the liberty to make mistakes without feeling judged and ridiculed, and without feeling that this will affect their value as individuals – a very important point in language lessons, given the link between language and identity (e.g. Edwards, 2009). It also means allowing learners to 'speak as themselves' (Ushioda, 2011) and incorporating their experiences and social identities in the language curriculum (Norton Peirce, 1995; Pellegrino Aveni, 2005). Being language learners is only one facet of these individuals' identities, who are also sons or daughters, siblings, friends, neighbours, music fans, sports players, budding (or accomplished) poets and so on – all these components of their identity being potentially rich sources of material and inspiration for language lessons. Accepting learners as individuals with intrinsic value irrespective of how many grammar or pronunciation mistakes they make, and helping them through their transition from what they are as L2 learners to what they would like to become, would also help alleviate the anxiety that characterises language learning and affects self-expression more than in any other subject (Horwitz, 1995).

While these suggestions will be familiar to anyone acquainted with movements in L2 pedagogy over the past half century, research shows that a focus on the language learner as a 'real person' is still rare in many educational contexts and this can have serious consequences for L2 learning achievement (Taylor, 2013). In order for such suggestions to have more persuasive value, further research is needed on the relational aspects of the self in social interaction – in particular, research combining the synchronic and diachronic perspectives that would provide better understanding of the developmental relationship between private self-beliefs and public self-presentations, on the one hand, and the relationship between contradictory self-presentations in various relational contexts and the impact these may have on the individual's perceptions, attitudes and wellbeing, on the other hand. As individuals play multiple social roles and the main tool by which they construct their respective public selves is language, research that further explores the relationship between these complex identity processes and language acquisition/development is long overdue.

Recommended reading

Leary, M.R. (1995) *Self-Presentation: Impression Management and Interpersonal Behavior*. Madison, WI: Brown & Benchmark.

This is perhaps the key text in the self-presentation and impression-management literature, providing a solid social psychological background to the relational study of the self. It explores in detail the influence of one's private self on the public selves that one displays through self-presentation in various relational contexts, as well as the influence that these public selves can have on one's private self, behaviours and perceptions. A highly accessible text with examples that will strike a familiar chord with all readers.

Pellegrino Aveni, V. (2005) *Study Abroad and Second Language Use: Constructing the Self.* Cambridge: Cambridge University Press.

An excellent example of self-presentation theory applied to language learning in a study-abroad context. It emphasises the sometimes painful discrepancy between a language learner's perceived private self and their ideal self. It explores the relationship between language and social identity through grounded theory methods (interviews, observations, narratives).

Taylor, F. (2013) *Self and Identity in Adolescent Foreign Language Learning.* Bristol: Multilingual Matters.

This book considers language learners' identity as an aggregate of their private, ideal, public and socially imposed selves, combining the actual/ideal with the private/public perspectives in a relational study of the self. It presents evidence that language learners display public selves strategically in their various relational contexts. It shows that not only are these public selves different from one context to another, but they are often also different from the learners' private selves, with important consequences for their L2-declared achievement, perceived competence and motivation.

References

Andersen, S.M., Glassman, N.S. and Gold, D.A. (1998) Mental representations of the self, significant others, and nonsignificant others: Structure and processing of private and public aspects. *Journal of Personality and Social Psychology* 75 (4), 845–861.

Bartram, B. (2006) Attitudes to language learning: A comparative study of peer group influences. *Language Learning Journal* 33 (1), 47–52.

Baumeister, R.F. (1982) A self-presentational view of social phenomena. *Psychological Bulletin* 91 (1), 3–26.

Baumeister, R.F. (ed.) (1986) *Public Self and Private Self.* New York: Springer-Verlag.

Baumeister, R.F. (1997) Identity, self-concept, and self-esteem: The self lost and found. In R. Hogan and J.A. Johnson (eds) *Handbook of Personality Psychology* (pp. 681–710). San Diego: Academic Press.

Bennett, M. and Sani, F. (eds) (2004) *The Development of the Social Self.* New York: Psychology Press.

Covington, M.V. (1992) *Making the Grade: A Self-worth Perspective on Motivation and School Reform.* Cambridge: Cambridge University Press.

Cross, S. and Markus, H.R. (1991) Possible selves across the life span. *Human Development* 34 (4), 230–255.
Dörnyei, Z. (2005) *The Psychology of the Language Learner: Individual Differences in Second Language Acquisition*. Mahwah: Lawrence Erlbaum.
Dörnyei, Z. (2009) *The Psychology of Second Language Acquisition*. Oxford: Oxford University Press.
Dunkel, C.S. (2000) Possible selves as a mechanism for identity exploration. *Journal of Adolescence* 23 (5), 519–529.
Dunkel, C.S. and Kerpelman, J.L. (eds) (2006) *Possible Selves: Theory, Research and Applications*. New York: Nova Science.
Dunkel, C.S., Kelts, D. and Coon, B. (2006) Possible selves as mechanisms of change in therapy. In C.S. Dunkel and J.L. Kerpelman (eds) *Possible Selves: Theory, Research and Applications* (pp. 187–204). New York: Nova Science.
Dweck, C.S. (1999) *Self-Theories: Their Role in Motivation, Personality and Development*. Hove: Psychology Press.
Edwards, J. (2009) *Language and Identity*. Cambridge: Cambridge University Press.
Erikson, M.G. (2007) The meaning of the future: Toward a more specific definition of possible selves. *Review of General Psychology* 11 (4), 348–358.
Goldstein, T. (1997) *Two Languages at Work: Bilingual Life on the Factory Floor*. New York: Mouton de Gruyter.
Gollwitzer, P.M. and Kirchhof, O. (1998) The wilful pursuit of identity. In J. Heckhausen and C.S. Dweck (eds) *Motivation and Self-Regulation Across the Life Span* (pp. 389–423). Cambridge: Cambridge University Press.
Harter, S. (1999) *The Construction of the Self: A Developmental Perspective*. New York: Guildford Press.
Hattie, J. (1992) *Self-concept*. Hillsdale: Lawrence Erlbaum.
Higgins, T.E. (1987) Self-discrepancy: A theory relating self and affect. *Psychological Review* 94 (3), 319–340.
Higgins, T.E. (1996) The 'self digest': Self-knowledge serving self-regulatory functions. *Journal of Personality and Social Psychology* 71 (6), 1062–1083.
Higgins, T.E. (2006) Value from hedonic experience and engagement. *Psychological Review* 113 (3), 439–460.
Higgins, T.E., Roney, C.J.R., Crowe, E. and Hymes, C. (1994) Ideal versus ought predilections for approach and avoidance: Distinct self-regulatory systems. *Journal of Personality and Social Psychology* 66 (2), 276–286.
Horwitz, E.K. (1995) Student affective reactions and the teaching and learning of foreign languages. *International Journal of Educational Research* 23 (7), 573–579.
Juvonen, J. (1996) Self-presentation tactics promoting teacher and peer approval: The function of excuses and other clever explanations. In J. Juvonen and K.R. Wentzel (eds) *Social Motivation: Understanding Children's School Adjustment* (pp. 43–65). Cambridge: Cambridge University Press.
Leary, M.R. (1995) *Self-Presentation: Impression Management and Interpersonal Behavior*. Madison, WI: Brown & Benchmark.
Leary, M.R. and Allen, A.B. (2011) Self-presentational persona: Simultaneous management of multiple impressions. *Journal of Personality and Social Psychology* 101 (5), 1033–1049.
Leary, M.R. and Kowalski, R.M. (1990) Impression management: A literature review and two-component model. *Psychological Bulletin* 107 (1), 34–47.
Markus, H.R. and Nurius, P. (1987) Possible selves: The interface between motivation and the self-concept. In K. Yardley and T. Honess (eds) *Self and Identity: Psychosocial Perspectives* (pp. 157–172). Chichester: Wiley.
Markus, H.R. and Ruvolo, A.P. (1989) Possible selves: Personalized representations of goals. In L.A. Pervin (ed.) *Goal Concepts in Personality and Social Psychology* (pp. 211–241). Hillsdale: Lawrence Erlbaum.

McKay, S. and Wong, S.C. (1996) Multiple discourses, multiple identities: Investment and agency in second language learning among Chinese adolescent immigrant students. *Harvard Educational Review* 66 (3), 577–608.
Mercer, S. (2011) *Towards an Understanding of Language Learner Self-Concept*. Dordrecht: Springer.
Miller, J. (2003) *Audible Differences: ESL and Social Identity in Schools*. Clevedon: Multilingual Matters.
Noels, K.A. (2009) The internalisation of language learning into the self and social identity. In Z. Dörnyei and E. Ushioda (eds) *Motivation, Language Identity and the L2 Self* (pp. 295–313). Bristol: Multilingual Matters.
Noels, K.A., Pelletier, L.G., Clément, R. and Vallerand, R.J. (2003) Why are you learning a second language? Motivational orientations and self-determination theory. *Language Learning* 53 (S1), 33–64.
Norton, B. (1997) Language, identity and the ownership of English. *TESOL Quarterly* 31 (3), 409–429.
Norton, B. (2000) *Identity and Language Learning: Gender, Ethnicity and Educational Change*. Harlow: Pearson.
Norton Peirce, B. (1995) Social identity, investment, and language learning. *TESOL Quarterly* 29 (1), 9–31.
Oyserman, D. and Fryberg, S. (2006) The possible selves of diverse adolescents: Content and function across gender, race and national origin. In C.S. Dunkel and J.L. Kerpelman (eds) *Possible Selves: Theory, Research and Applications* (pp. 17–39). New York: Nova Science.
Oyserman, D., Bybee, D., Terry, K. and Hart-Johnson, T. (2004) Possible selves as roadmaps. *Journal of Research in Personality* 38 (2), 130–149.
Pavlenko, A. (2004) The making of an American: Negotiation of identities at the turn of the twentieth century. In A. Pavlenko and A. Blackledge (eds) *Negotiation of Identities in Multilingual Contexts* (pp. 34–67). Clevedon: Multilingual Matters.
Pavlenko, A. and Blackledge, A. (2004a) Introduction: New theoretical approaches to the study of negotiation of identities in multilingual contexts. In A. Pavlenko and A. Blackledge (eds) *Negotiation of Identities in Multilingual Contexts* (pp. 1–33). Clevedon: Multilingual Matters.
Pavlenko, A. and Blackledge, A. (eds) (2004b) *Negotiation of Identities in Multilingual Contexts*. Clevedon: Multilingual Matters.
Pavlenko, A. and Lantolf, J.P. (2000) Second language learning as participation and the (re)construction of selves. In J.P. Lantolf (ed.) *Sociocultural Theory and Second Language Learning* (pp. 155–177). Oxford: Oxford University Press.
Pavlenko, A., Blackledge, A., Piller, I. and Teutsch-Dwyer, M. (eds) (2001) *Multilingualism, Second Language Learning, and Gender*. Berlin: Mouton de Gruyter.
Pellegrino Aveni, V. (2005) *Study Abroad and Second Language Use: Constructing the Self*. Cambridge: Cambridge University Press.
Pfeifer, J.H., Masten, C.L., Borofsky, L.A., Dapretto, M., Fuligni, A.J. and Lieberman, M.D. (2009) Neural correlates of direct and reflected self-appraisals in adolescents and adults: When social perspective-taking informs self-perception. *Child Development* 80 (4), 1016–1038.
Rogers, C. (1951) *Client-Centred Therapy*. Boston: Houghton-Mifflin.
Rogers, C. and Dymond, R. (1954) *Psychotherapy and Personality Change*. Chicago: University of Chicago Press.
Ruvolo, A.P. and Markus, H.R. (1992) Possible selves and performance: The power of self-relevant imagery. *Social Cognition* 10 (1), 95–124.
Schlenker, B.R. (1986) Self-identification: Toward an integration of the private and public self. In R.F. Baumeister (ed.) *Public Self and Private Self* (pp. 21–62). New York: Springer.
Schlenker, B.R. (2003) Self-presentation. In M. R. Leary and J. P. Tangney (eds) *Handbook of Self and Identity* (pp. 492–518). New York: Guildford Press.

Schlenker, B.R. and Weigold, M.F. (1992) Interpersonal processes involving impression regulation and management. *Annual Review of Psychology* 43 (1), 133–168.

Schlenker, B.R., Dlugolecki, D.W. and Doherty, K. (1994) The impact of self-presentations on self-appraisals and behavior: The power of public commitment. *Personality and Social Psychology Bulletin* 20 (1), 20–33.

Schwartz, S.J., Luyckx, K. and Vignoles, V.L. (eds) (2011) *Handbook of Identity Theory and Research*. New York: Springer.

Seifert, T.L. and O'Keefe, B.A. (2001) The relationship of work avoidance and learning goals to perceived competence, externality and meaning. *British Journal of Educational Psychology* 71 (1), 81–92.

Strahan, E.J. and Wilson, A.E. (2006) Temporal comparisons, identity, and motivation: The relation between past, present, and possible future selves. In C.S. Dunkel and J.L. Kerpelman (eds) *Possible Selves: Theory, Research and Applications* (pp. 1–15). New York: Nova Science.

Taylor, F. (2010) A Quadripolar Model of Identity in Adolescent Foreign Language Learners (Unpublished PhD thesis). University of Nottingham.

Taylor, F. (2013) *Self and Identity in Adolescent Foreign Language Learning*. Bristol: Multilingual Matters.

Taylor, F., Busse, V., Gagova, L., Marsden, E. and Roosken, B. (2013) Identity in foreign language learning and teaching: Why listening to our students' and teachers' voices really does matter. *British Council ELT Research Papers*. Available from http://www.teachingenglish.org.uk/publications

Tice, D.M. and Wallace, H.M. (2003) The reflected self: Creating yourself as (you think) others see you. In M.R. Leary and J.P. Tangney (eds) *Handbook of Self and Identity* (pp. 91–105). New York: Guildford Press.

Toohey, K. (2000) *Learning English at School: Identity, Social Relations and Classroom Practice*. Clevedon: Multilingual Matters.

Ushioda, E. (2009) A person-in-context relational view of emergent motivation, self and identity. In Z. Dörnyei and E. Ushioda (eds) *Motivation, Language Identity and the L2 Self* (pp. 215–228). Bristol: Multilingual Matters.

Ushioda, E. (2011) Motivating learners to speak as themselves. In G. Murray, X. Gao and T. Lamb (eds) *Identity, Motivation and Autonomy in Language Learning* (pp. 11–24). Bristol: Multilingual Matters.

Van Hook, E. and Higgins, T.E. (1988) Self-related problems beyond the self-concept: Motivational consequences of discrepant self-guides. *Journal of Personality and Social Psychology* 55 (4), 625–633.

Vignoles, V.L., Schwartz, S.J. and Luyckx, K. (2011) Introduction: Towards an integrative view of identity. In S.J. Schwartz, K. Luyckx and V.L. Vignoles (eds) *Handbook of Identity Theory and Research* (Vol. 1, pp. 1–27). New York: Springer.

Vohs, K.D., Baumeister, R.F. and Ciarocco, N.J. (2005) Self-regulation and self-presentation: Regulatory resource depletion impairs impression management and effortful self-presentation depletes regulatory resources. *Journal of Personality and Social Psychology* 88 (4), 632–657.

Williams, M., Burden, R. and Lanvers, U. (2002) 'French is the language of love and stuff': Student perceptions of issues related to motivation in learning a foreign language. *British Educational Research Journal* 28 (4), 503–528.

Wurf, E. and Markus, H.R. (1991) Possible selves and the psychology of personal growth. In D.J. Ozer, J.M. Healy Jr. and A.J. Stewart (eds) *Perspectives in Personality* (Vol. 3, pp. 39–62). London: Kingsley.

Zentner, M. and Renaud, O. (2007) Origins of adolescents' ideal self: An intergenerational perspective. *Journal of Personality and Social Psychology* 92 (3), 557–574.

8 Imagined and Possible Selves: Stories We Tell Ourselves About Ourselves

Stephen Ryan and Kay Irie

Introduction

All of us create and share stories. This is something we start from a young age, in our earliest social interactions, and continue throughout our lives. One of the key stories that follows us over the course of that lifespan is the story we tell to ourselves: the story of the self. This story affects how we interpret our pasts, how we see ourselves now, and the paths we envision for our futures; 'humans are storytelling organisms who, individually and socially, lead storied lives' (Connelly & Clandinin, 1990: 2).

In order to tell this story, we need to be able to create and project images of ourselves beyond our actual experience or environment, a uniquely human quality (Taylor *et al.*, 1998). This ability to generate internal representations of the self outside an immediate physical or social environment facilitates the planning and regulation of our own behaviour; the experience of 'participating' in mental simulations of events can function as a form of internal rehearsal that enables us to anticipate the actions or reactions of others and to guide our own behaviour accordingly. There is a broad consensus within the psychology literature 'that generating mental images of future success can sometimes increase achievement motivation, effort, and performance' (Vasquez & Buehler, 2007: 1392).

In this chapter, we consider how this ability applies to, and is applied by, language learners. As Pavlenko and Norton (2007: 670) observe, 'the learning of another language, perhaps more than any other educational activity, reflects the desire of learners to expand their range of identities and to reach out to wider worlds'. If we regard identity as 'an individual's sense of self in relation to a particular social context or community of practice' (Mercer,

2012: 11–12), then for many language learners, especially those with little or minimal opportunity for actual contact with speakers of a target language, the imagination is a key site in which the individual negotiates identities (Yashima, 2013). We aim to show that for some learners, possible and imagined selves are integral and essential to the language learning process, and a greater understanding of the workings of the imagination may prove to be an invaluable resource for both teachers and learners.

Although this chapter is primarily conceptual in nature, we present the imagination as an essential, practical tool for language learning. In the first part, we consider how the imagination and possible futures connect to self-concept in the psychology literature. We then identify a relative lack of interest, until very recently at least, in the power of the imagination on the part of second language acquisition (SLA) researchers. Although there has been some scholarly interest in concepts such as imagined and possible selves, the imagination remains very much on the margins of the SLA research agenda. In the final part of the chapter, we move away from the theoretical discussion to consider ways in which teachers may incorporate an understanding of imagined selves into their teaching, not as a mere 'optional extra' but in ways that may exploit some of the potential of the imagination as the 'workhorse' of learning (Egan, 2005).

Imagining the Self

An obvious starting point for understanding what we mean by the term 'self' would be to consider the answers individuals come up with when they ask themselves the question 'Who am I?' However, although this provides a useful base, it also represents a somewhat static portrayal of the self, very much rooted in the here and now. For this reason we intend to align ourselves with McAdams's (1996, 2001) notion of a 'storied self': the self as an ongoing internal narrative of who we think we have been, who we think we are, who we would like to be, and the person(s) we are afraid of becoming. As in many of the best stories, there are numerous simultaneous plot lines. It is a dynamic story, constantly being revised and retold. Through the telling and retelling of the story, the narrative is developed, with key events and characters being manipulated to serve the demands of that narrative.

Stories are created through interaction between a narrator and an audience. In the case of the story of the self, the self functions as both narrator and audience. The self is probably the most demanding audience of all; it is an audience that has heard the story many times before. The self as narrator is constantly tailoring the story to the demands of the self as audience. The demands of the audience shape the form and content of the story and how we choose to frame the current version of the story affects subsequent re-tellings.

Integrating past and present within the self-concept

There is a tendency, when discussing imagined or possible selves, to focus on future states or outcomes. This overlooks the key role that the imagination plays in the construction of the current self-concept; how we see ourselves now is very much a function of how we interpret or process past events and experiences. Mental simulations – imagining – are an integral part of our interpretations of past events, which in turn help us form theories of the current self. Based on a series of studies exploring how we distinguish between events that actually happened and those that have been mentally simulated, Johnson, together with various colleagues (Johnson, 1988; Johnson & Raye, 2000; Johnson et al., 1988), proposed the concept of 'reality monitoring'. A key finding of these studies, and central to the concept of reality monitoring, is that people sometimes struggle to differentiate the two; what we believe to be memories of actual events are often mental simulations of those events. In other words, they are imagined versions of what happened. It is important to note that these are neither false memories nor delusions; our interpretations of events, through the ongoing internal narrative of the self, are continually changing. Our sense of experience, and by extension our sense of who we are, comes from subjective, malleable interpretations of events rather than the actual events themselves. As an illustration, let us imagine a young language learner who comes into contact with a second language (L2) speaker. This is one of her first encounters with an actual, living speaker of the target language, and through a combination of misunderstandings, gestures, and a great deal of patience, the two manage to have a mutually satisfactory social exchange. This exchange makes a considerable impression on our young language learner and over time she mentally replays the scene, focusing on certain aspects while gradually discarding others. As she replays the scene in her mind, she may try out different conversational strategies or lexical items to those actually used. Through repeated mental simulation, retelling the story to herself, an awkward or limited social encounter may evolve into a smooth, successful exchange of ideas, which may go on to function as a key formative episode in the development of this learner's L2 self-concept. In such a case, it is the internally edited version of herself as a successful language user, rather than actual events, that informs her self-concept.

The above example illustrates how we process and re-interpret past events through mental simulations in order to construct our current self-concept. It also suggests links to other key concepts in educational psychology. One such concept is attributions, i.e. our internal explanations for perceived successes and failures. In this example, we observe the learner coming to perceive the interaction as a success only after repeated mental replaying and internal editing of the event. She will also come up with explanations for this success, perhaps a personality trait such as her outgoing nature or a belief that she has an innate ability to 'pick up' languages. Another key psychological concept suggested by the example is self-efficacy (see Mills, Chapter 2, this volume), which represents an assessment of our current ability to perform a given task within a given context and has been described as 'the most important building block in one's self-concept' (Bong & Skaalvik, 2003: 10–11). In this case, the young woman is likely to believe that she is capable of engaging in social interactions with strangers in the L2 and feel confident approaching such situations in the future. It is interesting to note that while her attributions and feelings of self-efficacy are very real, many of the events that produced them have occurred only in her imagination.

However, it is not only imagined versions of ourselves in the past that shape our current self-concept; how we envisage ourselves in the future also plays a major role in how we regard ourselves now. In the next section, we focus on how learners use their imaginations to guide them towards desirable future outcomes.

Agency in future-directed selves

Possible selves and self-discrepancy

A key concept in explaining how people represent themselves outside their immediate physical or temporal settings and into some future state is that of possible selves, which was introduced by Markus and Nurius (1986). Put simply, possible selves represent people's ideas of who they might become, who they would like to become or who they are afraid of becoming; they form 'a bridge of self-representations between one's current state and one's desired or hoped-for state' (Markus & Ruvolo, 1989: 211). These mental self-representations guide individuals towards becoming the person they would like to be, a *hoped-for self*, or away from outcomes they seek to avoid, a *feared self*.

Contemporaneously to Markus and colleagues' theorisations of possible selves, Higgins (1987) was developing his *Self-Discrepancy Theory*. Three sets of self guides were proposed: the *ideal self*, the *ought self*, and an *actual self*. In this model, the ideal self is the key motivational component of the self, 'the core mechanism for self-regulation and intrinsic motivation' (Boyatzis & Akrivou, 2006: 625), emerging from desires, hopes, dreams, and aspirations. Individuals are motivated to reduce discrepancies between this ideal self and the actual self, the individual's assessment of the current self. Higgins also proposes a third component, the ought self, which, crucially, adds a social dimension to the model. The ought self is a function of the expectations and perceived obligations to others; the ought self is how an individual perceives other people's views of who he or she should be.

One area of theoretical fuzziness concerns where the ideal self and ought self overlap. Almost all of us belong to various social groups and the act of belonging to those groups imposes some degree of obligation to conform to group norms. At what point does the pressure to conform to models of group identity compromise deeper personal dreams or aspirations? There may be times when there is harmony between the ideal and ought selves, but there may also be times of conflict, where other people's versions of what an individual's ideal self should be – the ought self – differs from that of the individual. The ideal self is 'both privately conceptualised and socially influenced' (Boyatzis & Akrivou, 2006: 625) and it is through the ought self that many of these external influences are regulated, with some of them eventually being internalised to such an extent that they become a part of the individual's ideal self.

Experienced meaning and agency within the vision

Although we earlier described possible selves as emerging from hopes, fears, and aspirations, Erikson (2007) warns against too loose a definition of the term; 'all hopes and fears are not possible selves' (Erikson, 2007: 350). So what is it that distinguishes mere hopes and fears from possible selves? According to Erikson, possible selves must contain some degree of experienced meaning and be sufficiently close or relevant to the current self-concept. Possible selves are more than mere representations of ourselves in some future state; they contain an element of experiencing ourselves in that future state. As discussed earlier, many of our so-called memories are actually mental simulations of past events, yet we can come to conceive of these as actual lived experiences; in the same way it is possible to 'experience' ourselves in future states.

It is through this experiential component that we create meanings relevant to the self, and Erikson goes on to identify agency as 'a fundamental feature of possible selves' (Erikson, 2007: 352). For the purposes of this discussion, we will regard agency as the power to act or influence outcomes, 'a subjective sense of the self as intentionally acting within the world' (Markus & Kitayama, 2004: 5). Wurf and Markus (1991: 39) characterise a possible self as 'a compelling vision or conception of the self in a future state' and it would seem that the 'compelling' element distinguishing a possible self from a mere vision of oneself in a future state is this sense of agency within the vision. If agency is a capacity to act volitionally and affect outcomes, then we can extrapolate that any vision largely dependent upon outside forces for its realisation is unlikely to become a compelling one. A sense of agency within possible selves performs a vital regulatory role, linking possible selves to the current self-concept; if a possible self is too remote from the current self-concept then an individual may not experience the requisite sense of agency.

Imagination and action

Erikson's emphasis on the crucial role of agency in the construction of possible selves is consistent with research looking at how the brain processes mentally simulated images. Decety and Grèzes (2006) describe how advances in neuro-imagery technology, by which we mean the various techniques that allow us to produce images of the structure and functioning of the brain, have expanded our knowledge of the workings of the human mind. In a review of the literature on mental imagery, they discuss numerous imaging studies that show 'a simulated action can elicit perceptual activity that resembles the activity that would have occurred if the action had actually been performed' (Decety & Grèzes, 2006: 5); in other words, the brain processes imagined events or actions in the same way that it processes actual ones. This finding is an important one that suggests imagining performing an action allows individuals to incorporate this experience into the self-concept, and this is equally true when we rehearse possible future outcomes as when we replay past events.

Different types of mental simulation

We need to take care not to group together all mental simulations under a single clumsy heading; humans use the imagination in many different ways. In this next section, we consider some of the different ways in which we imagine and their likely behavioural consequences.

Goal-directed mental simulation

Perhaps the most obvious way in which the imagination connects to behaviour is through the construction and articulation of goals. It is interesting to note how in popular discourse the word 'dream' is readily understood to mean life goal. However, dreams, or mental simulations, are not simply manifestations of pre-existing goals, they also help us envision steps towards achieving these goals. Additionally, mental simulations provide an extra sensory element containing 'tangible images related to achieving the goal' (Dörnyei & Kubanyiova, 2014) that enhance motivation. When we imagine doing something, we also 'experience' the action and feel emotionally involved. Just as we are able to utilise actual life experiences to improve future performance, imagined experiences enable us to predict how we may behave in certain situations, where we may succeed and where we may fail. This knowledge then facilitates the construction of problem-solving strategies and specific plans to achieve these goals (Taylor et al., 1998). Using the language of conventional goal-setting theory, we can say that the imagination contributes to the setting of distal goals – those long-term, far-off goals we set ourselves (for an overview of goal-setting theory, see Locke & Latham, 1994, 2006) – and more proximal goals, the more immediate and achievable goals that represent steps towards the eventual distal goal. However, regarding imagined or possible selves as simple goals fails to acknowledge their all-encompassing nature. As Pizzalato (2006: 58) explains, possible selves 'are related to a long-term developmental goal involving goal setting, volition (via adherence to associated schemas), and goal achievement, but are larger than any one or combination of these constructs'. Goals within a possible-selves framework represent a form of self-definition, an essential part of who one is, rather than some distant, desired future outcome.

Process or outcome

One key distinction in the nature of our mental simulations is their focus or content. For example, let us now picture another imaginary language learner. This learner has to make a presentation in the L2 in front of a large audience and is very nervous about doing so. Although the actual date of the presentation is some way off, he finds himself constantly thinking about it. At times, he pictures himself triumphant after making a successful presentation to the sound of thunderous applause, and in such a vision the focus of his imagination is very much on an outcome. At other times, he may imagine himself working on his presentation late into the night fuelled by endless cups of coffee; in this case, the focus of his imagination is on the process, on the steps required to achieve the successful outcome. There is a growing awareness that mental images focusing on how an individual may achieve a given outcome, the process, are more productive than those focusing on that outcome itself (Pham & Taylor, 1999; Taylor *et al.*, 1998). It is not enough to simply have clear visions of who or what one wants to become; an individual needs to simulate in detail how to become that person.

Fantasy or expectation

The idea that positive images of the self in some desired future state can motivate the individual to achieve that state is a highly attractive one; we would all like to believe that our dreams may one day come true. However, at this point, it may be pertinent to consider some of the possible negative behavioural outcomes associated with the imagination. In some cases, the imagination can provide a template for future action, whereas in others it merely provides the individual with a vicarious experience that bypasses any need for effort (Oettingen & Hagenah, 2007); mental simulations can turn into implausible fantasies that the individual has no intention of realising. A further indirect consequence of a mental simulation that drifts into fantasy may be that it distracts the individual from important tasks that require immediate attention or effort (Oettingen *et al.*, 2001).

Mental simulations do not always lead to self-regulated, goal-directed behaviour. In many cases, fantasies provide a reward in themselves; it can be very pleasant to temporarily immerse oneself in a fantasy that is unlikely to ever be realised. Fantasies can represent a short-lived escape from the current self and its limitations. For the workings of the imagination to have meaningful behavioural consequences, there must be some expectation that a vision may be realised. The notion of plausibility in future-oriented visions of the self is crucial and again we find the notion of a storied self to be helpful. For a mental self-representation to be plausible as a possible self, it must fit the current narrative of the self and not break with the trajectory of existing plot lines.

First-person or third-person mental images

A further interesting distinction made in the literature concerns the perspective from which we construct our mental imagery. Perhaps the most conspicuous way in which people construct mental images is to simply visualise themselves performing a given task; a first-person perspective. If we go back to the example of the language learner giving an important presentation in the L2, then he may picture himself approaching the podium, arranging notes, looking out at the audience, feeling his heart pounding from nerves, and taking a deep breath before commencing. However, another way to imagine this scene would be from a third-person perspective; for example, the learner could imagine being a member of the audience watching that presentation, observing himself and the reactions of others.

In a series of studies investigating how mental imagery influenced the motivation of university students, Vasquez and Buehler (2007: 1394) found that it was images from a third-person perspective that were more likely to enhance motivation, that a 'third-person perspective prompts people to construe events in a manner that heightens their personal meaning and significance'. In essence, what they are arguing is that the third-person perspective empowers the individual to gain distance from the self and construe events with a higher level of abstraction. This higher level of abstraction (Vallacher & Wenger, 1985) should make the action seem more important to the individual as it highlights its wider significance; in contrast, a lower level of abstraction would focus more on specific, concrete features of the action.

The finding that third-person perspectives enhance motivation is a challenging one, offering a fascinating contrast to much of the possible selves literature, which is very much based on the motivational effects of first-person experiential mental imagery. The obvious implication of this finding is that learners may benefit from some degree of detachment from imagined or possible selves, rather than immersion in them.

Summary

In this section we have considered the crucial role that the imagination plays in the formation of the self-concept. People spend a significant part of their lives imagining. They imagine in different ways, for different reasons, and with different outcomes. Some of these mental simulations become integral to the self-concept, while others are discarded. A storied-self approach offers an accessible explanation of how individuals incorporate imagined versions of themselves into their current self-concepts; people are able to assimilate those mental representations that fit within a currently operational narrative of the self.

Possible Selves and the Imagination in the SLA Literature

Educators tend to have a somewhat ambivalent relationship with the imagination. On the one hand, we tend to regard it as generally a 'good thing', something to be encouraged in learners, but, on the other, we are reluctant to recognise it as a core component of the learning experience, relegating it to a peripheral, 'optional' role. This is a pattern replicated in the SLA literature, which has, until very recently, been disinclined to consider a central role for the imagination in second language learning. However, in recent years, there has been a growing realisation that language learning is more than simply the gradual acquisition of discrete items of language: instead it is 'a process of becoming, or avoiding becoming a certain person, rather than a simple accumulation of skills and knowledge' (Pavlenko & Norton, 2007: 670). The central thesis underlying this chapter is that since so much of 'becoming a certain person' is contained within the imagination, a greater understanding of the workings of the imagination is essential to an understanding of language learning. We will begin this section by considering two established themes within the SLA literature, imagined communities and possible selves, which connect the self to language learning. We will then move on to suggest possible links between the imagination and other SLA concepts.

Imagined communities

The concept of imagined communities was originally developed by Anderson (1991) as an explanation for how people felt a sense of nationhood or common identity with others that they had never known or were unlikely to ever meet, and it was introduced to the field of SLA, via Wenger's (1998) notion of communities of practice, by Norton (2001). Norton's original concern was with immigrant learners' struggles to belong to language communities that were not immediately accessible; these struggles were theorised to have a significant impact on their identity construction and language learning. Since its initial, somewhat narrow, theorisation, the concept of imagined communities of language learners has been expanded to include other language learning contexts (see Murray, 2011) and to explain how language learners reach out and connect with people beyond their immediate social networks. As an illustration, Murray describes the case of learners of English using information from popular films and television programmes as models for their own emerging English-speaking identities; as a part of this process, they picture themselves interacting with others as members of the kinds of communities featured in these films and programmes. Imagining themselves belonging to these communities serves as a guide for both the kinds of social situations in which they might envision themselves using English, and the appropriate language to use in those situations. For many language learners, their membership and participation in these imagined communities is an important part of who they are. Belonging to an imagined community is neither escapist nor unregulated; it represents a vital form of self-realisation. As with all communities, there are membership requirements and these requirements function as self-guides for individuals participating in imagined communities.

Dörnyei's L2 motivational self system

Within the SLA literature, the most systematic application of the possible selves construct is found in Dörnyei's L2 Motivational Self System (Dörnyei, 2005, 2009; see Ushioda, Chapter 9, this volume). The L2 motivational self system represents an L2-specific version of Higgins's self-discrepancy framework and includes two principal sets of self-guides: the *ideal L2 self* and the *ought-to L2 self*. A third, experiential, component, the *L2 learning experience*, emerging from learners' perceptions of their own previous language-learning successes and failures, is also built into the framework. Possibly the most exciting aspect of the L2 Motivational Self System is that it offers an explanation for how visions of the self energise motivation. According to Dörnyei (2009), the ideal L2 self is more than simply a vision of oneself in a desired future state; it must be accompanied with the knowledge of 'how to get there' in order to function as an effective motivator. Dörnyei outlines four key steps: constructing the vision, strengthening the vision, substantiating the vision, and activating the ideal L2 self. Although employing different terminology, these steps to realising an ideal L2 self have clear echoes to the earlier discussion of process-focused mental imagery.

Links to other concepts in the SLA literature

The discussion of the L2 Motivational Self System reminds us that imagined and possible selves are already receiving some attention within the field of SLA. In this section, we would like to expand upon this and point to connections with other concepts elsewhere in the SLA literature, with the aim of highlighting the central role of the imagination in the language learning process and attracting more attention to this fascinating area.

Another area of motivation theory that has already been applied within SLA is *Self-Determination Theory* (SDT) (see Deci & Ryan, 1985, 2002; Ushioda, Chapter 9, this volume). A key concern of SDT is how individuals come to internalise external responsibilities and demands on the self. The imagination has a role to play here. Let us picture a language learner feeling considerable pressure from her parents and teachers to do well on a particular test. She may not see success in this test as relevant to her current L2 self-concept. However, since the test is such a dominant part of her current language learning experience, she may find herself, perhaps unwittingly at first, including success on this test within a visualisation of her future self. Over time and with repeated retelling of the story, success in this test may come to gain a more central role and become core to her L2 self-concept. Here we observe the imagination acting as a catalyst for the internalisation of what was once a remote, external obligation; pressure from others to succeed on a test is gradually incorporated into the self-concept through repeated mental simulations.

In our earlier discussion of the ways in which people imagine, we touched upon the importance of third-person mental imagery. The idea of stepping back or detaching from the self has echoes in the notion of critical reflection, which is central to metacognition. Another primary component of metacognition is planning, and this is closely related to the idea of process-oriented mental simulation, in that language learners are required to envision the various steps and strategies necessary for successful learning. The unique contribution the imagination offers is that it can provide an element of virtual experience or participation that may facilitate 'the ability to make one's thinking visible' (Anderson, 2012: 170). Mental simulations add a vital sensory and emotional experience that takes metacognition beyond conventional conceptualisations of coolly cognitive reflection.

We do not intend to suggest that SDT, reflection, and metacognition are the only areas in which there are overlaps with our discussion of imagined and possible selves. We have simply highlighted these as they represent clear illustrations of the connections between the current discussion and other concepts in SLA. This suggests that a greater understanding of the imagination may reveal areas of untapped potential for both theory and practice.

Methodological challenges researching the imagined selves of language learners

A key theme running through this chapter is that the distinction between imagined events and actual events is a blurred one; that imagined versions of ourselves are integral to our self-concept. This poses huge challenges for researchers. Within mainstream psychology, the dominant approach to the study of the imagination has been quantitative analysis of experimental studies. Such an approach provides insights into broad tendencies or patterns but is of little practical value to educators. Educators need to know more about the real stories learners tell themselves and how these are incorporated within their self-concept. The extent to which events, actual or imagined, are incorporated into the self-concept is very much an individual subjective judgement. This suggests that it may be more profitable for researchers to investigate this subjective dimension, rather than adhere to notions of objective investigation. One interesting approach to the study of possible selves is the use of Q-methodology (Kerpelman, 2006; Pittman *et al.*, 2009). Q-methodology represents a scientific approach to the study of individual subjectivity, people's viewpoints, beliefs, and attitudes through a unique data collection technique (Q sorts) followed by a set of statistical procedures and interpretation processes that offer a narrative-like qualitative detail (Brown, 1993). Q studies aim to identify existing viewpoints among a group of individuals and understand them holistically. A particular strength of Q-methodology is that it may enable us to investigate how some possible selves become more salient than others and how individuals organise and prioritise various available possible selves.

Our focus on the storytelling nature of the self-concept suggests that narrative inquiry (see Czarniawska-Joerges, 2004) may be another promising approach to researching the imagined or possible selves of language learners. One reason we describe this approach as promising is that it offers links to an already established body of research (see Duff & Bell, 2002; Pavlenko, 2002, 2007) within SLA. If we subscribe to the view that 'teachers and learners are storytellers and characters in their own and other's stories' (Connelly & Clandinin, 1990: 2), then a methodology focusing on the narrative dimension to human experience may be particularly suited to providing insights into the 'story of the self'.

Pedagogic Applications

One of the most rewarding aspects of being a language teacher is helping students realise their aspirations and dreams of using a language. In this chapter, we have aimed to stress the practical dimension to understanding learners' imaginations and we find the notion of a storied self very helpful in this respect, not least because stories are such a fundamental aspect of language use; the sharing of stories seems uniquely suited to the field of language learning. Encouraging learners to construct their 'storied self' from various angles and with different focuses may enable us to harness the potential of the imagination and do so in a way that is firmly grounded in the realities of the language classroom.

Attribution retraining

In the first part of this chapter, we observed how the constant telling and retelling of the story of the self causes us to re-interpret certain past events. This seems to offer an interesting opening for attribution retraining. This refers to interventions designed to encourage learners to reconsider their internal explanations for perceived successes and failures. Attributions, as discussed earlier in this chapter, are key to learners' feelings of being in control of their use of the L2, and have also been shown to influence motivation and approaches to learning (Hsieh, 2012).

If we regard attributions as a part of the story we tell ourselves, then attribution retraining becomes a matter of trying to help learners tell a more positive, more empowering story about themselves to themselves. If retelling a story allows us to re-interpret past events, then it should be possible for teachers to design activities that encourage learners to look at key events in their learning experience from various angles and perspectives. In doing so, learners may feel a greater sense of ownership of inferences emerging from stories that they have constructed for and about themselves. We hypothesise that this greater sense of ownership may make it easier for learners to challenge established attributions and integrate new ideas into the self-concept.

Let us consider a tricky example for any teacher: the case of a relatively successful language learner who attributes that success primarily to the influence of a good teacher. The aim of attribution retraining here would be to encourage this learner to focus more on factors contributing to her perceived successes that are within her own control. As part of the retraining, we could ask her to tell the story of one of her perceived successes while learning the language and in the telling of that story focus on some of the concrete challenges she faced and decisions she took to overcome those challenges. By highlighting the learner's agency in her own successes, the aim is that she may incorporate these elements into future versions of the story of her success, and, by extension, attribute that success to her own efforts rather than those of the teacher.

Maintaining connections to the current self-concept

As we observed earlier, keeping mental imagery sufficiently close to the current self-concept is crucial to maintaining a sense of agency within those visions. This requires well-intentioned language teachers to be mindful of some of the possible unintended consequences of uncritically encouraging learners to unleash their imaginations. In cases where mental simulations become too distant from the current self-concept, they are more likely to deteriorate into implausible fantasy than forge motivating visions. This presents a precarious balancing act for language teachers; on the one hand, they do not wish to crush the dreams or hopes of learners, but there is also a need to guide learners away from the kind of mental imagery that may result in maladaptive behaviour, such as the setting of unrealistic or impractical goals. As an extreme example, let us picture a beginner adult learner joining a class that meets only once per week. This individual has suddenly been inspired to learn a language after watching a major sporting event and dreams of becoming an interpreter for world-class athletes. Such a goal is too far removed from the learner's current proficiency and not feasible given the limitations of the learning situation. In the initial stages, this vision may provide the impetus for action, but it may become problematic as the learner encounters the frustrations of actually learning a language to maintain this enthusiasm and effort, the second essential element of motivation; a sudden realisation of the scale of the task ahead may cause this learner to give up altogether.

Teachers should encourage learners to believe in their dreams, but they must also persuade those learners to 'keep it real'. One way to do this is through the sharing of their stories of the self with peers, through making their mental imagery explicit. In a discussion of how we transform our mental images into goal-directed behaviour, Van der Helm (2009: 102) states that 'there is a need to make a vision explicit, and to use words, metaphors, and images to describe and share our idealised future. From a practical point of view, developing a vision requires communicating the vision'. The fact that the act of communication is an essential part of realising a vision suggests that language learning may be an area especially well suited to the sharing of personal visions and an interesting example of this in practice is provided by Murphey et al. (2012), who describe a series of activities that allowed learners of English to share their ideal L2 selves with other learners. The great advantage of this approach, beyond the fact that it offers an excellent opportunity for self-relevant language practice, is that it encourages learners to articulate their stories in an environment that is tied to the realities of their learning, an environment that may also offer feedback, support, and encouragement.

Process-focused imagination

One of the key distinctions we have discussed relating to how people imagine is on the focus of mental imagery: are mental simulations focused on outcome or process? The general consensus within the literature is that process-focused mental imagery leads to more successful outcomes. The challenge for language teachers is to come up with activities that encourage learners to explore their imaginations, but to do so in a systematic fashion based on an understanding of the relevant research. One attractive approach is that described by Hock et al. (2006), and further discussed by Dörnyei (2009) and Dörnyei and Kubanyiova (2014). They report on a *Possible Selves Program* used with university and middle-school students in the US. The programme consists of six stages: discovering, thinking, sketching, reflecting, growing, performing. What immediately struck us as practising language teachers were the similarities between some of the activities described in the programme and those – such as eliciting vocabulary, describing past events, and sharing reflections – that are already an integral part of language classes. Although research into interventions designed to enhance specifically L2-related self-images is limited, Magid and Chan (2012) describe highly encouraging findings from two such programmes conducted in very different learning contexts. Their findings suggest that it may be possible to tailor elements of this approach to the specific needs of the language classroom, situating the imagination and the sharing of personal visions at the centre of the language-learning experience.

Third-person perspectives

So far, the SLA literature dealing with imagined and possible selves has focused on first-person perspectives and the motivational effects of experiencing the self as an agent of a desired future outcome. We would like to propose a complementary third-person perspective that encourages learners to step back and observe themselves within their own mental simulations. The literature indicates that a third-person perspective may enhance motivation, which, using our storied-self framework, suggests that learners may benefit from activities that highlight their role as the audience in the developing story of the self. The detachment provided by this audience perspective may enable learners to step back and observe the 'big picture'.

Conclusion

'[P]eople spend an enormous amount of time envisioning their futures. We now know that this imaginative work has powerful consequences' (Markus, 2006: vii). As language teachers and continuing language learners, we have frequently been struck by the gulf between the central role that imagination plays in language learning and the dearth of serious discussion in this area. A more systematic understanding of how the imagination functions as part of the learning process should enable educators to identify pedagogic interventions that might harness the power of the imagination and facilitate learning. We conclude with the assessment that it is currently possible to regard the glass as both half full and half empty. It is half empty in the sense that we still know so little about how language learners use their imaginations. It is half full in the sense that we are now beginning to understand the potential of this area and that a storied self-conceptualisation of the imaginations of language learners seems like a promising place to begin integrating possible and imagined selves into actual classroom practice.

Recommended reading

Dunkel, C. and Kerpelman, J. (eds) (2005) *Possible Selves: Theory, Research and Applications*. New York: Nova Science.

This book is a collection of research on possible selves in a wide range of fields. Collectively, it provides an accessible overview of how possible selves are being conceptualised, examined, and applied in various contexts.

Murray, G. (2011) Imagination, metacognition and the L2 self in a self-access learning environment. In G. Murray, X. Gao and T. Lamb (eds) *Identity, Motivation and Autonomy in Language Learning* (pp. 75–90). Bristol: Multilingual Matters.

This chapter provides a succinct account of how the imagination and possible selves have been theorised and researched within the SLA literature. It also describes a rare, mixed-methods study into the role imagination played in a self-directed English course at a Japanese university.

Dörnyei, Z. and Kubanyiova, M. (2014) *Motivating Learners, Motivating Teachers: Building Vision in the Language Classroom*. Cambridge: Cambridge University Press.

This is a book that expands upon some of the theoretical issues discussed in this chapter. What particularly marks this book out is its valuable focus on practical pedagogic applications, offering a range of actual classroom activities developed in various language-learning contexts.

References

Anderson, B. (1991) *Imagined Communities: Reflections on the Origin and Spread of Nationalism.* London: Verso.
Anderson, N.J. (2012) Metacognition: Awareness of language learning. In S. Mercer, S. Ryan and M. Williams (eds) *Psychology in Language Learning: Insights from Research, Theory and Practice* (pp. 10–25). Basingstoke: Palgrave Macmillan.
Bong, M. and Skaalvik, E.M. (2003) Academic self-concept and self-efficacy: How different are they really? *Educational Psychology Review* 15 (1), 1–40.
Boyatzis, R.E. and Akrivou, K. (2006) The ideal self as the driver of intentional change. *Journal of Management Development* 25, 624–642.
Brown S.R. (1993) A primer on Q methodology. *Operant Subjectivity* 16 (3/4), 91–138.
Czarniawska-Joerges, B. (2004) *Narratives in Social Science Research*. Thousand Oaks: Sage Publications.
Connelly, F.M. and Clandinin, D.J. (1990) Stories of experience and narrative inquiry. *Educational Researcher* 19 (5), 2–14.
Decety, J.G. and Grèzes. J. (2006) The power of simulation: Imagining one's own and other's behavior. *Brain Research* 1079 (1), 4–14.
Deci, E.L. and Ryan, R.M. (1985) *Intrinsic Motivation and Self-Determination in Human Behavior*. New York: Plenum Publishing.
Deci, E.L. and Ryan R.M. (eds) (2002) *Handbook of Self-Determination*. Rochester: University of Rochester Press.
Dörnyei, Z. (2005) *The Psychology of the Language Learner*. Mahwah: Lawrence Erlbaum.
Dörnyei, Z. (2009) The L2 Motivational Self System. In Z. Dörnyei and E. Ushioda (eds) *Motivation, Language Identity and the L2 Self* (pp. 9–42). Bristol: Multilingual Matters.
Dörnyei, Z. and Kubanyiova, M. (2014) *Motivating Learners, Motivating Teachers: Building Vision in the Language Classroom*. Cambridge: Cambridge University Press.
Duff, P.A. and Bell, J.S. (2002) Narrative research in TESOL: Narrative inquiry: More than just telling stories. *TESOL Quarterly* 36 (2), 207–213.

Egan, K. (2005) *An Imaginative Approach to Teaching*. San Francisco: Jossey-Bass.
Erikson, M.G. (2007) The meaning of the future: Toward a more specific definition of possible selves. *Review of General Psychology* 11 (4), 348–358.
Higgins, E.T. (1987) Self-discrepancy: A theory relating self and affect. *Psychological Review* 94, 319–340.
Hock, M.F., Deshler, D.D. and Schumaker, J.B. (2006) Enhancing student motivation through the pursuit of possible selves. In C. Dunkel and J. Kerpelman (eds) *Possible Selves: Theory, Research and Application* (pp. 205–221). New York: Nova Science.
Hsieh, P.H. (2012) Attribution: Looking back and ahead at the 'Why' theory. In S. Mercer, S. Ryan and M. Williams (eds) *Psychology in Language Learning: Insights from Research, Theory and Practice* (pp. 90–102). Basingstoke: Palgrave Macmillan.
Johnson, M.K. (1988) Reality monitoring: An experimental phenomenological approach. *Journal of Experimental Psychology* 117 (4), 390–394.
Johnson, M.K. and Raye, C.L. (2000) Cognitive and brain mechanisms of false memories and beliefs. In D.L. Schacter and E. Scarry (eds) *Memory, Brain, and Belief* (pp. 35–86). Cambridge: Harvard University Press.
Johnson, M.K., Foley, M.A., Suengas, A.G. and Raye. C.L. (1988) Phenomenal characteristics of memories for perceived and imagined autobiographical events. *Journal of Experimental Psychology* 117 (4), 371–376.
Kerpelman, J.L. (2006) Using Q methodology to study possible selves. In C. Dunkel and J. Kerpelman (eds) *Possible Selves: Theory, Research and Application* (pp. 163–186). New York: Nova Science Publishers.
Locke, E.A. and Latham. G.P. (1994) Goal setting theory. In H.F. O'Neil and M. Drillings (eds) *Motivation: Theory and Research* (pp. 13–29). Hillsdale: Lawrence Erlbaum Associates.
Locke, E.A. and Latham, G.P. (2006) New directions in goal-setting theory. *Current Directions in Psychological Science* 15 (5), 265–268.
Magid, M. and Chan, L.H. (2012) Motivating English learners by helping them visualise their Ideal L2 Self: Lessons from two motivational programmes. *Innovation in Language Learning and Teaching* 6(2), 113–125.
Markus, H. (2006) Foreword. In C. Dunkel and J. Kerpelman (eds) *Possible Selves: Theory, Research and Application* (pp. xi–xiv). New York: Nova Science Publishers.
Markus, H. and Kitayama, S. (2004) Models of agency: Sociocultural diversity in the construction of action. In V. Murphy-Berman and J.J. Berman (eds) *Cross-cultural Differences in Perspectives on the Self: Nebraska Symposium on Motivation, Vol. 49* (pp. 1–57). Lincoln: University of Nebraska Press.
Markus, H. and Nurius, P. (1986) Possible selves. *American Psychologist* 41, 954–969.
Markus, H. and Ruvolo, A. (1989) Possible selves: Personalized representations of goals. In L.A. Pervin (ed.) *Goal Concepts in Personality and Social Psychology* (pp. 211–241). Hillsdale: Lawrence Erlbaum.
McAdams, D.P. (1996) Personality, modernity, and the storied self: A contemporary framework for studying persons. *Psychological Inquiry* 7 (4), 295–321.
McAdams, D.P. (2001) The psychology of life stories. *Journal of General Psychology* 5 (2), 100–122.
Mercer, S. (2012) Self-concept: Situating the self. In S. Mercer, S. Ryan and M. Williams (eds) *Psychology in Language Learning: Insights from Research, Theory and Practice* (pp. 10–25). Basingstoke: Palgrave Macmillan.
Murphey, T., Falout, J., Fukada, Y. and Fukuda, T. (2012) Group dynamics: Collaborative agency in present communities of imagination. In S. Mercer, S. Ryan and M. Williams (eds) *Psychology in Language Learning: Insights from Research, Theory and Practice* (pp. 220–238). Basingstoke: Palgrave Macmillan.

Murray, G. (2011) Imagination, metacognition and the L2 self in a self-access learning environment. In G. Murray, X. Gao and T. Lamb (eds) *Identity, Motivation and Autonomy in Language Learning* (pp. 75–90). Bristol: Multilingual Matters.
Norton, B. (2001) Non-participation, imagined communities and the language classroom. In M. Breen (ed.) *Learner Contributions to Language Learning: New Directions in Research* (pp. 150–171). Harlow: Pearson Education.
Oettingen, G. and Hagenah, M. (2007) Fantasies and the self-regulation of competence. In A.J. Eliot and C.S. Dweck (eds) *Handbook of Competence and Motivation* (pp. 647–665). New York: The Guilford Press.
Oettingen, G., Pak, H. and Schnetter. K. (2001) Self-regulation of goal-setting: Turning free fantasies about the future into binding goals. *Journal of Personality and Social Psychology* 80 (5), 736–753.
Pavlenko, A. (2002) Narrative study: Whose story is it, anyway? *TESOL Quarterly* 36 (2), 213–218.
Pavlenko, A. (2007) Autobiographic narratives as data in Applied Linguistics. *Applied Linguistics* 28 (2), 163–188.
Pavlenko, A. and Norton, B. (2007) Imagined communities, identity, and English language learning. In J. Cummins and C. Davison (eds) *International Handbook of English Language Teaching* (pp. 669–680). New York: Springer.
Pham, L.B. and Taylor, S.E. (1999) From thought to action: Effects of process-versus outcome-based mental simulations on performance. *Personality and Social Psychology Bulletin* 25 (2), 250–260.
Pittman, J. F., Kerpelman, J.L., Lamke, L.K. and Sollie. D.L. (2009) Development and validation of a Q-sort measure of identity processing style: The identity processing style Q-sort. *Journal of Adolescence* 32 (5), 1239–1265.
Pizzolato, J.E. (2006) Achieving college student possible selves: Navigating the space between commitment and achievement of long-term identity goals. *Cultural Diversity and Ethnic Minority Psychology* 12 (1), 57–69.
Taylor, S.E., Pham, L.B., Rivkin, I.D. and Armor. D.A. (1998) Harnessing the imagination: Mental simulation, self-regulation, and coping. *American Psychologist* 53 (4), 429–439.
Vallacher, R.R. and Wegner, D.M. (1985) *A Theory of Action Identification*. Hillsdale: Erlbaum.
Van der Helm, R. (2009) The vision phenomenon: Towards a theoretical underpinning of visions of the future and the process of envisioning. *Futures* 41 (2), 96–104.
Vasquez, N.A. and Buehler, R. (2007) Seeing future success: Does imagery perspective influence achievement motivation? *Personality and Social Psychology Bulletin* 33 (10), 1392–1405.
Wenger, E. (1998) *Communities of Practice: Learning, Meaning, and Identity*. Cambridge: Cambridge University Press.
Wurf, E. and Markus, H. (1991) Possible selves and the psychology of personal growth. In D. Ozer, J.M. Healy and A.J. Stewart (eds) *Perspectives in Personality* (Vol. 3, pp. 39–62). London: Jessica Kingsley Publishers.
Yashima, T. (2013) Individuality, imagination and community in a globalizing world: An Asian EFL perspective. In P. Benson and L. Cooker (eds) *The Applied Linguistic Individual: Sociocultural Approaches to Identity, Agency and Autonomy* (pp. 46–58). Sheffield: Equinox Publishing.

9 Motivational Perspectives on the Self in SLA: A Developmental View

Ema Ushioda

Motivation and Self-Related Cognitions: An Introductory Overview

If one picks up any comprehensive textbook on motivation in education and thumbs through the pages or peruses the index (e.g. Anderman & Anderman, 2010; Schunk *et al.*, 2008; Stipek, 2002), a key term found in almost every chapter is *self*. While early theories sought to explain motivation in terms of largely unconscious drives, emotions and instincts shaping human behaviour, the cognitive revolution in psychology in the second half of the 20th century brought to the science of motivation a focus on the conscious mental processes of the self, such as goals, beliefs, expectations and interpretations of events (e.g. experiences of success or failure). Cognitive theories of motivation seek to explain human behaviour through the prism of these mental processes that are seen as instrumental in shaping the person's decision to engage (or not engage) in certain actions. Almost invariably, these mental processes involve cognitions not just *by* the self, but specifically *about* the self, whereby motivation to act (or not act) is perhaps explained in terms of beliefs and perceptions one has about oneself based on past or current experience or future 'imagined' selves (see Ryan & Irie, Chapter 8, this volume); or reflects a desire to enhance or protect one's self-concept (see Rubio, Chapter 4, this volume); or expresses the agency (or lack of agency) of the self (see Norton, Chapter 5, this volume).

Thus, for example, motivation to engage in certain tasks requiring skill and competence may be shaped by *self-efficacy beliefs* – i.e. people's beliefs in their capability to carry out the task or not (Bandura, 1986, 2001; see also Mills, Chapter 2, this volume; and Sampasivam & Clément, Chapter 3, this volume, on the associated area of linguistic self-confidence). On the other hand, the need to protect their self-concept or *self-worth* may motivate people to engage in *self-handicapping strategies* (such as purposely not studying before a test) so that their poor performance may be attributed to lack of effort rather than low ability (Covington, 1992). More generally, people will feel differently motivated depending on whether they perceive their motivation to be *self-determined* and *self-regulated*, or to be externally controlled and regulated by others, as in the typical 'carrot-and-stick' approach to motivation (Deci & Ryan, 1985; Ryan & Deci, 2002).

It is not just within the academic learning domain that self-related cognitions are a significant feature of motivation. Such cognitions permeate the psychology of human motivation in diverse areas of life such as addiction and recovery, health, management, parenting, social relationships and sport (see e.g. Boekaerts *et al.*, 2005 and Deci & Ryan, 2002, on self-regulatory and self-determination perspectives on motivation in various life domains). Nevertheless, as Pajares and Schunk (2002) observe, it is perhaps in the context of academic learning in particular that self-related constructs of one kind or another have become effectively core to theories of motivation; and here we might add that they have also become core to theories of motivation in second language acquisition (SLA).

A conceptual challenge this raises for the analysis of motivational perspectives on the self is that such perspectives inevitably cut across most, if not all, the self-related concepts under discussion in this volume, as signalled by the numerous cross-references so far. In order to sustain some measure of focus in this chapter and minimise incursions into the conceptual territory of other chapters, I will not attempt a comprehensive overview of self-related cognitions relevant to motivation in SLA. Instead, I plan to approach the topic from a *developmental* angle and explore the processes whereby language learning motivation becomes (or does not become) an integral part of the self, and how such processes of integration and internalisation relate to the interactions between the self and the surrounding social context. With this developmental angle in mind, I think it is helpful to begin this exploration by mapping motivation and L2 learning onto a schematic timeline, in order to locate factors relevant to motivation within and outside the self and their points of interaction along the L2 learning trajectory.

Motivation and Second Language Learning Timeline

Figure 9.1 is an adaptation of a schematic framework I developed previously to represent second language (L2) motivation from a temporal perspective (Ushioda, 1998: 82). In this figure, the long diagonal arrow represents the process of L2 learning in a particular sociocultural environment, while circles A and B represent different learners at different stages of L2 learning, or conceivably the same learner at different points in time. The motivation characterising learners' progression along the L2 learning timeline has a forward-looking dimension, directed towards future goals and purposes. These may be long-term goals (e.g. future career plans), interim short-term objectives and incentives (e.g. passing this month's test), or more immediate targets or regular objectives (e.g. doing tonight's homework or learning ten new words each day). The motivation characterising learners' progression along the L2 learning timeline also has a historical and experiential dimension, shaped by past and ongoing experiences of L2 learning and use, as well as other relevant personal experiences such as cultural and social encounters, visits abroad or critical events. These cumulative experiences may be positive or negative or more likely a mixture, affecting motivation in different ways. The overall motivational balance between cumulative experiential perspectives and goal-directed perspectives will vary from learner to learner and at different stages of L2 learning, as represented schematically by the different positioning of circles A and B in relation to these temporal perspectives in Figure 9.1. Thus, the motivation of learner B is more strongly goal-focused than that of learner A, for whom motivation is shaped more by ongoing experiential factors. For example, we might imagine learner A as someone who engages in L2 learning primarily because of personal interest and enjoyment, and learner B as someone who needs to acquire L2 skills for professional purposes.

Turning our attention now to self-perspectives, the quality of motivation sustaining progression along the L2 learning timeline will vary considerably

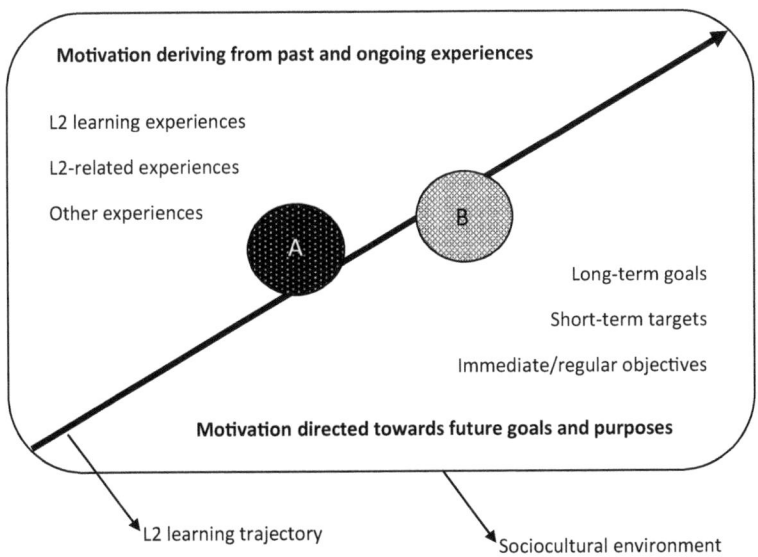

Figure 9.1 Motivation and L2 learning timeline (adapted from Ushioda, 1998: 82)

depending on the extent to which its goal-focused and experience-related processes are internalised and integrated within the self or not. For example, our imaginary learner A who is engaged in L2 learning because of personal interest and enjoyment may be described as having intrinsic motivation – i.e. motivation deriving from the affective rewards of engaging in a satisfying activity for its own sake (Deci & Ryan, 1985). Intrinsic motivation does not depend on any social-environmental influences but is located within the self and the self's interaction with the activity in question. By contrast, our imaginary learner B may have little personal interest in L2 learning but may be required to develop skills in language X because of a job transfer overseas. Learner B's motivation may thus be largely regulated by social-environmental factors (employer goals and requirements, L2 course demands and pressures) rather than fully internalised within the self. These differences in degree of internalisation are represented schematically in Figure 9.1 in the degree of shading in the circles for A and B – the darker shading representing fuller internalisation of motivation within the self. For example, we might imagine another learner C positioned exactly as learner B in Figure 9.1, yet who has deeply held reasons for L2 learning relating to personal goals and aspirations and whose motivation is thus more strongly internalised within the self.

How then might we characterise or theorise such differences in internalisation of motivation in SLA, and what kinds of processes may mediate the internalisation of motivation within the self? As a way into exploring these issues, I will first discuss the relationship between motivational factors external and internal to the self and how this has been theorised and researched in our field.

Motivational Factors Within and Outside the Self

In analyses of motivation in SLA as well as the field of motivational psychology more broadly, the factors shaping individual motivation are commonly classified according to whether they are internal or external to the self. This internal–external classification is, for example, the organising principle of Williams and Burden's (1997: 138–140) comprehensive theoretical framework of L2 motivation, which set out to summarise the range of motivational factors relevant to L2 learning. Factors internal to the self include the various self-related cognitions briefly mentioned earlier (i.e. cognitions by the self and cognitions about the self), as well as attitudinal and affective factors (e.g. enjoyment, anxiety) and individual characteristics (e.g. gender, developmental age, personality). On the other hand, factors external to the self comprise the broad complex of social, cultural and contextual factors that may influence individual motivation, such as interactions with significant others (e.g. teachers, parents, peers), specific features of the learning environment (e.g. classroom tasks and materials) or less visible aspects of the wider sociocultural context (e.g. educational values and cultural beliefs).

If we consider the relationship between internal and external factors, models of motivation that have been particularly influential in the SLA field have generally assumed the implicit influence of social-environmental factors on motivation of the self. For example, this assumption underpins the long-established social-psychological analysis of L2 motivation based on the individual's cultural and ethnolinguistic attitudes (Gardner, 1985; Gardner & Lambert, 1972). These attitudes are assumed to be socially formed, grounded in 'cultural beliefs' in the surrounding milieu (Gardner, 1985: 146–147), though the processes whereby these invisible environmental influences become internalised in the self are not explicitly theorised or empirically explored within the social-psychological paradigm. The theoretical and empirical focus falls instead on the already internalised beliefs and attitudes of the L2 learner self, as operationalised through self-report questionnaire measures of individual attitudes and motivation, typified by the Attitude-Motivation Test Battery (AMTB) developed by Gardner and his associates (Gardner, 1985). The AMTB gathers self-report data on how much L2 learners agree or disagree with, rate the importance of, or perceive to be true for themselves, certain statements reflecting particular cultural attitudes (e.g. 'French Canadians are a very sociable, warm-hearted and creative people'), learning attitudes (e.g. 'French is an important part of the school programme'), future goals (e.g. 'Studying French can be important to me because I think it will someday be useful in getting a good job'), parental attitudes (e.g. 'My parents feel that because we live in Canada, I should learn French'), as well as personal learning intentions and behaviours (Gardner, 1985: 178–180). Contextual motivational factors external to the self are thus not empirically measured and analysed in themselves, but are implicitly reflected in the individual's self-reported attitudes and cognitions. This conceptual and methodological focus on the self's motivational cognitions and perceptions is characteristic of much research on motivation in SLA since its social-psychological origins, and mirrors of course the psychometric heritage of the wider field of cognitive motivation in mainstream psychology.

This is not to say that context in a broad sense has been neglected in SLA research on motivation. On the one hand, comparative replication studies of L2 motivation in different cultural, linguistic and educational settings have been a hallmark of research in the field, reflecting the rigorous pursuit of generalisable motivation constructs and models across diverse contexts (see e.g. the meta-analysis of L2 motivation studies involving 75 independent samples and 10,489 learners in various Canadian and non-Canadian settings in Masgoret & Gardner, 2003; see also Taguchi *et al.*, 2009, for a comparative analysis of L2 motivation in Japanese, Chinese and Iranian educational settings). On the other hand, context as an external background variable has also been implicated in research that has sought to investigate culture-specific perspectives on L2 motivation, such as non-individualistic forms of motivation that may be characteristic of Chinese Confucian culture (e.g. Chen *et al.*, 2005). Nevertheless, in both comparative and culture-specific analyses of this kind, the methodological focus on learner perspectives (through self-report questionnaire data) means that the processes whereby invisible contextual or cultural influences shape and become integrated into the motivation of the self are not the subject of empirical exploration.

At a localised level, external factors of a more visible and tangible kind (such as social, physical and instructional features of the learning environment) have received more explicit theoretical attention in L2 motivation research since the 1990s. Prompted by Crookes and Schmidt's (1991) call for research on motivation more relevant to language teachers, this decade saw an increasing interest in classroom-based analyses of L2 motivation, focusing on specific features of the learning environment such as task design, classroom participation structures, instructional methods or teachers' motivational strategies or communicative styles (for an overview of research, see Dörnyei & Ushioda, 2011). Yet here too, the empirical analysis tends to focus on learners' perceptions of these classroom features, and the relationship between these perceptions and their self-reported motivation. Thus, for example, Noels *et al.* (1999) found a statistically significant link between students' perceptions of their teachers' autonomy-supportive communicative style in the L2 classroom and their reported levels of intrinsic motivation. Similarly, Bernaus and Gardner (2008) identified a significant relationship between students' self-reported levels of motivation and attitudes, and their perceptions of how frequently teachers used certain motivational strategies in the L2 classroom.

Interestingly, in this latter study, teachers' own reported frequency of using motivational strategies was not found to be linked to students' reported motivation, suggesting that it is the learner's *perceptions* of external factors (rather than external factors in themselves) that mediate motivational growth within the self. In this respect, therefore, Bernaus and Gardner's findings would seem to provide evidence to justify the dominant methodological focus on learner self-report data in L2 motivation research, including learner perceptions of external contextual factors. In effect, this focus on the self's perspectives is fundamental to the cognitive paradigm of motivation theory outlined at the beginning of this chapter, whereby human behaviour is explained through the prism of internal cognitive processes that interpret experience and shape motivation and behaviour.

Nevertheless, questions remain as to how and why learner perceptions of external factors may lead to qualitative changes in their motivation. Returning to our motivation and L2 learning timeline (see Figure 9.1), what are the developmental processes whereby external motivational factors and influences in the surrounding sociocultural environment become integrated and internalised within the self to shape a person's motivation? And what are the processes that may impede such integration and internalisation of motivation? It is to the discussion of these issues that we now turn.

The Internalisation of Motivation Within the Self

Within the SLA field, two influential theoretical frameworks in particular have helped characterise the distinction between internalised and less internalised forms of L2 motivation: *self-determination theory* (e.g. Noels *et al.*, 2000) and more recently, Dörnyei's (2005, 2009) *L2 Motivational Self System*. Both frameworks theorise the relationship between motivation and self-concept – the former with a stronger focus on current self-states and experiences along the L2 learning timeline, and the latter with a particular focus on projected future self-states. Moreover, both frameworks provide an analysis of how social-environmental motivational influences may be internalised to varying degrees within the self-concept.

Future self-states and internalisation of motivation

Dörnyei's L2 Motivational Self System offers an approach to conceptualising L2 motivation from a self-perspective, with specific reference to future representations of the self. It draws on the psychological theory of possible selves, where possible selves represent people's ideas of what they might become, what they would like to become or what they are afraid of becoming (Markus & Nurius, 1986, 1987; see also Ryan & Irie, Chapter 8, this volume). As Markus and Nurius (1987: 158) explain, the range of possible selves within a person's self-system constitute cognitive representations of deep-seated personal strivings, aspirations, fears and threats that serve to channel motivation, and possible selves thus 'provide an essential link between the self-concept (or identity) and motivation'. Clearly, future self-representations that are highly desirable are likely to channel motivation more strongly than future self-images that are less attractive or less personally valued.

In Dörnyei's (2005, 2009) L2 Motivational Self System, these differences in the self-relevant value of particular future self-representations are theorised as differences in degree of internalisation. On the one hand, the *ideal L2 self* represents a strongly valued and cherished future possible self whose desirable attributes include L2 proficiency for personal, social or vocational purposes. Thus, the motivation to strive towards this ideal end state is fully internalised within the self. On the other hand, the *ought-to L2 self* represents a more externally imposed future image of oneself with a level of proficiency in the L2, shaped by the need perhaps to comply with the expectations of others (e.g. teachers, parents), bow to social pressures and demands, or avoid possible negative consequences. In this respect, the motivation channelled by the ought-to L2 self is theorised to be less internalised within the self, and directed more by external factors in the sociocultural environment.

This contrast between internally driven and externally driven motivation is captured in the theoretical distinction between the *promotion* focus of the ideal L2 self (i.e. aspiration towards a desired end state) and the *prevention* focus of the ought-to L2 self (i.e. avoidance of feared or negative end states) (Dörnyei, 2009: 28; see also Higgins, 1998). Nevertheless, as individuals progress along the L2 learning timeline (see Figure 9.1), it seems conceivable that developmental changes may occur whereby a future self-image dictated by external pressures and obligations becomes gradually aligned and integrated with one's personal values and aspirations, leading to greater internalisation of motivation within the self. This may entail a process of transformation of the ought-to self into an ideal self, as elaborated by Kim (2009) in his comparative case study analysis of the motivation and English learning experiences of two Korean English as a second language (ESL) learners in Canada. Alternatively, it may entail the development of a promotion (as well as prevention) focus to the ought-to self, whereby fulfilling significant others' expectations for oneself in the future becomes fully endorsed and internalised within the self as a desirable obligation (see Ushioda & Chen, 2011, for some research evidence in relation to Taiwanese senior high school students' motivation towards learning English).

Current self-states and internalisation of motivation

However, in order to understand better how and why these processes of internalisation may happen, we need to consider not just the future-oriented dimension of the self-concept, but also current self-states and the ongoing experiences and social-environmental influences that mediate developmental changes in motivation. In Dörnyei's (2005, 2009) L2 Motivational Self System, this experiential dimension along the L2 learning timeline is characterised in broad terms under the heading of *L2 Learning Experience*. As Dörnyei (2009: 29) concedes, this dimension of his framework is conceptualised at a rather different level from the future self-components, and the question of how L2 learning experience shapes the development and internalisation of future possible selves remains under-theorised (though see Hadfield & Dörnyei, 2013, for practical pedagogical perspectives on this question).

Self-determination theory (SDT), on the other hand, focuses more explicitly on current self-states and experiences in the analysis of motivation, and sheds light on the processes whereby motivation becomes internalised within the self. Specifically, SDT provides an analysis of how developmental processes of motivation are a function of social-environmental conditions and influences. SDT originates within mainstream psychology as a general theory of motivation and human growth, associated with the work of

Edward Deci and Richard Ryan (e.g. Deci & Ryan, 1985; Ryan & Deci, 2000, 2002). Within the SLA field, SDT perspectives on L2 motivation have been developed principally by Kim Noels and her colleagues (e.g. Noels, 2001, 2009; Noels *et al.*, 1999, 2000).

As Ryan and Deci (2002) explain, an underlying assumption in SDT is that humans have an innate tendency towards psychological growth, the exploration and mastery of new experiences and challenges, the development of skills, potentialities and capacities, and the integration of these into an increasingly elaborated yet coherent and unified sense of self. According to SDT, this natural propensity towards an integrated and authentic sense of self shaping human motivation and behaviour may be enabled or constrained by particular social-environmental conditions. The development of motivation is thus viewed in 'dialectical' terms (Ryan & Deci, 2002: 6) as emerging in the interactions between self and context. Critical to these interactions is the extent to which the social-environmental conditions support the person's sense of *competence, autonomy* and *relatedness*, which are regarded as three basic psychological needs or 'nutriments' (Ryan & Deci, 2002: 7) underpinning the healthy growth and internalisation of motivation. *Competence* means feeling effective in one's interactions with the environment, and has long been considered fundamental to human motivation (see White, 1959). *Autonomy* is the sense that actions and behaviours are self-determined as an authentic expression of the self and the self's internal values, even when these actions, behaviours and values may be influenced by external sources. In this latter respect, autonomy is linked (rather than opposed) to *relatedness*, referring to the sense of belonging and connectedness with others, which entails alignment with, and integration of, relevant social influences and values.

Research evidence suggests that social-environmental conditions that support all three psychological needs of the self are likely to promote healthy internalisation of motivation (e.g. see the empirical studies in Deci & Ryan, 2002). In other words, when people experience feelings of autonomy and relatedness and engage in optimal challenges that enhance their sense of competence, their motivation will be increasingly internalised and self-regulated. By contrast, social-environmental conditions that undermine people's sense of competence, autonomy or relatedness will generate forms of motivation that are less internalised, less integrated into the self or aligned with its values, and more externally regulated by environmental influences, pressures and controls. For example, if the learning challenge is too great and students do not feel competent to undertake it, they will not develop any intrinsic motivation for doing so and will feel that they are acting under coercion (i.e. lacking autonomy) if obliged to try. On the other hand, when students are engaged in setting and achieving optimal challenges and thus cultivating a sense of competence as well as personal agency (i.e. autonomy), they are likely to enhance their intrinsic interest in the learning activity in question (for research evidence, see e.g. Bandura & Schunk, 1981).

As these examples suggest, supporting students' sense of competence and autonomy seems particularly important for the development of *intrinsic* forms of motivation (i.e. interest in a skill-based activity for its own sake). This was the case too in the earlier-cited study by Noels *et al.* (1999), which found a relationship between L2 learners' reported levels of intrinsic motivation and how far they perceived their teachers to support their feelings of autonomy and provide them with informational competence-related feedback. On the other hand, research evidence suggests that for the development of internalised forms of *extrinsic* motivation (i.e. pursuit of short-term or long-term goals contingent on the learning process, such as achieving a qualification or gaining entry to university), autonomy and relatedness are the twin critical factors. For example, a study by Ryan *et al.* (1992) shows that children are more likely to accept and internalise curriculum goals and values when the social learning environment supports their sense of autonomy and involves them in some of the decision-making processes that shape their learning (for an insightful practitioner perspective, see Dam, 1995; see also Ushioda, 2003 on the role of autonomy and social influences in mediating motivation). Regarding relatedness, research reported by Ryan *et al.* (1994) suggests that children who feel more secure in their relationships with teachers and parents are more likely to internalise the motivation for positive school-related behaviours and values endorsed by these significant others.

In short, returning to our motivation and L2 learning timeline in Figure 9.1, self-determination theory offers a useful analysis of how current self-states, experiences and social-environmental factors may interact with one another to promote (or obstruct) the development of intrinsic motivation and the internalisation of socially valued goals and forms of motivation within the self.

Metacognition and internalisation of motivation

However, intrinsic interest and fully internalised goals and values are unlikely to be sufficient to sustain motivation when faced with the increasing cognitive and linguistic challenges of L2 learning. In the earlier stages of learning a new language, a sense of developing competence may be relatively transparent as learners' progress from a zero state to the acquisition of basic skills and vocabulary. But as they proceed further along the L2 learning timeline, the cognitive and linguistic demands increase exponentially, while actual gains in L2 proficiency seem slower and less tangible. This is the stage in the L2 learning trajectory when intrinsic interest and internalised motivation may not be enough, because the challenges to motivation lie in not knowing how to advance further or how to cope with growing cognitive and linguistic difficulties in L2 learning. In other words, motivation needs to be directed not simply towards setting goals, exerting effort, practising skills or sustaining focus, but also towards marshalling the necessary metacognitive strategies for dealing with increasingly complex tasks and challenges in one's learning. In effect, a further important developmental process along the motivation and L2 learning timeline is the integration of motivation with metacognitive know-how within the self.

In the literature on self-regulated learning, this integration of motivation and metacognitive know-how is commonly termed 'will and skill' (McCombs & Marzano, 1990), where 'will' refers to willingness or motivation, and 'skill' refers to the metacognitive and strategic thinking processes that regulate complex learning. As Bronson (2000: 55) comments, self-regulated learning can occur only when the ability to control strategic thinking processes is accompanied by the wish to do so. In the SLA literature, there have been quite a few studies that have explored the relationship between motivation and use of metacognitive strategies (e.g. MacIntyre & Noels, 1996; Schmidt & Watanabe, 2001; Vandergrift, 2005). In keeping with the methodological tradition of motivation research in SLA, such studies naturally tend to use self-report measures to assess levels of motivation and frequency or range of strategy use. However, while research of this kind provides evidence to support the relationship between motivation and metacognitive strategy use, it cannot shed light on the developmental question of how 'will and skill' evolve – i.e. how this important motivational dimension of self-regulated L2 learning emerges and becomes internalised within the self.

From a developmental perspective, an important prerequisite in the exercise of 'will and skill' is the learner's recognition of the 'self-as-agent' in constructing the thoughts, beliefs and expectations that shape motivation (McCombs, 1994; McCombs & Marzano, 1990). Learners need first to recognise their cognitive agency in this way so that they can then be brought to recognise their potential to have control over their thoughts and thus control over their own motivation and learning. Integrating will and skill to regulate motivation and learning depends on this higher-order metacognitive self 'who steps outside the boundaries of thoughts or beliefs and exercises control at a higher level of awareness, perspective taking and choosing to redirect thinking processes in healthier ways' (McCombs, 1994: 55).

As I have discussed elsewhere (Ushioda, 2007, 2010), the key to helping learners in this regard would seem to lie in problem-focused dialogue or interactions (among peers or with the teacher) that serve to make thoughts tangible, explicit and an object for analysis, development and redirection. This perspective is of course influenced by a Vygotskian sociocultural paradigm, with its emphasis on the role of talk or interaction in mediating learning. According to sociocultural theory (Vygotsky, 1978), the goal of learning is self-regulation, where self-regulation is understood to mean metacognitive control and independent strategic functioning in relation to a particular type of task. A central principle of the theory is that the origins of self-regulation are social and dialogic, realised in the problem-focused interactions through which the teacher scaffolds the learner's attempts to accomplish the task. The purpose of scaffolding is not simply to help the learner complete the task, but to promote her capacity to think strategically and so achieve metacognitive control or self-regulation. Importantly, research evidence suggests that the explicit transfer of the self-as-agent regulatory role is critical in the dialogue, whereby the learner is *motivated* to do the thinking instead of simply responding to instructions and directives (e.g. see the research reported by Diaz *et al.*, 1990). In short, this transfer of the self-as-agent role seems pivotal in promoting the internalisation of motivation for metacognition and self-regulation.

In this respect, as I have suggested elsewhere (Ushioda, 2010; see also Ushioda, 2012), there is clearly scope within SLA research on motivation for studies that go beyond self-report perspectives, and that focus on the microgenetic analysis of how motivational and metacognitive processes may develop through dialogic interactions around particular cognitive or linguistic problems in the L2 learning process. Central elements in this analysis would be the linguistic features of the dialogue that support and stimulate the transfer of the self-as-agent role to the learner, particularly when the target language is not only the focus of metacognitive attention but also the medium through which strategic thinking processes are verbalised, discussed and internalised.

Concluding Remarks

In this chapter, I have sought to explore developmental aspects of how processes of motivation become internalised within the self, taking into account the various experiential factors, social-environmental influences and future-oriented dimensions that may shape (or impede) these processes of internalisation and motivate (or inhibit) progression along the L2 learning timeline. In doing so, I have drawn on a range of theoretical perspectives that help capture different aspects of the relationships and interactions between the self and social-environmental factors that seem relevant in this regard. However, I should like to conclude by acknowledging that, in using a schematic framework of the L2 learning timeline as the organising principle for my discussions, I have not tried to take account of dynamic complexities in the organic relationship between self and context (see Ushioda, 2009), or the relational complexities of the various self-systems with which the L2 learning self interacts (see Ushioda, 2012), since other chapters in this volume (in particular: Mercer, Chapter 11; Taylor, Chapter 7, this volume) address such complexities at length.

> **Recommended reading**
>
> Dörnyei, Z. (2009) The L2 Motivational Self System. In Z. Dörnyei and E. Ushioda (eds) *Motivation, Language Identity and the L2 Self* (pp. 9–42). Bristol: Multilingual Matters.

This chapter provides a detailed account of Dörnyei's currently influential model of L2 motivation in terms of self-perspectives. It offers a clear theoretical analysis of the model, discusses relevant empirical evidence and outlines implications for pedagogy.

McCombs, B.L. and Marzano, R.J. (1990) Putting the self in self-regulated learning: The self as agent in integrating will and skill. *Educational Psychologist* 25 (1), 51–69.

This classical article is essential reading for understanding the role of motivation and 'self-as-agent' in the development and exercise of metacognitive processes in self-regulated learning.

Noels, K.A. (2009) The internalisation of language learning into the self and social identity. In Z. Dörnyei and E. Ushioda (eds) *Motivation, Language Identity and the L2 Self* (pp. 295–313). Bristol: Multilingual Matters.

This chapter offers an insightful analysis of L2 motivation and social identification from the perspective of self-determination theory, and critically explores some of the limits of this perspective.

References

Anderman, E.M. and Anderman, L.H. (2010) *Classroom Motivation*. Upper Saddle River: Merrill.
Bandura, A. (1986) *Social Foundations of Thought and Action: A Social Cognitive Theory*. Englewood Cliffs: Prentice-Hall.
Bandura, A. (2001) Social cognitive theory: An agentic perspective. *Annual Review of Psychology* 52, 1–26.
Bandura, A. and Schunk, D. (1981) Cultivating competence, self-efficacy, and intrinsic interest through proximal self-motivation. *Journal of Personality and Social Psychology* 41, 586–598.
Bernaus, M. and Gardner, R.C. (2008) Teacher motivation strategies, student perceptions, student motivation, and English achievement. *The Modern Language Journal* 92 (3), 387–401.
Boekaerts, M., Pintrich, P.R. and Zeidner, M. (eds) (2005) *Handbook of Self-Regulation* (First published 2000). San Diego: Elsevier Academic Press.
Bronson, M. (2000) *Self-Regulation in Early Childhood: Nature and Nurture*. New York: Guilford Press.
Chen, J.F., Warden, C.A. and Chang, H.T. (2005) Motivators that do not motivate: The case of Chinese EFL learners and the influence of culture on motivation. *TESOL Quarterly* 39 (4), 609–633.
Covington, M. (1992) *Making the Grade: A Self-Worth Perspective on Motivation and School Reform*. Cambridge: Cambridge University Press.
Crookes, G. and Schmidt, R. (1991) Motivation: Reopening the research agenda. *Language Learning* 41, 469–512.
Dam, L. (1995) *Learner Autonomy 3: From Theory to Classroom Practice*. Dublin: Authentik.

Deci, E.L. and Ryan, R.M. (1985) *Intrinsic Motivation and Self-Determination in Human Behavior.* New York: Plenum.

Deci, E.L. and Ryan, R.M. (eds) (2002) *Handbook of Self-Determination Research.* Rochester: The University of Rochester Press.

Diaz, R.M., Neal, C.J. and Amaya-Williams, M. (1990) The social origins of self-regulation. In L. Moll (ed.) *Vygotsky and Education: Instructional Implications and Applications of Sociohistorical Psychology* (pp. 127–154). New York: Cambridge University Press.

Dörnyei, Z. (2005) *The Psychology of the Language Learner: Individual Differences in Second Language Acquisition.* Mahwah: Lawrence Erlbaum.

Dörnyei, Z. (2009) The L2 Motivational Self System. In Z. Dörnyei and E. Ushioda (eds) *Motivation, Language Identity and the L2 Self* (pp. 9–42). Bristol: Multilingual Matters.

Dörnyei, Z. and Ushioda, E. (2011) *Teaching and Researching Motivation* (2nd edn). Harlow: Pearson.

Gardner, R.C. (1985) *Social Psychology and Second Language Learning: The Role of Attitudes and Motivation.* London: Edward Arnold.

Gardner, R.C. and Lambert, W.E. (1972) *Attitudes and Motivation in Second Language Learning.* Rowley: Newbury House.

Hadfield, J. and Dörnyei, Z. (2013) *Motivating Learning.* London: Longman.

Higgins, E.T. (1998) Promotion and prevention: Regulatory focus as a motivational principle: In M.P. Zanna (ed.) *Advances in Experimental Social Psychology* (Vol. 30, pp. 1–46). New York: Academic Press.

Kim, T.-Y. (2009) The sociocultural interface between ideal self and ought-to self: A case study of two Korean students' ESL motivation. In Z. Dörnyei and E. Ushioda (eds) *Motivation, Language Identity and the L2 Self* (pp. 274–294). Bristol: Multilingual Matters.

MacIntyre, P. and Noels, K.A. (1996) Using social-psychological variables to predict the use of language learning strategies. *Foreign Language Annals* 29, 373–386.

Markus, H. and Nurius, P. (1986) Possible selves. *American Psychologist* 41, 954–969.

Markus, H. and Nurius, P. (1987) Possible selves: The interface between motivation and the self-concept. In K. Yardley and T. Honess (eds) *Self and Identity: Psychosocial Perspectives* (pp. 157–172). Chichester: John Wiley and Sons.

Masgoret, A-M. and Gardner, R.C. (2003) Attitudes, motivation and second language learning: A meta-analysis of studies conducted by Gardner and his associates. *Language Learning* 52 (Suppl 1), 167–210.

McCombs, B.L. (1994) Strategies for assessing and enhancing motivation: Keys to promoting self-regulated learning and performance. In H.F. O'Neil Jr and M. Drillings (eds) *Motivation: Theory and Research* (pp. 49–69). Hillsdale: Lawrence Erlbaum.

McCombs, B.L. and Marzano, R.J. (1990) Putting the self in self-regulated learning: The self as agent in integrating will and skill. *Educational Psychologist* 25 (1), 51–69.

Noels, K.A. (2001) New orientations in language learning motivation: Towards a contextual model of intrinsic, extrinsic, and integrative orientations and motivation. In Z. Dörnyei and R. Schmidt (eds) *Motivation and Second Language Acquisition* (pp. 43–68). Honolulu: University of Hawaii Press.

Noels, K.A. (2009) The internalisation of language learning into the self and social identity. In Z. Dörnyei and E. Ushioda (eds) *Motivation, Language Identity and the L2 Self* (pp. 295–313). Bristol: Multilingual Matters.

Noels, K.A., Clément, R. and Pelletier, L.G. (1999) Perceptions of teachers' communicative style and students' intrinsic and extrinsic motivation. *The Modern Language Journal* 83 (i), 23–34.

Noels, K.A., Pelletier, L.G., Clément, R. and Vallerand, R.J. (2000) Why are you learning a second language? Motivational orientations and self-determination theory. *Language Learning* 50, 57–85.

Pajares, F. and Schunk, D.H. (2002) Self and self-belief in psychology and education: A historical perspective. In J. Aronson (ed.) *Improving Academic Achievement: Impact of Psychological Factors of Education* (pp. 3–21). New York: Academic Press.

Ryan, R.M. and Deci, E.L. (2000) Self-determination theory and the facilitation of intrinsic motivation, social development, and well-being. *American Psychologist* 55, 68–78.

Ryan, R.M. and Deci, E.L. (2002) Overview of self-determination theory: An organismic dialectical perspective. In E.L. Deci and R.M. Ryan (eds) *Handbook of Self-Determination Research* (pp. 3–33). Rochester: The University of Rochester Press.

Ryan, R.M., Connell, J.P. and Grolnick, W.S. (1992) When achievement is not intrinsically motivated: A theory of internalization and self-regulation in school. In A. Boggiano and T.S. Pittman (eds) *Achievement and Motivation: A Social-Developmental Perspective* (pp. 167–188). Cambridge: Cambridge University Press.

Ryan, R.M., Stiller, J. and Lynch, J.H. (1994) Representations of relationships to teachers, parents and friends as predictors of academic motivation and self-esteem. *Journal of Early Adolescence* 14, 226–249.

Schmidt, R. and Watanabe, Y. (2001) Motivation, strategy use, and pedagogical preferences in foreign language learning. In Z. Dörnyei and R. Schmidt (eds) *Motivation and Second Language Acquisition* (pp. 313–359). Honolulu, HI: University of Hawaii Press.

Schunk, D.H., Pintrich, P.R. and Meece, J. (2008) *Motivation in Education: Theory, Research and Applications* (3rd edn). Upper Saddle River: Pearson/Merrill Prentice Hall.

Stipek, D. (2002) *Motivation to Learn: Integrating Theory and Practice* (4th edn). Boston: Allyn & Bacon.

Taguchi, T., Magid, M. and Papi, M. (2009) The L2 Motivational Self System among Japanese, Chinese and Iranian learners of English: A comparative study. In Z. Dörnyei and E. Ushioda (eds) *Motivation, Language Identity and the L2 Self* (pp. 66–97). Bristol: Multilingual Matters.

Ushioda, E. (1998) Effective motivational thinking: A cognitive theoretical approach to the study of language learning motivation: In E.A. Soler and V.C. Espurz (eds) *Current Issues in English Language Methodology* (pp. 77–89). Castelló de la Plana: Universitat Jaume I.

Ushioda, E. (2003) Motivation as a socially mediated process. In D. Little, J. Ridley and E. Ushioda (eds) *Learner Autonomy in the Foreign Language Classroom: Teacher, Learner, Curriculum and Assessment* (pp. 90–102). Dublin: Authentik.

Ushioda, E. (2007) Motivation, autonomy and sociocultural theory. In P. Benson (ed.) *Learner Autonomy 8: Teacher and Learner Perspectives* (pp. 5–24). Dublin: Authentik.

Ushioda, E. (2009) A person-in-context relational view of emergent motivation, self and identity. In Z. Dörnyei and E. Ushioda (eds) *Motivation, Language Identity and the L2 Self* (pp. 215–228). Bristol: Multilingual Matters.

Ushioda, E. (2010) Motivation and SLA: Bridging the gap. *EUROSLA Yearbook* 10, 5–20.

Ushioda, E. (2012) Motivation: L2 learning as a special case? In S. Mercer, S. Ryan and M. Williams (eds) *Psychology for Language Learning: Insights from Research, Theory and Practice* (pp. 58–73). Basingstoke: Palgrave Macmillan.

Ushioda, E. and Chen, S-A. (2011) Researching motivation and possible selves: The need to integrate qualitative inquiry. *Anglistik: International Journal of English Studies* 22 (1), 43–61.

Vandergrift, L. (2005) Relationships among motivation orientations, metacognitive awareness and proficiency in L2 listening. *Applied Linguistics* 26, 70–89.

Vygotsky, L.S. (1978) *Mind in Society: The Development of Higher Psychological Processes*. Cambridge: Harvard University Press.

White, R.W. (1959) Motivation reconsidered: The concept of competence. *Psychological Review* 66, 297–333.

Williams, M. and Burden, R.L. (1997) *Psychology for Language Teachers*. Cambridge: Cambridge University Press.

10 Brain and Self: A Neurophilosophical Account

Georg Northoff

Introduction: Concept of Self

You read these lines. You find them boring and your experience is marked by boredom. Who experiences this boredom? You. You are the subject of the experience of boredom. Without you as subject of this experience, you could not experience anything at all, not even boredom. This subject of experience has been described as the 'self'. Your 'self' makes it possible for you to experience things. In other words, it is a necessary condition for experience and thus also consciousness. It is clear, therefore, that there is much at stake when it comes to the self. We thus need to discuss how to characterize and define the concept of self.

Usually, we assume that somebody must have consciousness. Somebody speaks a language. Somebody writes a letter. And somebody acquires a second language when moving to a new country. Without 'somebody', we remain unable to do all of these things. But who or what exactly is this somebody? This is what is traditionally called 'self'. This chapter seeks to provide some answers to questions of the self by discussing ways of understanding the self. In what follows, I will outline four ways of conceptualizing the self: the mental self, the empirical self, the phenomenal self and the minimal self. I will then consider how the self can and has been researched experimentally in respect to the brain, before concluding with a discussion of the relevance of these points for language learning.

Concepts of Self

Any empirical research relies and is based on certain presuppositions. This also holds for current neuroscientific research on the self, which aims to reveal the neuronal mechanisms underlying our experience or sense of self. However, before examining the neuroscientific findings, we need to briefly shed some light on the concept of self and how it has been defined in philosophical discussions. There are mainly four different concepts of self discussed in current philosophy. First, the *'mental self'* is based on our thoughts and a specific mental substance. Second, in the *'empirical self'*, the self is assumed to no longer be based on a mental substance, but is rather thought of as representing and reflecting the biological processes in one's body and brain. Third, the *'phenomenal self'* starts from what we can experience in our consciousness. Our consciousness comes with an awareness of our self, referred to as pre-reflective self-awareness or phenomenal self. Finally, most recently, philosophers speak of a *'minimal self'* that is based on our body and its physiological processes. I will now discuss each of these in turn in more detail.

Concept of self: Mental self

What is the self? What must it look like in order to presuppose experience and be the subject of our experience? The self has often been viewed as a specific 'thing'. Stones are things and the table on which your laptop stands is a thing. And in the same way that the table makes it possible for the laptop to stand on it, the self may be a thing that makes experience and consciousness possible. In other words, metaphorically speaking, these stand on the shoulders of the self. However, another question is whether the self is a thing or, as philosophers such as Rene Descartes suggest, a substance? A substance is a specific entity or material that serves as a basis for something like a self. For instance, the body can be traced back to a physical substance, while the self is associated with mental workings, for example mental substance.

Is our self real and thus does it exist? Or is it just an illusion? Let us compare the situation with perception. When we perceive something in our environment, we sometimes perceive not a real thing but an illusion that in reality does not exist. The question of what exists and is real is what philosophers call a *metaphysical question*. Earlier philosophers, such as Rene Descartes, assumed that the self is real and exists. However, he also assumed that the self is different from the body. Hence, self and body exist but differ in their existence and reality. Thus, from this perspective, the self cannot be a physical substance but is rather a mental substance: it is a feature not of the body but of the mind, and thus a mental entity rather than physical substance.

However, the characterization of the self as a mental entity has been questioned. For example, the Scottish philosopher David Hume argued that there is no self as a mental entity. There is only a complex set or 'bundle' of perceptions of interrelated events that reflect the world in its entirety. There is no additional self in the world; instead, there is nothing but the events we perceive. Everything else, such as the assumption of a self as mental entity, is nothing but an illusion. The self as mental entity and thus as a mental substance does not exist and is therefore not real.

The rejection of the self as mental substance and dismissing the self as a mere illusion is currently popular. One major proponent of such a view is the German philosopher Thomas Metzinger (2003). In a nutshell, he argues that, through our experience, we develop models of the self, so-called 'self-models'. These self-models are nothing but information processes in our brain. However, since we do not have direct access to these neuronal processes (e.g. all those processes and activities of the cells, neurons, in the brain), we tend to assume the presence of an entity that must underlie our own self-model. This entity is then characterized as the self.

As depicted in Figure 10.1, the self is determined as mental substance (left) that is distinguished from the body (and brain) as a mere physical substance (right). Thereby, the self as 'mental self' controls and directs the body as proposed, for example, by the French philosopher Descartes. This is denied in current empirical approaches to the self (e.g. vertical red lines). They reject the notion of the self as mental substance and claim that such a mental self does not exist. Instead, all that exists according to them is the body as physical substance with the brain allowing for the representation of both body and brain in the brain's neural activity. Such self-representation may then amount to what can be described as the empirical self.

According to Metzinger, the assumption of the self as a mental entity results from an erroneous inference from our experience. We cannot experience the neuronal processes in our brain as such. Nobody has ever experienced their own brain and its neuronal processes. Therefore, the outcome of our brain's neuronal processes, the self, cannot be traced back to its original basis, the brain, in our experience. Where then does the self come from? We assume that it must be traced back to a special instance different from the brain. This leads us to assume that a mind and the self is a mental entity rather than a physical, for example, neuronal, entity originating from the brain itself. Metzinger argues that any such self as a mental entity simply

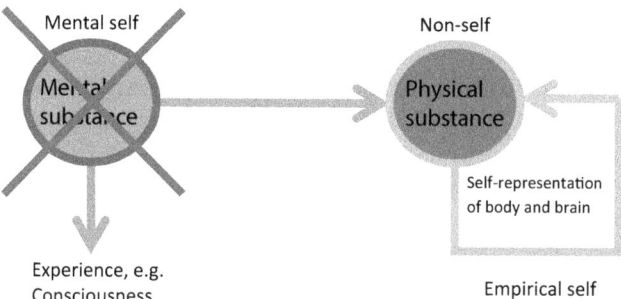

Figure 10.1 Concepts of self: Mental self and its replacement by an empirical self

does not exist. Therefore, Metzinger (2003) concludes, selves do not really exist. Hence, the title of his book *'Being No One'*.

Concept of self: From the metaphysical to the empirical self

What then is the self if not a mental entity? Some current authors, such as Metzinger (2003) and Churchland (2002), argue that the self as mental substance or entity does not exist. How though do we come up with the idea of a self or the 'self-model' as Metzinger (2003) calls it? The model of our own self is based on summarizing, integrating and coordinating all the information from our own body and own brain. In more technical terms, our own brain and body are represented in the neuronal activity of the brain. And such representation is the model of your self. The self-model is therefore nothing but an inner model of the integrated and summarized version of your own brain and body's information processing.

The original mental self, the self as mental substance or entity, is replaced in this line of thinking by a self-model. This implies a shift from a metaphysical discussion of the existence and reality of self to the processes that underlie the representation of body and brain as an inner model, for example, as a self-model. Since such representation is based on the coordination and integration of the various ongoing processes in brain and body, it is associated with specific higher-order cognitive functions, such as working memory, attention, executive function and memory, among others.

What does this imply for the characterization of the self (presupposing a broader concept of self beyond the self as mental substance)? The self is no longer characterized as a mental substance but as a cognitive function. Methodologically, this implies that the self is no longer investigated in metaphysical terms with regard to its existence and reality. Instead, we need to search for the cognitive processes underlying the special self-representation, thereby implying empirical rather than metaphysical investigation. The question for the self is consequently no longer an issue of philosophy, but rather one of cognitive psychology and ultimately of cognitive neuroscience. In short, the self is no longer a metaphysical matter, but a possible subject of empirical investigation.

Concept of self: Phenomenal self

One may now wonder about the proposition that we never experience any such substance or meta-representation that is supposed to account for the self. We are not conscious of any such substance or meta-representation. Our consciousness does not even provide us access to something like that. Therefore, instead of speculating about something that lies beyond the scope of our experience, why not start with experience itself and thus with consciousness? Rather than looking at what lies 'outside' our consciousness, like a substance or meta-representation, the self may be found within that very consciousness itself. However, such location 'outside' is denied in a particular branch of philosophy, phenomenological philosophy, that focuses on consciousness itself and what lies 'inside' our experience. More specifically, phenomenological philosophy is interested in investigating the structure and organization of our experience from a first-person perspective and thus is concerned with consciousness.

How does the phenomenal approach determine the self? Currently, it is argued that the self is an integral part of experience itself (Northoff, 2012). The self is not present in the experience as distinct and separate content as is the case with objects, events or other persons. Instead, it is always present and manifest in the phenomenal features of our experience, such as intentionality (e.g. the directedness of our consciousness towards specific contents), qualia (e.g. the qualitative character of our experience; what it is like), etc., without which the self would remain impossible. Consequently, phenomenological philosophers, such as Zahavi (2005), consider the self to be an inherent part of consciousness itself. In other words, the self is always already accompanied by some kind of consciousness of the external world, even if we are not aware of the self being part of that experience. Phenomenological philosophers therefore speak of what they call pre-reflective self-awareness (or pre-reflective self-consciousness).

What does the concept of pre-reflective self-consciousness mean? Pre-reflective means that the experience of the self does not stem from any reflection or cognitive operation. Instead it is already always there as part of our experience such that we cannot avoid it. The self is thus pre-reflective. It is simultaneously an inherent part of our experience and thus of our consciousness. The self is consequently no longer outside of our consciousness but an integral part of it, hence the second term, self-consciousness. Such an approach suggests an intimate and even stronger intrinsic link between self and consciousness.

As depicted in Figure 10.2, the phenomenal self no longer claims to be outside and prior to any experience. Instead, the phenomenal self is supposed to be 'located' within or part of the experience itself in the gestalt of

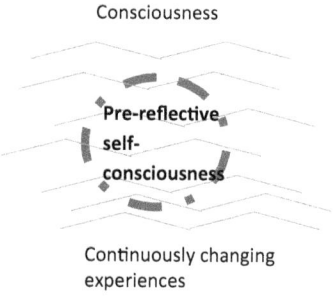

Figure 10.2 Concepts of self: Phenomenal self as pre-reflective self-consciousness

pre-reflective self-consciousness. This is indicated by the insertion of the circle within the midst of the experience, for example, consciousness itself.

Characterizing the self in terms of self-consciousness implies a significant shift. The self is no longer metaphysical as Descartes proposes. Nor is it empirical as advocated by Hume and others such as Metzinger (2003) and Churchland (2002). Instead, the self is part of the experience and of consciousness itself and can therefore be characterized as the 'phenomenal self'. Such a phenomenal self is thus open to systematic investigation of the phenomenal features of our experience that would complement the metaphysical, empirical and logical approaches to the self.

Concept of self: Minimal self

How can we describe the pre-reflective self-consciousness in more detail? It is always already there in every experience so that we cannot avoid it or separate it from the experience. The self is always present in our consciousness and thus in our subjective experience. Even if we do not focus on the self as such, we cannot avoid or remove its presence. Hence, the term pre-reflective self-consciousness describes an implicit or tacit experience of our self in our consciousness.

Since the self as pre-reflectively experienced is the basis of all phenomenal features of our experience, it must be considered as essential for any subsequent cognitive activity. Such a basic and fundamental self occurs in our experience before any reflection. For instance, when reading the lines of this book, you experience the contents and, in addition, you also experience your self as reading these lines. Hence, your immediate experience, for example, consciousness, comes with both the content and your own self. Since the experience of such self occurs prior to any reflection and recruitment of higher-order cognitive functions, such a concept of self is sort of a minimal version of the self. Current phenomenological philosophers, such as Gallagher (2000) or Zahavi (2005), speak therefore of a 'minimal self' when referring to the self as implicitly, tacitly and immediately experienced in consciousness.

How can we describe the concept of the 'minimal self'? The minimal self refers to a basic form of self that is part of any experience. The self in this sense is not extended across time; this distinguishes the self from personal identity that can be characterized by experience of continuity of the self across time. Instead, the minimal self describes a basic sense of self at any particular given moment in time, but does not yet provide a link between different moments in time and thus continuity across time. How can such continuity across time be constituted? Cognitive functions such as memories and autobiographical memories in particular may be central here. The self may then become more complex and one may speak of a cognitive, extended or autobiographical self, as, for instance, the Portuguese–American neuroscientist, Damasio does (see e.g. Damasio, 1999, 2010).

Another important feature of the minimal self is that although we experience it, we may not be aware of it as such, nor able to reflect upon it in order to gain knowledge of it. We are, to put it in technical terms, only pre-reflectively aware of the minimal self but not yet consciously reflective aware of it. How can we become reflectively aware of the minimal self? That is possible when all different time moments are put together and, as philosophers say, represented as such. For such representation, cognitive functions are needed that make it possible to put and link together the different time points.

Finally, the minimal self may also occur prior to and precede verbalization and thus linguistic expression. Rather than being tied to specific linguistic concepts as is the case with more cognitive concepts of the self, the minimal self must be considered pre-linguistic. It is an experience, a sense of self that can barely be put into concepts. We can experience it as self, but are not really able to describe these experiences in terms of concepts and thus articulate them in a linguistic way. Thus, the minimal self is pre-linguistic and pre-conceptual and will therefore, speculatively, not be affected by second language acquisition. It is the kind of experience, an implicit sense of self, which most likely subjects will take with them, remaining more or less stable when moving to a new country where they have to acquire a new language. However, at the same time, such a self provides the essential basis upon which more cognitive forms of self are developed, and which are then central and instrumental in providing the ability to learn a second language.

Methodological Approaches to the Experimental Investigation of the Self

How then can we investigate the self? In order to experimentally address the self, we need some quantifiable and objective measures that can be observed from a third-person perspective as distinguished from the subjective experience of the first-person perspective. How can we obtain such measures? Psychologists focusing on memory observed that items related to ourselves were better remembered than those unrelated to the person (see Northoff *et al.*, 2006). For instance, living in Ottawa, I recall much better the recent thunderstorm that wiped away several houses locally than you do as the reader, perhaps living in Germany, who just heard about it in the news.

There is thus superiority in recall of those items and stimuli that are related to one's own self. This is described as *self-reference effect* (SRE). The SRE has been well validated in several psychological studies (Northoff *et al.*, 2006). Most interestingly, it has been shown to operate in different domains. Not only in respect to memory, but also in relation to emotions, sensorimotor functions, faces, words, etc. In all these different domains (see below for details), stimuli related to one's own self, for example, self-specific stimuli, show much better recall than those that are unrelated to one's own self, for example, non-self-specific stimuli.

How is the SRE possible? Numerous investigations (see e.g. Klein, 2012; Klein & Gangi, 2010 for summaries) show that the SRE is mediated by different psychological functions. These range from personal (e.g. autobiographical memories), over memories of facts (e.g. semantic memories), to those cognitive capacities that allow for self-reflection and self-representation as introduced above (e.g. the processes in one's own brain and body). Hence, the SRE is by itself not a unitary function, but rather a complex multifaceted psychological composite of functions and processes.

How can we link the SRE to the brain? Before the introduction of functional imaging techniques, such as functional magnetic resonance imaging (fMRI) at the beginning of the 1990s, most studies conducted focused on the effect of dysfunction or lesions in specific brain regions caused, for instance, by brain tumours or stroke. These revealed that, for instance, lesions in medial temporal regions that are central in memory recall, such as the hippocampus, change and, ultimately, abolish the SRE effect.

With the introduction of brain imaging techniques such as fMRI, we could then transfer the experimental paradigms of comparing self- and non-self-specific stimuli to the scanner and investigate the underlying brain regions. The basic premise here is that if self-specific stimuli are better recalled than non-self-specific ones, they must be processed in the brain in a different way, such as, for instance, by higher degrees of neural activity and/or different regions.

This led to the investigation of numerous experimental designs of SRE-like paradigms in the fMRI scanner. For example, subjects were presented trait adjectives that were either related to themselves (such as for me, my hometown, Ottawa) as opposed to (Sydney, an unrelated city for me). Or the participant's own face was presented and compared with faces of other people. Also autobiographical events from the subject's past were compared with those from other people. One's own movements and actions could also be compared with those of other people implying what is called ownership (e.g. my movements) and agency ('I myself caused that action').

The stimuli belonged to different domains such as memory, faces, emotions, verbal, spatial, motor or social. Most of the stimuli were presented either visually or auditorily, and the presentation of these stimuli was usually accompanied by an online judgment about whether the stimuli are related, for example, personally meaningful or not to the research subject.

Spatial patterns of neural activity during self-reference

What results did the various imaging studies yield in fMRI? Two different kinds of regions showed up. First, one could see that the regions specific for the respective domain like emotions or faces were recruited. For instance, there is a region in the back of the brain that processes specifically faces (as distinguished from say houses); this is called the fusiform face area. This region is obviously active during the presentation of faces no matter whether it is one's own face or another person's face. Importantly, clear differences between self- and non-self-specific stimuli could not be observed in these domain-specific regions in most of the studies (Northoff et al., 2006).

What about other regions that are not specific for a particular domain like emotions or faces, for example, domain-independent regions involved in the neural processing of the self? Meta-analyses of the various studies demonstrated the involvement of a particular set of regions in the middle of the brain. These regions include the perigenual anterior cingulate cortex (PACC), the ventro- and dorso-medial prefrontal cortex (VMPFC, DMPFC), the supragenual anterior cingulate cortex (SACC), the posterior cingulate cortex (PCC) and the precuneus. Since they are all located in the midline of the brain, they have been coined 'cortical midline structures' (CMS). The self-specific stimuli, for example, those that were personally relevant for the subjects, induced higher neural activity in these regions than non-self-specific ones, for example, those that remained irrelevant und unrelated to the person. This was observed in the various domains for faces, trait adjectives, movements/actions, memories and social communication. Therefore, the CMS seem to show a special significance to the self, for example, self-reference.

However, there is also some differentiation within the CMS. The self-specific stimuli may be presented in different ways to the subject in the scanner. If subjects have to make judgments requiring cognitive involvement, the dorsal and posterior regions, such as the SACC, DMPFC and PCC, are recruited to a stronger degree. If, in contrast, stimuli are merely perceived without any judgment and thus without any cognitive component, the ventral and anterior regions, such as the VMPFC and PACC, were strongly involved.

The left-hand side of Figure 10.3a depicts all the imaging studies on the self as plotted in their location on one brain. This includes self-referential stimuli in various domains or functions such as memory, social, spatial, etc., as indicated in the lower text with the colours as shown below and on the right of the figure. On the right, three different coordinates (x, y, z) are shown that determine the direction (medial-lateral, inferior-superior) of the location in the brain. One can see that all of the studies are located in the midline regions of the brain (left image) as seen in the x-coordinates that describe the medial-lateral location (right image).

Figure 10.3b shows the anatomical regions in the midline of the brain. This led to the assumption that the different regions mediate different aspects of self-reference. The ventral and anterior regions, such as the PACC and VMPFC, may be more involved in the representation of the degree of self-reference in the stimulus. However, dorsal regions, such as the SACC and

(a)

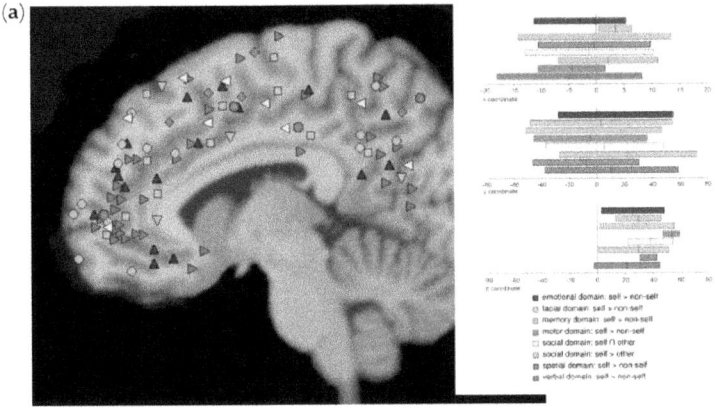

▲ emotional domain: self > non-self
▽ facial domain: self > non-self
▢ memory domain: self > non-self
◆ motor domain: self > non-self
◁ social domain: self ∩ other
◯ social domain: self > other
✢ spatial domain: self > non-self
▷ verbal domain: self > non-self

(b)

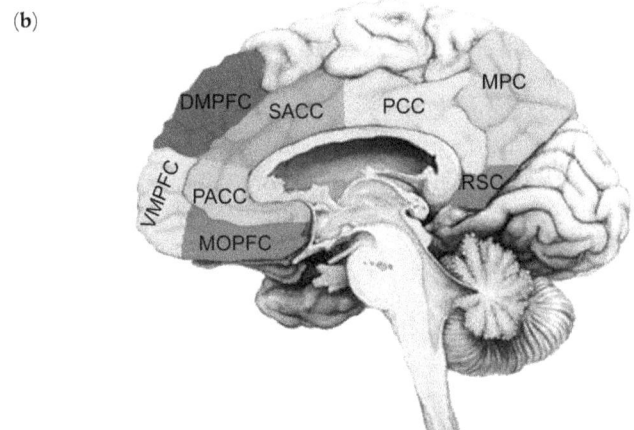

Figure 10.3 Cortical midline structures and the self. (a) Distinction between self and non-self: cortical midline structures and domain independence; (b) cortical midline structures – anatomical definition. The figure demonstrates the results of a meta-analysis on imaging studies of self-reference (Northoff *et al.*, 2006) (a) and anatomical illustration of the midline regions (b) MOPFC: medial orbital prefrontal cortex; PACC: perigenual anterior cingulate cortex; VMPFC, DMPFC: ventro- and dorso-medial prefrontal cortex; SACC: supragneual anterior cingulate cortex; PCC: posterior cingulate cortex; MPC: medial parietal cortex; RSC: retrosplenial cortex

the DMPFC, may be related to monitoring and reflection of the stimulus and its self-reference when we become aware of the stimulus as self-specific. Finally, the posterior regions, such as the PCC, may be implicated in integrating the stimulus and its degree of self-reference into the autobiographical memory of the respective person. These regions have been shown to be implicated in the recall and retrieval of especially personally relevant and autobiographical information from the past of that person. Thus, it can be concluded that specific regions in the midline of the brain, the cortical midline structures, seem to be involved in the neural processing of self-reference, for example, attributing personal relevance or self-relevance to stimuli.

Neurophilosophical Reflection

Psychological and experimental specificity

Most of the fMRI above compared self- versus non-self-specific stimuli, such as a grand piano for a professional pianist compared with a saw for a carpenter. In addition to the mere perception, subjects were required to make a judgment after each stimulus, to judge whether it was self- or non-self-specific. This raises the question about what exactly the study is measuring – the perception or the judgment of the stimulus? Is it thus capturing the effect of the stimulus itself or the task related to that stimulus?

Most likely the results reflect a mixture between stimulus-related and task-related effects. This, therefore, casts some doubt on whether the midline regions show psychological specificity for the self. The judgment about self-specificity requires various cognitive functions, such as attention, working memory and autobiographical memory retrieval. Some authors, such as the French neuroscientist D. Legrand, therefore argue that the midline regions may be more related to what she describes as 'general evaluation function', rather than being specific to the self and self-specific stimuli.

What about when research investigates self in relation to more basic functions such as movements and actions? Even when subjects perform some motor tasks, we face the same confusion of different functions: The self-components such as ownership, for example, is the movement my own movement, as well as agency, for example, whether I am the agent of the movement, may be confounded by the neural mechanisms underlying the execution of the movement/action by the person.

Such psychological unspecificity highlights the need in neuroscience to specify the experimental design and measures. We need measures that are specific to the self as distinguished from the various associated sensorimotor, affective and cognitive functions. And we need experimental designs to segregate stimulus-related and task-related effects, for example, by spacing perception and judgment temporally apart from each other.

Self-specificity and other functions

Finally, one needs to discuss the relationship between self and other functions. Recent imaging studies demonstrated strong neural overlap between self and reward, self and emotions, and self and decision making. For example, when receiving a reward in relation to a specific stimuli, such as money, regions of the reward system like the ventral striatum (VS) and the VMPFC become active (Northoff, 2012). These same regions are also active when the same stimulus is conceived as self-specific rather than non-self-specific by the respective subject. The same effects can be observed in emotions where emotional and self-specific stimuli have been shown to overlap in especially the anterior midline regions. Finally, the same effect can be observed in decision making: if external cues are provided when making a decision (such as a higher or lower price of the same kind of apples), lateral cortical regions become active. If, in contrast, no such external cues are provided, we need to come up with some internal criterion to guide and make our decision about which apples to purchase (Nakao *et al.*, 2012). Such internal criterion can only stem from our self. Studies comparing both kinds of decision making show predominant involvement of the midline regions in internally guided, when compared with externally guided, decision making (Nakao *et al.*, 2012).

Together such neural overlap between self and other functions, such as reward, emotions and decision making, raises questions about the relationship between them. Different models could be imagined. Self and self-specificity could be an independent function just like attention, working memory, emotion, sensorimotor, etc. However, in that case, one would expect specific regions in the brain and specific psychological functions to subserve specifically and exclusively self-specificity. However, at this point in time, this cannot be supported empirically.

Finally, one could also suggest that self and self-specificity are basic functions that underlie and provide the basis for all other functions, for example sensorimotor, affective, cognitive, social. In this sense, self and self-specificity would occur prior to the recruitment of the other functions. Self-specificity would then always be present, making its involvement and manifestation in the various functions unavoidable. Rather than searching for self-specificity in relation to specific functions, such as language, one would then need to look for more basic functions that must occur prior to sensorimotor, affective or cognitive functions. One could, for instance, imagine that the strong involvement of the self in language acquisition requires the recruitment of midline regions. Such involvement of midline structures may be implicitly presupposed in many of the tasks or paradigms as described above when presenting self-relevant and non-self-relevant words, for example, trait adjectives. While the linguistic tasks themselves seem to involve more the lateral cortical regions, the latter's degree of activity may, nevertheless, be dependent upon the midline regions and their high resting state activity. Hence, future studies may want to investigate the relationship between midline regions and lateral networks implicated in language, which psychologically may correspond to the relationship between self and language.

Phenomenal specificity of the self

The assumption of self-specificity brings us back to the concept of the self as 'minimal self' outlined above in which the self was considered fundamental. To recap, the minimal self describes a basic sense of self that occurs immediately and is always already part of our experience of the world. The question now is how the concept of the minimal self is related to the neuroscientific results discussed above. For that, we briefly have to shed light on the experience of the minimal self as manifest in pre-reflective self-consciousness.

Consciousness can be characterized by various phenomenal features such as qualia (what our experience is like for us) and first-person perspective. All your experiences presuppose a specific point of view, your individual one, which is different from that of other persons. This individually specific point of view is supposed to give your experience a specific quality, qualia. The first-person perspective refers to the fact that we can experience the world only from a first-person perspective, while any experience remains impossible from a third-person perspective where we can only observe but not experience.

If the self, for example, the minimal self, is part of any experience (rather than being outside of it), the self should be manifest in these phenomenal features too. What experiential and thus phenomenal features does the self add? One may assume that the self first and foremost makes possible the generation of qualia. Without self, there is no point of view and hence no qualitative features in our experience, for example, qualia. Phenomenological philosophers assume that the special contribution of the self consists in what they describe as *'belonginess'* or *'mineness'* (Gallagher, 2000; Zahavi, 2005): the contents of our experience are experienced as belonging to a particular self; they are experienced as mine. For instance, I experience the laptop on which I write here in front of me as my laptop going along with an experience of being related to my self. However, such experience is not possible for the person sitting besides me who though looking at the same laptop does not experience any relation to the self. Instead, they may experience mineness or belonginess of the CD lying besides the laptop, because they are a composer and it is a CD of their work.

Such relation to one's own self is particularly important when one needs to acquire a second language. The foreign language could appear as totally strange, as having no relation to one's own self and thus no self-relevance would be detected in any of the words. Why? Because none of the new words are yet associated with any experiences in specific contexts and situations. The words thus do not yet elicit any sense of relation to the self. However, once one immerses oneself more and more into a new culture or learning context and gains new experiences, the novel words will become associated with self-relevance, thus inducing a sense of self. In short, the novel language will increasingly become associated with one's own self and become part of it. It is to be supposed that this self-relevance of language may also facilitate the acquisition and learning of the new language.

Phenomenal specificity and phenomenal limits

In order to account for phenomenal specificity, neuroscience needs to show the neuronal mechanisms underlying the experience of mineness and belonginess and also to distinguish those neuronal mechanisms underlying other phenomenal features of experience, intentionality, unity, first-person perspective, qualia and spatiotemporal continuity. One would therefore require distinct experimental measures and designs for each of these phenomenal features. Only then would we be able to achieve phenomenal specificity and to clearly distinguish the phenomenal or minimal self from phenomenal consciousness. In short, we need to experimentally distinguish between self-specific and non-self-specific phenomenal measures.

However, the phenomenological philosopher may want to raise the following question: is such phenomenal specificity with the experimental distinction between self-specific and non-self-specific phenomenal measures really possible at all? The minimal self is considered part of the experience and thus of consciousness in general. Any consciousness of the world goes along with an experience of the self in a pre-reflective way. And the converse holds too. Any experience of the self is part of an experience of the world. Both experience of self and experience of world are thus intrinsically linked.

What does such an intrinsic link between experience of self and experience of the world imply for the phenomenal specificity of the self? It means that we will remain unable to properly and clearly segregate experimental measures for the minimal self from those of our experience in general, for example, experience of the world. More specifically, this means that we will be unable to account experimentally for the relation to the self distinct and separate from other spatiotemporal features, such as spatiotemporal continuity, unity, first-person perspective and qualia.

Why? Because these phenomenal features are always already 'infected' by the self, for example, in the same way as they are encoded and ingrained into the self. Hence, the requirement of maximal experimental and phenomenal specificity may here have reached its phenomenal limits. If so, we may be forced to acknowledge that there may be principal limitations in what we can and cannot investigate experimentally when it comes to the minimal self.

Minimal self and body

What about self and body? We can experience our own body as our own body. This leads us to a characteristic feature of the body, namely, that it can be experienced in consciousness. The body is not only an objective body that can be observed from a third-person perspective. This is the body the neuroscientist and the doctor investigate. It can also be experienced from a first-person perspective. This is the body we consciously experience, which is therefore characterized as a 'lived body'. This is the body that we experience as our body, as my body as distinguished from others' bodies. Hence, we experience the lived body in relation to our self. Thus, the experience of the body, the lived body, may be regarded as the first and most fundamental manifestation of the phenomenal or minimal self. Our self in its most basic and minimal form is thus essentially a bodily self.

Such relation to the self is also reflected in what we described earlier as ownership and agency. Ownership describes the fact that I experience my body as my body rather than some other body. Neuroscientifically, the ownership of the body has been associated with neuronal activity in specific regions of the brain, such as the sensory cortex and the parietal cortex with the parietal cortex mediating the spatial position of the body in the world. Agency is the experience that I, rather than some other person, originated and caused the subsequent action and movement. For example, I, my self, am the agent of the lines I am currently writing here on my laptop. The action and the movements are thus mine since they were caused by me as agent. Neurally, regions such as the premotor cortex and the motor cortex have been associated with agency; these are regions that are implicated in generating movement and action in general.

Conclusion: Self and Language

How do the concepts of the self and their neurobiological underpinnings relate to language production and language learning? The empirical self, as suggested by Metzinger (2003) and Churchland (2002), is based on the monitoring and representation of one's own body and brain's neuronal and physical processes. Such re-representation of our experiences involves higher-order cognitive functions among which language is central. Language is a fundamental tool to re-represent, for example, access, and express one's own body and brain in another higher-order layer so that we can reflect upon it. The concept of the empirical self is, thus, essentially a cognitive self and, as such, always a linguistic self. This though, given the above consideration, is only a secondary self, a reflective or cognitive self, which is based on and builds upon a more basic one, a pre-reflective pre-cognitive self that is communicated in a non-verbal way, such as, for instance, via sensorimotor and affective functions.

Neurobiologically, the empirical self is associated with specific regions (e.g. the ventro- and dorsolateral prefrontal regions), which are active, for example, during self-recognition or self-reflection. The very same regions are also implicated in linguistic functions, thus, further supporting the potentially strong ties between the empirical self and language. Within the brain, the language network includes mainly lateral regions in the prefrontal and the parietal and temporal cortex. These differ from the medial regions, the midline structures, supposedly involved in the self and self-reference. However, there is much interaction between the two that may reciprocally modulate each other. This means that if the one is more active, the other becomes less active. While the exact mechanisms remain unclear at this point in time, including how self and language interact on a neuronal level, there is much potential in exploring understandings of the self and language in the brain, given the centrality of both to human experience.

What about the pre-reflective self and the minimal self as related to the bodily self? Both are assumed to occur prior to the acquisition of specific cognitive functions including language. They are thus pre-cognitive and pre-linguistic. We can experience and feel our pre-reflective self or minimal self but we are not yet able to verbalize them as such. This corresponds well to their underlying neural regions, the subcortical regions and cortical midline structures, which themselves are not implicated in linguistic functions. The pre-reflective self or minimal self may, thus, be a kind of self that occurs prior to language and may, speculatively, remain more or less independent of it. Rather than expressing it in our language and its concepts, such a self may be accessed, in our experience, as manifest in a sense of self with mineness or belongingness.

This demonstrates that there is a sense of self via presumably self-related processing prior to the occurrence of language. However, any subsequent cognitive and thus linguistic function is based on and builds upon the prior pre-cognitive and pre-linguistic processing. This implies for second language acquisition (SLA) that a high degree of personal relevance and importance, for example, self-reference of the new language, may ease and facilitate subsequent learning and acquisition. If personal relevance and thus a high degree of self-relatedness are associated with the new language, it may be acquired more easily than in the case of low personal relevance. Why? Because this is the way our brain relates extrinsic stimuli to its own neural processing in the subcortical and cortical midline regions. Therefore, newly acquired language may ultimately and ideally become part of a person's sense of self. This will be manifest in the experience of belongingness or mineness of the respective concepts and their associated environmental context and events. Unfortunately, to the best of my knowledge, this remains to be researched fully; however, in addition to the relevance for furthering understandings in the neurosciences, the findings of such studies could have considerable importance also for language learning education.

> **Recommended reading**
>
> Metzinger, T. (2003) *Being No One*. Cambridge/Mass: MIT Press.
>
> This is a central book about one of the current concepts of self that denies its existence as such. Instead, the self is considered to be an illusion. The book provides a nice overview of the state of the art.
>
> Zahavi, D. (2005) *Subjectivity and Selfhood: Investigating the First-Person Perspective*. London: MIT press.
>
> This book presents a phenomenological philosophical viewpoint on the self – the self as pre-reflective self-consciousness. It provides an excellent overview with many links to the philosophy of mind.
>
> Northoff, G., Heinzel, A., de Greck, M., Bermpohl, F., Dobrowolny, H. and Panksepp, J. (2006) Self-referential processing in our brain- a meta-analysis of imaging studies on the self. *Neuroimage* 31 (1), 440–457.
>
> This article gives an overview of empirical findings on the self in imaging studies and how they relate to the different concepts of self discussed in both psychology and philosophy.

References

Churchland, P.S. (2002) Self-representation in nervous systems. *Science* 296 (5566), 308–310.
Damasio, A.R. (1999) How the brain creates the mind. *Scientific American* 281 (6), 112–117.
Damasio, A.R. (2010) *The Self Comes to Mind*. New York: Viching.
Gallagher, S. (2000) Philosophical conceptions of the self: Implications for cognitive science. *Trends Cognitive Science* 4 (1), 14–21.
Klein, S.B. (2012) Self, memory, and the self-reference effect: An examination of conceptual and methodological issues. *Personality and Social Psychology Review: An Official Journal of the Society for Personality and Social Psychology* 16 (3), 283–300.
Klein, S.B. and Gangi, C.E. (2010) The multiplicity of self: Neuropsychological evidence and its implications for the self as a construct in psychological research. *Annals of the New York Academy of Sciences* 1191, 1–15.
Metzinger, T. (2003) *Being No One*. Cambridge: MIT Press.
Nakao, T., Ohira, H. and Northoff, G. (2012) Distinction between externally vs. internally guided decision-making: Operational differences, meta-analytical comparisons and their theoretical implications. *Frontiers in Neuroscience* 6, 31.
Northoff, G. (2012a) Autoepistemic limitation and the brain's neural code: Comment on 'neuroontology, neurobiological naturalism, and consciousness: A challenge to scientific reduction and a solution' by Todd E. Feinberg. *Physics of Life Reviews* 9 (1), 38–39.
Northoff, G. (2012b) *Das undisziplinierte Gehirn. Was nun Herr Kant?* München: Isiriana/Random House.

Northoff, G. (2012c) Immanuel Kant's mind and the brain's resting state. *Trends in Cognitive Sciences* 16 (7), 356–359.

Northoff, G., Heinzel, A., de Greck, M., Bermpohl, F., Dobrowolny, H. and Panksepp, J. (2006) Self-referential processing in our brain – a meta-analysis of imaging studies on the self. *Neuroimage* 31 (1), 440–457.

Zahavi, D. (2005) *Subjectivity and Selfhood: Investigating the First-Person Perspective.* London: MIT Press.

11 The Self from a Complexity Perspective

Sarah Mercer

Introduction

It is perhaps stating the obvious to say that the self is complex. Reflecting briefly on the question of 'who you are' leaves you with a multitude of self-descriptions, incorporating a range of self-related cognitions, beliefs, emotions, motives, roles, relationships, memories, dreams and goals, as well as expressions of who you feel you are not. The self is the hub at the centre of all our lived experiences. It is, therefore, unsurprising that it has been a principal goal for researchers in many fields to better understand the nature, composition and development of the self.

However, the starting point for any valid, reliable research is a clear, operationalisable definition of constructs. And herein lies the inherent problem in researching the self. Clearly, something as multifarious as the self defies a neat, tidy definition. Yet, in order to meet the exigencies and demands of research, attempts have been made to constrain, set boundaries and make the self measurable and quantifiable. In the dominant experimental paradigm in psychology-based research, this has meant tightening and narrowing down definitions of constructs in order to strengthen correlational scores and increase the reliability of quantitative studies. However, phenomenologically, we have an intuitive sense of self, which encompasses a much broader range of beliefs, feelings and motivations than many of the self-constructs are able to capture. In this chapter, I propose a conceptualisation of self that can help unite diverse perspectives on the self and which can prompt fresh thinking about the self in a way that enables greater recognition of its inherent complexity, situatedness and dynamism.

Integrative Perspectives on the Self

In addition to the traditional research conducted using a variety of conceptually distinct self-constructs, some researchers in both psychology and second language acquisition (SLA) have begun to embrace more holistic, dynamic conceptualisations of the self. In psychology, for example, there have been various attempts at taking more integrative approaches to the self, which stretch across diverse theories of the self, disciplinary boundaries and methodological approaches (see e.g. Deaux & Perkins, 2001; Neisser, 1988; Osborne, 1996). Such works essentially bring together multiple theories and findings to create a coherent, unified theory or understanding of the self based on a range of perspectives. The subsequent theories tend to comprise conceptualisations of the self as composed of multiple, interconnected types of self-beliefs, motives and emotions, which are intimately interconnected with contexts and are differently dynamic across time and place; characteristics that are reminiscent of those of complex dynamic systems.

An explicit dynamic systems perspective on the self has been advocated in psychology by Mischel and Morf (2003). They propose an integrative model of the self which they argue is not uniquely 'theirs' but instead represents 'an effort to integrate diverse already existing contributions' (Mischel & Morf, 2003: 16). They conceptualise the self as a 'psycho-social dynamic processing system'. Central to understanding their model is the idea that the self is not a collection of static attributes, but a coherent, organised system of cognitive-affective 'units' that are interconnected with each other and form a unique network for each person. They suggest that individual differences in the self can be understood in relation to the different organisational structures of these units in the network. In terms of dynamics, they conclude that the self-system is responsive to contexts and continuously adapts to and accommodates different features of social environments and interactions, depending on which situational factors are especially salient for a particular individual. Despite acknowledging and indeed stressing the idea of process and dynamics in their model, they also caution that the self-system as they conceive it is also relatively stable in two possible ways: first, in terms of how the structure of the network is organised for an individual, and second, in terms of the types of self-related processes typically activated for particular individuals in certain contexts.

Others in psychology have also proposed explicitly dynamic systems approaches to the self (see e.g. Nowak *et al.*, 2000; Nowak *et al.*, 2005; Vallacher & Nowak, 1997; Vallacher *et al.*, 2002a). In 2002, a special issue of the *Personality and Social Psychology Review* was dedicated to dynamical perspectives and approaches to studying personality. In their introductory article to that volume, Vallacher *et al.* (2002b: 264) argue that 'the subject matter of personality and social psychology is inherently dynamic' and conclude that 'no one would argue with the suggestion that human social experience is complex and dynamic, nor would most observers deny the potential relevance and utility of non-linear dynamical systems to personal and interpersonal phenomena' (Vallacher *et al.*, 2002b: 268).

Within SLA, the whole field of learner individual differences has steadily been moving towards one of increased complexity and dynamism across contexts and time (Mercer, 2011a; Mercer *et al.*, 2012). In respect to the self explicitly, a more holistic, integrative perspective has been offered by van Lier (2004) in his ecological model of the self. He argues that the self is dialogically and socially constructed and highlights the close connection between language and the construction of self. Importantly, he also draws attention to the ongoing nature of self-construction throughout the life time as people continually seek to establish their place in the world (van Lier, 2004: 131). A key characteristic of an ecological perspective is the importance of embodied views of the self, in other words that our bodies are an integral part of our self, and thus the inseparable connection between body and mind (van Lier, 2004: 107). It also emphasises the concept of emergence, meaning that the self becomes a different entity through its experiences and development from one that can be deduced from its component parts or its prior state.

Self as a Complex Dynamic System

Following this trend towards integrative perspectives, I wish to describe how the self can be conceptualised as a complex dynamic system (see also Mercer, 2011a, 2011b). The first key characteristic of a complex dynamic system is that it is composed of multiple interrelated components. In respect to the self, these components have been differently defined such as in terms of the traditional constructs of self-efficacy, domain-specific self-concepts, such as maths self-concept or EFL self-concept, relational selves, identities, etc. Alternatively, it has been defined in terms of processes or relationships of specific cognitive-affective units (e.g. Mischel & Morf, 2003). It is important to note that components of the system can be systems in their own right, while simultaneously being part of a larger system. As a result, it becomes difficult to separate systems as no system can be thought of as being fully self-contained. So, for example, the individual self can be viewed as a complex dynamic system in its own right; however, within a classroom collective, it can also be understood as a component part of the larger classroom system. Thus, a learner's sense of self influences the character and dynamics of the classroom group through their participation, but, at the same time, how they see themselves as an individual is also influenced by their interaction in the group (cf. Morin, 2008). Complex dynamic systems are therefore often referred to as being 'open systems' in reference to the influence of other systems on the particular system under investigation.

The second core characteristic of a complex dynamic system concerns the nature of its dynamics. Within a system, everything is conceived as being in a state of flux, which can lead to various types of dynamics. For example, a system can change by constantly adapting and maintaining equilibrium known as 'dynamic stability' (Larsen-Freeman & Cameron, 2008: 43) or 'homeostasis' (cf. Nowak *et al.*, 2005: 354). However, the system can also change in more dramatic or sudden ways, such as through potentially small influences at critical points, often referred to as 'the butterfly effect', as well as gradually through cumulative change over time. As all the components in the system are interdependent, changes in one part of the system will lead to changes in other parts of the system in ways that are not entirely predictable and hence complex systems are typically described as being non-linear. As Dörnyei and Ushioda (2011: 37) explain, 'because of the multiple interactions of the system constituents – which also involve environmental factors – the system is constantly in flux, but the direction of change cannot be ascribed to any single variable in isolation as it is a function of the overall state of the system'. Therefore, there is no one single cause of change and consequently simple cause-and-effect models cannot capture the kinds of dynamics inherent in such systems.

Such non-linear dynamics also point to another key characteristic, namely, emergence. This refers to changes in a system's state so that its emergent properties are different to those of its previous state and cannot be reduced to or explained by its individual components or the sum of the separate components. In other words, the collective functioning of the system as one organic whole cannot be deduced from an understanding of the individual components. Thus, the properties of the system as a whole are more than merely the sum of its separate parts (Mason, 2008: 33) or at least different to the sum of its parts (Lewin, 1951 cited in Ehrman & Dörnyei, 1998: 14). Another way of talking about this emergent quality is in terms of self-organisation, which refers to the process whereby the system organises itself into a new state rather than some external force acting as the organising agent. In respect to the self, the concept of emergence mirrors understandings of more global self-structures, such as self-esteem, which cannot be understood in terms of the component elements of the self individually in isolation, but rather as emerging from the interaction of multiple forms and sources of self-relevant information that are weighed and evaluated in a variety of processes leading to the macro-level emergent sense of global self-esteem (see e.g. Mruk, 2006).

Considering these characteristics, the self can be thought of as a coherently organised dynamic system encompassing all the beliefs, cognitions, emotions, motives and processes related to and concerning oneself. This implies the self can be understood as an ongoing process that is never completed, but is continually in a state of development and self-organising emergence. As an open system, the self should not be thought of as situated exclusively within the mind of the individual. Instead, in line with embodied perspectives, the self is intimately connected to the physical world through actions, behaviours and physical senses, thereby uniting body, mind and environment. A useful distinction proposed by Schwartz (2007: 97) distinguishes between 'self as an organism' and a person's 'sense of self'. He argues that 'self as an organism' captures the idea of a unified, coherent whole being integrating mind and body into 'a single, integrated, organised system', whereas a person's 'sense of self' reflects 'the individual's experience of himself as a coherent being' (Schwartz, 2007: 99). From a complexity perspective, this enables the self as a whole being to be thought of as a complex dynamic system, with a central, core component of this system represented by a person's sense of self. It is then this sense of self that is most likely to be accessed in research as the conscious sense of self that individuals are at least partially aware of and able to articulate through self-report data.

Dynamic and Emergent Self

One of the characteristics of the self that has caused perhaps the most controversy and debate concerns its dynamism. Research findings have been at times viewed as contradictory in suggesting that the self is both stable and dynamic, as well as consistent and inconsistent (e.g. Harter, 1999; Markus & Kunda, 1986; Markus & Wurf, 1987; Mercer, 2009, 2011b; Onorato & Turner, 2004). From traditional perspectives that argued an either/or perspective on the dynamism of the self, the findings were deemed to be incompatible; however, from a complexity perspective, these characteristics of the self are to be expected and could, indeed, potentially be predicted from models of system dynamics.

Early debates around the self argued about whether the self was an intrinsically mental, static construct or dynamic and socially constructed. In recent years, it has become widely accepted that the self does not develop in a vacuum, but is influenced by experiences, environmental factors and interpersonal relationships. Indeed, the claim that the self is dynamic in respect to multiple contexts and experiences is doubtless intuitively familiar to people's own lived experiences of their sense of self. As Vallacher *et al.* explain:

> The sheer number and variety of factors identified as relevant to human experience guarantee that everything people think and do is constantly subject to change. Thoughts, feelings, and actions are influenced by a myriad of social stimuli that run the gamut from those that are momentary and trivial (e.g., a stranger's glance) to those that are persistent and significant (e.g., criticism from a loved one). This influence is central to everyday social interaction, with each person responding to the real or imagined thoughts, feelings, and actions of the other person. (Vallacher *et al.*, 2002b: 265)

However, it is not the unidirectional influence of contexts, feedback from others or experiences that leads to change in the self, but the self emerges from a series of concurrent processes as the self mediates external influences by selecting, evaluating, assessing and interpreting their relevance and significance for the self. This mediation can stem from a range of possible self-related motives, such as self-evaluation (to get an accurate sense of self), self-enhancement (to get an improved sense of self), self-protection (to maintain consistency in one's sense of self) or self-congruency (to maintain congruency between one's sense of self and behaviours) (see e.g. Osborne, 1996). Thus, the self-system is responsive and adaptive to contexts; however, when we enter any situation, we do so with an already established schema about ourselves as well as the types of people or the setting we find ourselves in. As Nowak et al. (2000: 39) point out, before we can engage in any self-relevant behaviour or processes, we must 'have a relatively coherent perspective on the vast number of features relevant to self-understanding'. In other words, the enormous range of self-relevant cognitions, emotions, goals, motives, identities, etc., must be organised together in some way, in order to provide us with a coherent, recognisable as opposed to fragmented sense of self. In this way, the self as a system can be thought of as having an underlying relative stability similar to the notion of equilibrium or homeostasis (Nowak et al., 2005: 354). As Nowak et al. (2005: 78) conclude, 'The notion of personality implies some form of stability in thought, emotion and action. At the same time, human experience is inherently dynamic and constantly evolving in response to external circumstances and events'. Questions, however, remain about how the different dynamics of the self-system are interconnected with each other and the nature of their development.

Researching the Dynamics of the Self

To contribute to our growing body of knowledge about the dynamics of the self in relation to language learning, a small pilot study was conducted with four female, tertiary-level EFL learners over the period of one semester, which is approximately four months. All of the students were attending an integrated language skills course at a university in Austria, had English at approximately B2 (upper intermediate) level and were aged on average 20 years old. When researching the dynamics of a system, it is important to attend to the potential different dynamics across different timescales. In this study, the self was investigated retrospectively at the macro level across a timescale of years using autobiographies and concurrently across the four-month duration of the course using three approximately equally spaced, in-depth interviews.

The study also examined a micro-level timescale of dynamics. Mid-way through the course the students engaged in two different speaking tasks in pairs that lasted in total approximately 20 minutes. The first task was a deliberately open-ended task in which students introduce themselves to each other based on prompt questions such as *'what book or film or TV show has your partner enjoyed recently?'*. The second task was a discussion task about problems in the city where they live in which they had to reach an agreement about perceived priorities. While they worked on these speaking tasks together, they were videoed. Immediately following the tasks, each participant was interviewed separately. They were shown the video and asked to evaluate their feelings of confidence. This self-construct was chosen because of its easy comprehensibility for the participants and relatively broad scope. However, it is clear that this represents only a fragment of their self-system, but for the practical feasibility of this research, such a boundary needs to be set while mindful of its partiality in the self-system as a whole (see also following discussion in 'Issues for Researching the Self as a Complex Dynamic System'). Students' responses about their perceived self-confidence were recorded using the idiodynamic software (MacIntyre & Legatto, 2011). This software allows the students, when retrospectively watching the video, to mark using the mouse on a scale perceived rises and falls in their confidence. An output graph of their perceived highs and lows is then printed and the participants then have the opportunity to comment on the graph as well as the video as a form of stimulated recall. The focus of the idiodynamic interview was on perceived reasons for any rises or falls in their self-confidence.

All of the data were digitalised, interviews were transcribed and all data were coded line-by-line in a series of coding phases until 'saturation' in the coding process and no new codes or combinations of codes could be assigned. The focus of the analysis was on possible dynamics in terms of the self, as well as perceived factors affecting the self during the interaction of the speaking tasks. All four participants gave their informed, signed consent to take part and were assigned pseudonyms to protect their identities.

Findings and discussion: Dynamics of the self

On the whole, there was notably less dynamism in the reported selves of these learners in these data sets across the timescale of one semester compared with my earlier study using longitudinal data covering three years (Mercer, 2011b). As has been suggested by Shapka and Keating (2005: 93), for any changes to be noted in self-beliefs at this age and level of proficiency, it may be necessary to generate data for a period of time, ideally longer than one year. Nevertheless, there are reported perceived changes in the self retrospectively in the autobiographical data. However, in this chapter owing to space limitations, I wish to focus my discussion on two other forms of dynamics evident in the data. The first concerns dynamics across time in respect to the certainty with which some of the participants held their self-beliefs regarding their foreign languages, which was the domain at the focus of this study. The second concerns situational dynamics arising, in particular, in the idiodynamic data during the speaking tasks.

Dynamics across time

When examining possible dynamics in the self across time, it is important not to simply focus on possible changes in terms of the content of self-beliefs or the positivity of the sense of self, but research also needs to consider changes that may take place in terms of quality, intensity or certainty with which beliefs or feelings are held. Of particular interest for dynamics is the certainty of self-beliefs, as it seems probable that the more certain you are about your sense of self, the less open to change this is likely to be. For example, Nora, who displays a strong, confident and certain sense of self, had more overall consistency to her beliefs throughout the semester and, indeed, also across contexts. In contrast, Olivia, for example, was relatively confident about her abilities but displayed more dynamism in her self-beliefs, also in the positivity of her beliefs, across time and contexts. However, most notably throughout the data, she expressed uncertainty about her self-beliefs and this did not appear to change during the study:

> I must admit that it is rather hard for me to describe myself as a foreign language learner. I mean I have been learning English for about ten years now and I must say that it is very hard for me to define my strengths and weaknesses as they have always changed over time. (Olivia, autobiography)

> Well, I think I have improved a bit, but ... it's quite hard to observe how much it is over a semester. (Olivia, final interview)

I would suggest that an important aspect of self-related work interested in dynamics may need to examine more fully the extent to which an individual feels certain in terms of their self-perceptions and evaluations. For example, Campbell (1990) proposes that individual self-concepts may not differ with respect to whether they are more or less positive or negative, but in terms of 'self-concept certainty' (SCC), which she defines as 'the extent to which the contents or self-beliefs are clearly and confidently defined' (Campbell, 1990: 539). Another perspective on self-certainty is proposed by Nowak et al. (2000) who suggest that self-certainty may be interconnected with the degree to which the self-system is integrated and coherent. Thus, establishing not only the content and degrees of positivity of a learner's sense of self, but also its clarity and certainty, may be crucial for understanding the dynamics and structures of learners' self-system.

Situational dynamics

The second key set of dynamics concerns changes that were contextual in nature and which reveal the context-dependency of self-beliefs and emotions. Throughout the speaking tasks, all four participants reported ups and downs in their levels of self-confidence during the interaction. Given complexity understandings of the self-system as being in a constant state of self-organising fluctuations, such dynamism is to be expected (cf. Verspoor et al., 2008). Nevertheless, caution must be exercised as the necessity of having to report on potential changes could lead participants to report more dynamism than they actually felt, in order to be seen to be active and attentive during the stimulated recall. While the graph data reveal differences across individuals, with some indicating greater and some fewer changes over time as well as differing degrees of intensity in their self-confidence (higher and lower peaks and troughs on the graphs), an interesting aspect of the graphs that requires a more detailed analysis is that there appear at first sight to be some loose overall patterns to each pair. These are not neat, exact matches, but there seems to be a general flow to the respective pairs of graphs that suggest there may be potential in exploring possible patterns in learners' responses and their interaction. To illustrate, Martha and Olivia's graphs for their pair work on the second speaking task are presented in Figures 11.1 and 11.2.

For example, both graphs have two clear spikes towards the end at a point in the discussion where they were sharing similar stories about a comparable experience they had both had. It was a period of the task that included extended dialogue for each participant and a segment of strong empathy and agreement between the two students. While it is beyond the scope of this chapter to explore this suggestion in depth here, work by Verspoor et al. (2008) suggest more detailed analytical procedures for comparing graph data and, thus, examining possible patterns between interactional partners as well as individual self-development patterns. Importantly, such an analysis would enable researchers to investigate possible interconnections between individual

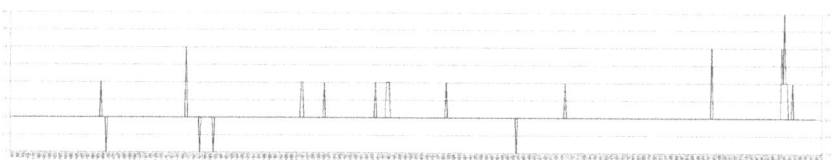

Figure 11.1 Martha's output graph for speaking task 2

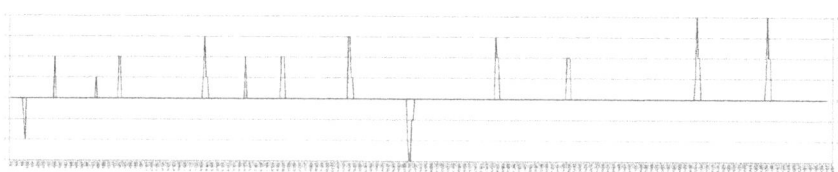

Figure 11.2 Olivia's output graph for speaking task 2

learner's self-systems during work in dyads or potentially even in groups. In terms of a complexity perspective, Shoda *et al.* (2002) suggest that selves are interdependent and that a dyad itself develops its own 'personality', which cannot be thought of as resulting from the cumulative sum of the two individuals involved, but which has an emergent character stemming from the interaction of these two unique self-systems. Conceptualising the self as a complex dynamic system means that it is understood as an 'open system', which can be influenced by other systems such as other individuals, contexts and groups. Such systems thinking may therefore offer a fresh way of thinking about the possible relationships between the individual, relational and collective selves (see e.g. Sedikides & Brewer, 2001).

A particularly interesting dimension to the situational dynamics concerns learners' own awareness of the context-dependency of their self-beliefs. All of the learners were able to articulate settings and contexts in which they felt their self-beliefs would be affected. For example:

> In general I would consider myself a person who feels more comfortable in spoken English than in written English, although there are exceptions e.g. when I'm really nervous during an oral exam. (Martha, autobiography)

> ...it's not hard for me to talk in English, but if the other person is not responding, it's a bit awkward at the moment, so that's when I get a bit less confident. (Nora, idiodynamic interview)

They were also able to articulate patterns regarding when they typically behaved in a certain way in particular settings or under specific conditions, for example:

> I think when we have some group-activities and we have to do some group-work, I'm usually the person who initiates the talk. So because sometimes you are sitting in a circle and four people looking at each other and I'm the one who starts 'What do you think about this?' (Olivia, first interview)

Recognition of patterns in their own behaviour was especially salient in the idiodynamic data. One reason for this may be that observing themselves on video may have facilitated processes of self-recognition. For example, Martha watched the video and recognised her use of fillers as an observable indicator of her lack of confidence:

> When I use fillers, like 'ähm', 'äh', ... I'm less confident. This is what I recognise when I see myself. (Martha, idiodynamic interview)

Whereas Patrizia recognised her nervous laugh, which she reports using to disguise the fact that she feels nervous and unsure of herself:

> What I can see, every time when I laugh, I want to hide my 'Unsicherheit' [*insecurity*]. (Patrizia, idiodynamic interview)

Such behaviours can be understood as an outward, embodied expression of the inner self and show the interconnections between the two. It implies that in combination with self-report data, there may also be potential in informed observational data if patterns in certain behaviours were to be established.

These situational dynamics mirror work by Mischel (2004), who refers to similar patterns in personality research as 'IF-THEN signatures'. In respect to the self, this means IF certain situations and factors come together, THEN I usually or typically feel this way or behave in a certain way. This suggests that although there is variation in self-beliefs and feelings across contexts and situations, there may also be patterns to this. Essentially, this implies that not all intra-learner variation may be random but, in line with complexity thinking, there could be patterns to the system's behaviour, which could reveal underlying characteristics of the self-system possibly reflecting certain consistencies to aspects of the self, such as beliefs, motives, goals and/or emotions. In this way, situational patterns in self-systems may help to explain the connection between situational dynamics of the self and what has been referred to as the core sense of self that appears to be more stable across time (see e.g. Mercer, 2011b).

Importantly, these data suggest we need a better understanding of the features of a setting or context and the ways in which these may be relevant for an individual's sense of self. It is insufficient to consider a context in a monolithic, static way as relevant for a learner's sense of self, such as in terms of 'a classroom' or 'a pair-work activity'. In line with complexity thinking, contexts themselves need to be conceptualised both as a complex dynamic system in their own right and simultaneously as an integrated part of the learner's self-system. It is not the setting or context per se that is important, but rather how the individual perceives and evaluates it. Thus, to understand the situational dynamics of the self, we also need to know what situational factors are perceived as relevant for an individual in a particular setting, how they appraise and interpret them, and any patterns to this behaviour. The next section will consider in more detail what some of those situational factors may be.

Factors in situational dynamics

Unsurprisingly, in the situational dynamics of their self-confidence, all of the learners assigned a strong role to their interactional partner.

The data indicate clearly how the individual's own self-confidence can be affected by how they perceive their partner, their level of English, their interactional exchanges, and the affective climate between them. Interestingly, all four learners commented on the importance for their confidence of their partners showing interest and listening to their comments:

> ... when I was talking about my travel in the summer, the confidence grew as I, well, I realised her face expressions that she was very interested in what I was doing. (Olivia, idiodynamic interview)

All of them also mentioned the importance of the affective quality of the relationship. However, in part, they chose to focus on different aspects of the interaction and interlocutor. For example, Nora and Martha stressed the importance of finding out that they had something in common:

> And there it got higher, the self-confidence because we saw from the beginning that we had some things in common we picked, so this was a bit easier. (Nora, idiodynamic interview)

Nora reported that her confidence was particularly affected by whether they were agreeing or disagreeing about a topic and whether they felt they had shared points of interest with each other:

> And there it [*my self-confidence*] got up because she agreed with me on that. (Nora, idiodynamic interview)

In contrast, Martha was unique in explaining that her self-confidence was affected by the perceived level of the partner's English in comparison with her own:

> Sometimes I think she used, in my opinion ... she used a wide range of vocabulary and sometimes when people talk to me and use a very good English, I'm less confident because I think 'I can't talk so well'. (Martha, idiodynamic interview)

In addition to the interlocutor, the participants also reported on other situational factors. For example, all of the learners reported that their confidence was influenced by the types of task and whether it was a topic they felt they could talk about easily:

> There I was quite confident because I could talk about something I'm really, really interested in. (Nora, idiodynamic interview)

They all also mentioned that their confidence increased as the time passed, simply as a result of becoming more familiar with the setting, the tasks and their partners:

> I just need some time to find my way in the conversation and so at the beginning I was less confident. (Olivia, idiodynamic interview)

Except for Nora, who has an exceptionally high level of English, the other participants all reported repeatedly that their confidence was affected by whether they were having difficulty in finding vocabulary or were uncertain about their use of grammar or their pronunciation, for example:

> Ah, there I lost a bit of my confidence because I had a sentence in my head, but I didn't end it and so the beginning and the ending of this sentence did not really correspond. (Olivia, idiodynamic interview)

Interestingly, only Martha commented on her confidence being negatively affected by the presence of the video camera. However, her discomfort at being observed or judged is a persistent theme for her across all of her interviews, and it is possible her confidence is particularly sensitive to this feeling of being observed or monitored as a contextual factor:

> ... at university I feel like being judged and the professors record and everything you say is analysed and I always have to think about what to say. (Martha, final interview)

Thus, although there are commonalities across all of the learners about factors in the context affecting their self-confidence, certain characteristics of the context played a particularly heightened role for certain individuals. For example, in Nora's data, as previously outlined, it is noticeable that she seeks agreement with her partner, points of commonality and a positive affective climate is important for her. These factors could be indicative of underlying personality characteristics such as agreeableness and a dislike of conflict. In line with a complexity perspective, a more holistic view of the self would incorporate both conscious and unconscious aspects of the self, thereby uniting personality and self-research. An interesting direction for future research will be to explore whether there could be patterns in terms of the types of contextual factors that are important for an individual, as these patterns too may also reveal features of a learner's underlying self-system. Essentially, all the data emphasise that if we want a full analysis of the dynamics of the self, we require a consideration of the actual self-beliefs and emotions in terms of content, quality, positivity, intensity and certainty, as well as a full appreciation of the relevant and personally significant contextual factors and their dynamics.

Issues for Researching the Self as a Complex Dynamic System

Researching the self from a complexity perspective is challenging to say the least. As Vallacher *et al.* (2002b: 266) state, 'the structure of human social experience is simply too intricate and multifaceted to admit to complete description, let alone precise prediction'. The impossibility of the task becomes apparent if one considers the complex network of multiple types and levels of self-related beliefs, emotions, motives, roles and processes stretching across time, place and domains – all of which are interrelated, not only with each other, but also with various contexts and other larger systems in complex, potentially changeable and unpredictable ways (cf. Mercer, 2012). While, ideally, research would seek to retain as much of a holistic perspective as is empirically feasible, in reality, boundaries need to be set and units of analysis selected. However, rather than returning to more tightly defined reductionist conceptualisations of the self, we perhaps need to explore more holistic ways of viewing the self. In my own case, I have chosen to distinguish between the whole being as the self-system in its entirety, and a focus on a learner's sense of self defined as the situated, embodied self-beliefs, motives and related emotions across a person's life, and various domains as a core component of the self-system. In the idiodynamic section of the study reported on in this chapter, it was necessary to select an even more tightly defined construct in order to focus the attention of the participants and communicate with them using a familiar, recognisable term. As a result, the term self-confidence was chosen; however, taking a complexity perspective implies the need to maintain an awareness and humility about the limits of our knowledge and research on the self. Thus, in relation to the data reported on here, it is clear that while the idiodynamic data provide rich insights into the dynamics of one aspect of the self-system, out of empirical necessity they represent only a fragment of the larger puzzle of the self. It will remain for meta-reviews and integrative approaches to bring together all of the fragments to create a fuller picture.

In terms of researching the dynamics of the self, we need to ensure we have a sufficiently broad understanding of dynamics as these can refer to processes that can potentially involve stability, dynamic stability, partial change, sudden change, cumulative changes and degrees of change. Furthermore, change need not only imply change in content, form and positivity of self-related beliefs, motives and emotions, but it can also involve changes in quality, quantity, intensity, certainty, as well as changes in the respective role of system components, their significance and interrelations in the system as a whole (see Mercer, 2009, 2011b).

In respect to methods, I have found that various qualitative approaches have much to contribute to furthering our understandings of the self from complexity perspectives in terms of the depth, detail and holistic perspectives they can employ (see e.g. Mercer, 2011b). In particular, this study has shown the potential in innovative new research approaches for dynamics, such as the use of the idiodynamic software and stimulated recall in respect to the short-term situational dynamics. As with any method, there are drawbacks, such as the usual self-report issues, memory bias and the potential problem of gaining an exaggerated view of a learner's dynamics during an interaction. However, such innovations in research tools can generate fresh ideas and help move forward our thinking towards an understanding of how long-term, temporal dynamics of the self may interconnect with micro-level, situational dynamics (for another innovative dynamics software design for the self, see also the 'mouse paradigm', Vallacher *et al.*, 2002a).

Implications for Practice

This chapter has shown that a learner's sense of self in relation to language learning is highly complex, personal and its development difficult to predict given the dynamic interaction of multiple internal and external processes across time and place. This means that it would be naïve and misleading to think, in the face of such complexity, that we can straightforwardly influence or easily predict how our learners' sense of self may change and develop. However, as teachers, we can attempt to create conducive, positive learning conditions and environments to help enhance their sense of self in respect to language-related domains. Specifically in respect to speaking tasks, which were the focus of this study, if we wish to promote such a positive setting, it is important to attend to factors, such as the interpersonal relationships between the interlocutors and their affective quality, as well as the role of interesting, personally relevant topics and time for learners to get familiar with each other. As teachers, our challenge is to ensure that learners can connect their language learning experiences in class with their underlying, continually emergent core sense of self in a positive way. Ultimately, we cannot tell or teach our learners how to feel and think about themselves as language learners, but we can appreciate and respect the unique, complex individuals we work with in our classes, and that in itself is likely to provide a good basis for future learning together.

> ### Recommended reading
>
> Mercer, S. (2011) The self as a complex dynamic system. *Studies in Second Language Learning and Teaching* 1 (1), 57–82.
>
> This article is an initial conceptual paper outlining the rationale for conceiving of the self in SLA as a complex dynamic system.

> Osborne, R.E. (1996) *Self: An Eclectic Approach*. Needham Heights: Allyn & Bacon.
>
> This is an excellent book taking an integrative approach to the self and bringing together many different strands of research and perspectives on the self.
>
> Mischel, W. and Morf, C.C. (2003) The self as a psycho-social dynamic processing system: A meta-perspective on a century of the self in psychology. In M.R. Leary and J.P. Tangney (eds) *Handbook of Self and Identity* (pp. 15–43). New York: The Guildford Press.
>
> This comprehensive chapter outlines some of the connections between self and personality and makes an explicit case for a dynamical systems perspective on the self.

References

Campbell, J.D. (1990) Self-esteem and clarity of the self-concept. *Journal of Personality and Social Psychology* 59 (3), 538–549.

Deaux, K. and Perkins, T.S. (2001) The kaleidoscopic self. In C. Sedikides and M.B. Brewer (eds) *Individual Self, Relational Self, Collective Self* (pp. 299–313). Philadelphia: Psychology Press.

Dörnyei, Z. and Ushioda, E. (eds) (2011) *Teaching and Researching Motivation* (2nd edn). Harlow: Pearson.

Ehrman, M.E. and Dörnyei, Z. (1998) *Interpersonal Dynamics in Second Language Acquisition*. Thousand Oaks: SAGE Publications.

Harter, S. (1999) *The Construction of the Self: A Developmental Perspective*. New York: Guildford Press.

Larsen-Freeman, D. and Cameron, L. (2008) *Complex Systems and Applied Linguistics*. Oxford: Oxford University Press.

Lewin, K. (1951) *Field Theory in Social Science*. New York: Harper & Row.

MacIntyre, P.D. and Legatto, J.J. (2011) A dynamic system approach to willingness to communicate: Developing an idiodynamic method to capture rapidly changing affect. *Applied Linguistics* 32 (2), 149–171.

Markus, H. and Kunda, Z. (1986) Stability and malleability of the self-concept. *Journal of Personality and Social Psychology* 51 (4), 858–866.

Markus, H. and Wurf, E. (1987) The dynamic self-concept: A social-psychological perspective. *Annual Review of Psychology* 38, 299–337.

Mason, M. (2008) What is complexity theory and what are its implications for educational change? In M. Mason (ed.) *Complexity Theory and the Philosophy of Education* (pp. 32–45). Chichester: Wiley-Blackwell.

Mercer, S. (2009) The dynamic nature of a tertiary learner's foreign language self-concepts. In M. Pawlak (ed.) *New Perspectives on Individual Differences in Language Learning and Teaching* (pp. 205–220). Poznań – Kalisz: Adam Mickiewicz University Press.

Mercer, S. (2011a) The self as a complex dynamic system. *Studies in Second Language Learning and Teaching* 1 (1), 57–82.

Mercer, S. (2011b) Language learner self-concept: Complexity, continuity & change. *System* 39 (3), 335–346.

Mercer, S. (2012) Self-concept: Situating the self. In S. Mercer, S. Ryan and M. Williams (eds) *Psychology for Language Learning: Insights from Research, Theory and Practice* (pp. 10–25). Basingstoke: Palgrave MacMillan.
Mercer, S., Ryan, S. and Williams, M. (eds) (2012) *Psychology for Language Learning: Insights from Research, Theory and Practice*. Basingstoke: Palgrave MacMillan.
Mischel, W. (2004) Toward and integrative science of the person. *Annual Review of Psychology* 55 (1), 1–22.
Mischel, W. and Morf, C.C. (2003) The self as a psycho-social dynamic processing system: A meta-perspective on a century of the self in psychology. In M.R. Leary and J.P. Tangney (eds) *Handbook of Self and Identity* (pp. 15–43). New York: The Guildford Press.
Morin, E. (2008) *On Complexity*. Cresskill: Hampton Press.
Mruk, C.J. (2006) *Self-Esteem Research, Theory, and Practice*. New York: Springer Publishing Company.
Neisser, U. (1988) Five kinds of self knowledge. *Philosophical Psychology* 1, 35–59.
Nowak, A., Vallacher, R.R., Tesser, A. and Borkowski, W. (2000) Society of self: The emergence of collective properties in self structure. *Psychological Review* 107 (1), 39–61.
Nowak, A., Vallacher, R.R. and Zochowski, M. (2005) The emergence of personality: Dynamic foundations of individual variation. *Developmental Review* 25, 351–385.
Onorato, R.S. and Turner, J.C. (2004) Fluidity in the self-concept: the shift from the personal to social identity. *European Journal of Social Psychology* 34 (3), 257–278.
Osborne, R.E. (1996) *Self: An Eclectic Approach*. Needham Heights: Allyn & Bacon.
Schwartz, A. (2007) Self-as-organism and sense of self: Toward a differential conception. *The Journal of Ayn Rand Studies* 9 (1), 93–111.
Sedikides, C. and Brewer, M.B. (eds) (2001) *Individual Self, Relational Self, Collective Self*. Philadelphia: Psychology Press.
Shapka, J.D. and Keating, D.P. (2005) Structure and change in self-concept during adolescence. *Canadian Journal of Behavioural Science* 37 (2), 83–96.
Shoda, Y., Tiernan, S.L. and Mischel, W. (2002) Personality as a dynamical system: Emergence of stability and distinctiveness from intra- and interpersonal interactions. *Personality and Social Psychology Review* 6 (4), 316–325.
Vallacher, R.R. and Nowak, A. (1997) The emergence of dynamical social psychology. *Psychological Inquiry* 8 (2), 73–99.
Vallacher, R.R., Nowak, A. and Froehlich, M. (2002a) The dynamics of self-evaluation. *Personality and Social Psychology Review* 6 (4), 370–379.
Vallacher, R.R., Read, S.J. and Nowak, A. (2002b) The dynamical perspective in personality and social psychology. *Personality and Social Psychology Review* 6 (4), 264–273.
van Lier, L. (2004) *The Ecology and Semiotics of Language Learning: A Sociocultural Perspective*. Norwell, Mass.: Kluwer Academic Publishers.
Verspoor, M., Lowie, W. and van Dijk, M. (2008) Variability in second language development from a dynamic systems perspective. *The Modern Language Journal* 92 (2), 214–231.

12 Concluding Reflections

Sarah Mercer and Marion Williams

Introduction

In putting together this collection of chapters, our primary aim has been to open dialogue about different perspectives on the self, provide a shared space to learn from each other and take steps towards a more comprehensive, integrative view of the self. It has not been our intention to attempt to settle questions about the self once and for all; far from it. Instead we hope to have provided readers with a multiplicity of perspectives from which to view the self in second language acquisition (SLA). We feel that for a construct as complex as the self, such diversity is necessary and indeed healthy. Given the breadth of the field, this volume cannot possibly claim to be comprehensive. In fact, while working on the book, we became aware of yet more additional perspectives on the self that could have been included, especially recent work on personality (cf. Mischel & Morf, 2003) and self-regulatory perspectives on the self that explore the functional significance of self-representations (see e.g. Higgins & May, 2001). In reviewing all of the chapters, while we are aware of the differences in the perspectives taken by the authors, various themes have emerged across the chapters and it is these we would like to engage with briefly in this final chapter.

Defining the Self

As the chapters in this volume attest, there are many different ways to conceptualise, define and thus measure the self. As a result, one of the greatest challenges facing researchers in the field concerns definitions of self-constructs. For empirical purposes, researchers need to make clear what facet of the self the study is focusing on. However, constructs are often poorly or not even explicitly defined, may overlap, and frequently researchers have used terms as if they are interchangeable. This has made it incredibly difficult to make comparisons across studies and sometimes researchers even remain unaware of the connections between their work as terminology separates their spheres of interest (Leary & Tangney, 2003). Although our intention with this volume has been, in part, to highlight the special understandings that different views of the self can offer, we also intended to show how, viewed together as a whole in one volume, they can be seen to complement each other and contribute to a more comprehensive picture of the self. By encouraging authors to be explicit about their understanding of self terms, we hope to have generated some definitional clarity and boundaries, and problematised the fragmented nature of the field. Yet, perhaps more importantly, we hope to have been able to enable the connections between perspectives to become apparent and thereby add a little more to the picture of the self in SLA.

To illustrate the interconnections between different perspectives on the self at least in part, let us follow a pathway through some of the chapters, beginning with self-concept and leading through motivation to implications about behaviour. In his chapter, Rubio illustrates how a person's sense of worthiness and sense of competence are interdependent and continually developing, forming both their self-concept and their interrelated sense of self-esteem. Norton then considers how the role of social factors can affect our sense of self, in particular settings, and she examines in detail the dimensions of learners' situated identities. Both self-concept and identities form the basis of the kinds of imagined selves we are able to construct, and, in their chapter, Ryan and Irie explore the key role that imagination can play in self-related goals and motivations in respect to language learning. Taking up the motivational aspect of the self, Ushioda goes on to show how both internal aspects of the self and external socio-environmental factors interact to generate a learner's motivational frame, which is also dynamic over time. Together, all these aspects of the self and related motives interact with contextual affordances to affect learners' self-regulatory behaviours, which are ultimately crucial for successful language learning both in formalised classroom contexts and in independent learning settings.

Essentially, all of the chapters share points of commonality and collectively provide a fuller picture of the self. While it can be useful to explore the differences between the constructs and perspectives, these need not be viewed as competing perspectives. Instead it is perhaps more helpful to concentrate on the areas of overlap and interconnections between the different facets of the self and explore how they combine to generate a more holistic view of the self. As editors, we have concluded that understanding the self is rather like viewing a jigsaw puzzle. If you want to see a full picture of the self, you need to bring all of the pieces together. If you focus your attention only on one corner or piece of the puzzle, you will get an incomplete and potentially distorted impression of the overall picture. Working out how the pieces fit together is the next key step for the field.

The Contextual Self

All of the chapters in this volume acknowledge, to differing degrees, that the self cannot be conceptualised as being abstracted and separated from contexts. This is a considerable step forward compared with debates that have long raged in psychology about the relative situatedness of the self. However, there remain differences in how this relationship between the self and contexts is understood. As such, conceptualisations of the self can perhaps be thought of as stretching along a continuum from those that are strongly situated, to those that are less situated (cf. Turner *et al.*, 2006: 13). For example, although self-efficacy is in some ways strongly tied to context through its focus on specific tasks, in respect to socially and contextually situated perspectives, it can perhaps be thought of as one of the least situated of the self-constructs; however, in her chapter, Mills shows how the construct is increasingly being defined in ways that attend to particular contextual dimensions, such as in using test items that refer to real tasks using rating scales that reflect typical formats for particular cultures in which the research is being conducted. Similarly, second language (L2) linguistic self-confidence is a construct that has traditionally not been researched using socially situated methods; however, in their chapter, Sampasivam and Clément explore in detail the different forms of contact space and interactions that language learners can engage with and highlight the importance of the nature and quality of these different contexts for a learner's L2 self-confidence. At the other end of the continuum are understandings of identity as reflected in the work by Norton and Hemmi, which both focus on the relation of the self to various contexts, cultures and communities of practice, and are strongly situated in nature. Combining perspectives but emphasising the role of relational contexts, Taylor, for example, examines the dynamic interplay between learners' private and public selves. In this book, one of our aims is to challenge the polarising dichotomy between a purely personally defined self and an entirely socially situated self. Instead, we hope that researchers will increasingly explore the interplay between both and consider the capacity of the self to encompass both highly situated and less contextually defined elements.

A particular feature of situated conceptualisations of the self is the recognition of the potential for intra-learner variation in the self, particularly across contexts. Indeed such contextual dynamism was one of the notable features of several of the chapters, such as that by Mercer who investigates the features of an interactional setting that can affect a learner's situational self-confidence. Several chapters, such as Ushioda's, also consider the ways in which external factors, social encounters and the environment are perceived, evaluated and interpreted through the lens of the current self. Thus, rather than assigning a unidirectional effect of contexts on a passive self, a more complex relationship involving the interplay of both internal and external processes is proposed.

In terms of context, whether it is at the more global level of national cultures or the more micro-level of a specific interaction, it seems likely that the self in all its forms will be affected by, and potentially will in turn influence, the settings leading to change both in the self and the context itself. These bidirectional relationships between the self and nested systems of contexts reflect the increasingly sophisticated understandings of the situated nature of the self and indicate the direction that the field appears to be moving in. Another major step will be to seek to clarify the nature of contexts and their particular relevance for individuals. This suggests replacing more monolithic conceptualisations and generalised understandings of contexts with more diverse, multifaceted, dynamic and individually meaningful representations of context.

The Temporal Self

Another type of dynamics evident across the chapters concerns the temporal dynamics of the self. These dynamics across time are divided into two main types; first, temporal dimensions that reflect changes across micro-level timescales in ways that are also connected to variation in contextual factors as well as the progression of time, and, second, long-term developmental perspectives across the lifespan. The latter of these, the long-term changes, are discussed by Rubio, who stresses that different life stages bring different demands and needs for the self. These affect self development, structure and also the relative significance of various contextual factors. For example, parents have a greater influence on their child's self-concept during early childhood, but this influence is thought to decrease during middle childhood and adolescence as other individuals, such as peers and teachers, begin to exert more influence.

A particular temporal dimension of the self that emerges from several of these chapters concerns how the self connects past experiences, present cognitions, emotions and motives, and future goals and visions. Ryan and Irie's chapter focuses in particular on the narrative construction of self in the present in order to make sense of the past and give direction to the future. They show that individuals connect the different temporal threads of the self to help construct a coherent sense of self in the present, and provide direction and motivation. Several chapters suggest that our current sense of self cannot meaningfully be separated from either our past experiences and interpretation of them, or our hopes and goals for the future. The self is continually evolving across time and, as such, is always a work in progress, rather than a finished product. It is possible that conceptualising the self in this way, as a temporally situated process, may lead to fresh insights concerning its development across time and its role in relation to goals and motivation.

Methodological Perspectives

A further dimension of this collection of chapters that we wish to draw attention to is the methodological diversity that the chapters represent. It is to be expected that the variety of perspectives on the self implies a similarly broad range of methodologies for investigating the self. For example, Northoff's chapter considers insights from neuroscience and how brain imaging techniques can offer unique perspectives on how the self is constructed and engaged in various areas of the brain. He also problematises the dilemma of consciousness and how our conscious self is experienced and the role of our subconscious. As yet, the vast majority of approaches to the self tend to be dependent on self-report measures, but if we wish to also explore the unconscious elements of the self, then alternative approaches, such as brain-based research, may prove invaluable. Another alternative approach, proposed by Mercer, involves using a combination of interview, stimulated recall using the idiodynamic software and observation to explore 'IF-THEN signatures', which are patterns in self behaviour that individuals may not always be immediately conscious of. Other problematic dimensions of the self for research include the blurred boundaries in memory between real and imagined events and our subsequent interpretation of them as highlighted by Ryan and Irie. Engaging with such challenges will require innovative approaches to research, which necessitate an openness to diverse methodological designs and an exploration of less common methodologies, such as working with Q-methodology as suggested by Ryan and Irie.

In more quantitatively oriented approaches to the self, survey methods have an important role to play in helping us to understand relationships between aspects of the self and other variables. For example, in respect to self-efficacy, the high degree of specificity of the construct is essential in order to ensure that strong correlational results emerge. As Mills points out, self-efficacy researchers are advised to measure self-efficacy with a specificity that corresponds to the task and domain being assessed. She shows how such research has afforded valuable insights into the connections between self-efficacy and other factors, such as motivation, achievement and anxiety.

In more situated and hence more typically qualitatively oriented studies, Norton, for example, shows the merits of using narrative-based research reported in the form of vignettes to highlight the contextualised and social nature of identity. Similarly, Hemmi, in her situated study, takes a grounded theory approach to the analysis of detailed interview data to investigate the socially constructed nature of the identities of bilingual women in Japan. Such interpretative and contextualised studies will continue to make important contributions in helping us to better understand the nature of the interrelations between self and multiple levels and dimensions of cultures and contexts.

In terms of mixed method studies combining insights offered by both qualitative and quantitative perspectives on the self, Taylor's study of public and private selves is a good illustration of the potential in bringing together different methodological viewpoints. Her research is able to explore correlations between private and public selves, but also illuminate the processes underlying the relationships between the two from the participants' perspectives.

Essentially, as understandings of the self become increasingly nuanced, situated, complex and dynamic, there will be a need for methodological innovation in order to meet the challenges these new perspectives offer. There cannot be only one best way to research the self. Just as there are a range of perspectives on and definitions of the self, so too there will also be a need for different ways of researching it; each in its own way providing particular insights that add to our growing picture of the self in SLA.

Pedagogical Implications

In a book in the field of SLA, we feel it is important to consider the pedagogical implications of the research and theories explored as far as this is possible. The majority of the chapters show that having a positive sense of self, irrespective of how that is defined, is invaluable for successful learning in terms of reducing anxiety, enhancing motivation, developing persistence and promoting autonomy, self-regulation and an effective, flexible use of strategies. Rubio, for example, shows that self-esteem can be enhanced by using co-operative learning structures and developing positive group dynamics. He cites Reasoner's model in highlighting the importance of fostering security, identity, belonging, purpose and competence in order to enhance self-esteem in learners. In Mills's chapter, she stresses that confidence in one's capabilities (self-efficacy) is a central element of academic success. She suggests that positive self-efficacy can be enhanced by facilitating mastery experiences, developing an awareness of a range of learning strategies, fostering internal, controllable attributions, and exploring positive, achievable role models that offer vicarious learning experiences. She also emphasises the key role of a low-anxiety learning environment and effective forms of feedback and praise from the teachers.

Another dimension of the self that has important pedagogical implications concerns how we can help learners to articulate and realise their future selves. Ushioda points to the importance of self-determination theory in this regard and the need for appropriate social-environmental conditions that promote a sense of competence, autonomy and belonging, and the mastery of new experiences and challenges. She explains that, 'when students are engaged in setting and achieving optimal challenges and thus cultivating a sense of competence as well as personal agency (i.e. autonomy), they are likely to enhance their intrinsic interest in the learning activity' (Chapter 9). Ushioda also argues in particular for problem-focused interactions among learners to make thoughts explicit as an object for analysis and redirection, and the need to scaffold learners' attempts to complete tasks in order to achieve metacognitive control and become self-regulated. In respect to future selves, Ryan and Irie highlight the potential of imagination and storytelling in constructing learners' visions for their futures; however, they stress the necessity for future visions to remain realistic and achievable without becoming 'implausible fantasy' (Chapter 8). Referring to Hock *et al.* (2006), they suggest that helping learners to focus on future selves in terms of processes, rather than outcomes, is likely to be more effective in the long run and is an approach that can comfortably be integrated with language learning goals.

Several authors also raise other important pedagogical issues regarding the self. For example, Norton raises the pedagogical question of power and the way in which the perceived power of the teacher (or tester) can affect the way in which a task is interpreted and the willingness and perceived ability of learners to communicate. She also draws attention to the importance of considering the identities students are negotiating in learning a new language, and asks teachers to consider whether the practices in their classrooms address the students' daily challenges and anxieties about the future. Hemmi also draws attention to the idea of multiple identities in learning and using different languages. She concludes that although multilingualism can engender positive emotions and reactions, it can potentially also raise negative emotions and challenges that teachers need to be sensitive to. The potential for internal conflicts within learners in regard to multiple selves is also a focus of Taylor's chapter. She too highlights the need for teachers to ensure their classrooms represent a supportive environment in which every learner feels comfortable and supported in 'speaking as themselves' (Ushioda, 2011) without feeling judged or ridiculed.

Essentially, all of the chapters highlight the complexity of the self and the close ties to emotions. As Mercer concludes in her chapter, an appreciation of the self implies an inherent respect for learner diversity and uniqueness, as well as a sensitivity to individuals' needs, hopes, fears and wishes for the future. Given the centrality of the self in the learning process, it is surprising that, at present, the pedagogical implications and classroom-based research on the self is relatively under-researched, and there remains considerable scope for further enquiry in this area.

Future Directions

The underlying rationale of this book has been to collect in one volume a variety of perspectives on the self in the hope that the total contribution of them will indeed be more than the sum of its parts (cf. Forgas & Williams, 2002: 2). This reflects a general move in self psychology towards integrative approaches that incorporate multiple self-constructs and perspectives, and consider the nature of their interactions (see e.g. Forgas & Williams, 2002; Sedikides & Brewer, 2001). While the majority of the chapters in this collection have focused on the self as an individual self-perception considering one key dimension of the self, a future approach could take more explicitly integrative or holistic perspectives, for example, considering the ways in which individual, relational and collective selves combine, such as in Sedikides and Brewer's (2001) tripartite self-model.

Another alternative, more integrative perspective on the self might also be offered by process-oriented models of the self, such as in self-categorisation theory (SCT) (Turner *et al.*, 1987). The majority of the chapters in this volume have tended to focus on describing the self as an organised entity. In contrast, SCT concentrates on the dynamic categorisation of the self in which instead of there being a 'preformed self-structure waiting to be activated; the content and meaning of self-categories are not determined prior to their use' (Onorato & Turner, 2001: 159). Such an approach switches the focus from the self as a structure or object, to self as a dynamic process, and is inherently integrative and contextually situated. It may be that such process-oriented perspectives on the self can open up fresh pathways for understanding possible relationships between various facets of the self and their development.

Further, all of the chapters in this volume set out from the perspective of the individual considering the self as a singular person. Even in those chapters such as those on identity, which explicitly focus on the role of self in relation to others and groups, the starting point remains the individual. However, in recent years, there has been a steady increase of interest in how groups function and how the self is related to and co-constructs the emergent 'character' of groups. Rather than the typical dualist separation of the individual and the group, an exciting way forward for the field that may explore more fully the dynamic interaction between individuals and groups, may be to commence research on the self by focusing on the groups in which the particular self functions, working our way from the group to the self instead of the other way round (cf. Postmes & Jetten, 2006).

In addition, while the focus has been on the learner in this volume, all of the discussions could equally apply to teachers. An important step for research on the self would be to extend such studies in relation to teachers, seeking to better understand how teachers' sense of self can affect their behaviours and relationships in class. In particular, it would be of interest to examine how learners and teachers interact to generate the classroom rapport considered so crucial to successful language learning in formalised learning contexts and the role that their respective selves play in these processes.

To conclude, we hope that this volume has contributed another piece to the puzzle of the self in SLA. It is a fundamental dimension of what it means to be human, a learner, a teacher, a linguist, bi/multilingual and to take part in human social interaction. Many questions remain and this exciting construct promises to continue to challenge our thinking and understandings of the processes and people involved in language learning and teaching. However, given the centrality of the self in all that we do, we must make it a priority to seek to better understand how the self, as experienced by learners and teachers, can facilitate or inhibit effective language learning.

References

Forgas, J.P. and Williams, K.D. (eds) (2002) *The Social Self: Cognitive, Interpersonal, and Intergroup Perspectives*. New York: Psychology Press.

Higgins, E.T. and May, D. (2001) Individual self-regulatory functions: It's not 'we' regulation, but it's still social. In C. Sedikides and M.B. Brewer (eds) *Individual Self, Relational Self, Collective Self* (pp. 47–67). Philadelphia: Psychology Press.

Hock, M.F., Deshler, D.D. and Schumaker, J.B. (2006) Enhancing student motivation through the pursuit of possible selves. In C. Dunkel and J. Kerpelman (eds) *Possible Selves: Theory, Research and Application* (pp. 205–221). New York: Nova Science.

Leary, M.R. and Tangney, J.P. (2003) The self as organizing construct in the behavioural and social sciences. In M.R. Leary and J.P. Tangney (eds) *Handbook of Self and Identity* (pp. 3–14). New York: The Guildford Press.

Mischel, W. and Morf, C.C. (2003) The self as a psycho-social dynamic processing system: A meta-perspective on a century of the self in psychology. In M.R. Leary and J.P. Tangney (eds) *Handbook of Self and Identity* (pp. 15–43). New York: The Guildford Press.

Onarato, R.S. and Turner, J.C. (2001) The 'I', the 'Me' and the 'Us': The psychological group and self-concept maintenance and change. In C. Sedikides and M.B. Brewer (eds) *Individual Self, Relational Self, Collective Self* (pp. 147–170). Philadelphia: Psychology Press.

Postmes, T. and Jetten, J. (2006) (eds) *Individuality and the Group: Advances in Social Identity*. London: Sage Publications.

Sedikides, C. and Brewer, M.B. (eds) (2001) *Individual Self, Relational Self, Collective Self*. Philadelphia: Psychology Press.

Turner, J.C., Hogg, M.A., Oakes, P.J., Reicher, S.D. and Wetherell, M.S. (1987) *Rediscovering the Social Group: A Self-categorization Theory*. Oxford: Blackwell.

Turner, J.C., Reynolds, K.J., Haslam, S.A. and Veenstra, K.E. (2006) Reconceptualizing personality: Producing individuality by defining the personal self. In T. Postmes and J. Jetten (eds) *Individuality and the Group: Advances in Social Identity* (pp. 11–36). London: Sage Publications.

Ushioda, E. (2011) Motivating learners to speak as themselves. In G. Murray, X. Gao and T. Lamb (eds) *Identity, Motivation and Autonomy in Language Learning* (pp. 11–24). Bristol: Multilingual Matters.

Index

Note: With grateful thanks to Stephen Ryan for his help in putting together the index.

acculturation, 10, 29–31
actual self, 47, 98–99, 112, 172
affect, 42, 47, 52, 180, 184
affective indicators, 8
agency, 4, 7, 61, 65, 112–113, 121, 127, 135, 137, 149, 152, 156, 183
anxiety, 9–10, 12–16, 19, 23–28, 30, 33–34, 41, 49, 54, 71, 79, 104, 130, 181–182
Attitude-Motivation Test Battery (AMTB), 24, 131
attributions, 2, 111–112, 120–121, 182
autobiographical memory, 152
autonomy, 11, 132, 135–136, 182–183

belonging, 46, 51, 53–54, 75, 80–85, 112, 118, 135, 154, 182
belongingness, 157
bilingual, 4, 27, 75, 77, 79–87, 89, 181
bilingualism, 79–81
brain, 4, 44, 113–114, 142–145, 147, 149–153, 155–159, 181
brain imaging techniques, 149, 181
brain regions, 149

carryover effect, 96
cognition, 6, 42
cognitive revolution, 127
cognitive-situated period, 6–7
collective self, 52
communicative apprehension, 49
community of practice, 77–78, 85, 109, 117, 179
competence, 7, 10, 13, 15, 24–27, 30, 36, 43–49, 52–54, 63, 99, 127, 135–136, 178, 182–183
complex dynamic systems, 162–164, 169–170, 173–174

complexity, 4, 50, 160–165, 167–174, 183
computer-mediated communication (CMC), 27–28
confidence (see self-confidence, linguistic self-confidence, second language confidence), 3, 9, 11, 13, 19, 26, 53, 166, 169, 171–172, 182
consciousness, 4, 79, 142–147, 154–156, 158, 181
contact, 3, 23–36, 44, 110–111, 179
contact space framework, 23, 31–33, 36
context, 4, 6, 13, 15, 17, 23–24, 26–36, 41–42, 47, 51, 53, 60, 62, 66–68, 71, 76–77, 80, 89, 92–93, 97–98, 101–102, 109, 112, 128, 131, 135, 138, 155, 157, 167, 169–170, 172, 179–180
contextual factors, 4, 43, 130, 132, 172, 180
cooperative learning, 52
cortical midline structures, 150–152, 157

discourse communities, 77
domain-specificity, 41, 51, 150, 162
double consciousness, 79
duality, 79–80, 85, 89
dynamic systems (see complex dynamic systems), 161, 163–164, 170, 174
dynamism, 5, 47, 54, 160, 162, 164, 166–168, 179

embodied self, 4
emergence, 162–163
emotions, 9, 11, 64, 78–79, 98, 127, 148–150, 153, 160–161, 163, 165, 168, 170, 172–173, 180, 183
empirical self, 142–145, 156–157
ethnolinguistic vitality, 30–31, 35

fantasy, 115, 121, 183
feared self, 112
first-person perspective, 116, 146, 148, 154–155, 158–159
foreign language (FL) anxiety (see anxiety), 12
foreign language acquisition, 27
frequency of contact, 25, 31, 33
functional magnetic resonance imaging (fMRI),149

hoped-for self, 112
humanism, 52

ideal self, 43–44, 98–99, 112–113, 118, 133–134
identity, 2–4, 6, 29–31, 36, 53–54, 59–71, 75–79, 86–87, 89, 93–96, 98, 100–101, 104, 109, 113, 117, 133, 138, 147, 179, 181–182, 184
idiodynamic software, 166, 174, 181
if-then signatures, 170, 181
imagined community, 62, 70, 117–118
imagined identities (see identity), 62, 70
imagined selves, 4, 110, 119, 123, 178
impression management, 102, 104
instrumental motivation, 6
integrative motivation, 6, 24
intrinsic motivation, 112, 130, 132, 135–136
integrative perspectives, 161–162, 173, 177, 184
internalisation, 96–97, 119, 128, 130, 133–136, 138
international posture, 35
investment, 3, 61–62, 69–71

L2 Motivational Self System (see Motivation), 10, 49, 99, 118, 133–134, 138
language learning strategies (see strategies), 11, 13, 18
language teaching, 1, 3, 52, 71
linguistic self, 156
linguistic self-confidence (see confidence, second language confidence), 9–10, 128
listening self-efficacy, 13, 17

mastery, 19, 135
mastery experiences, 8, 14, 17, 182
mediation, 165

mental self, 112, 116, 142–145
mental simulation, 111, 114–115, 119
metacognition, 13, 119, 136, 138
metacognitive strategies, 14, 43, 136–137
mineness, 154, 157
minimal self, 142–143, 147–148, 154–157
motivation, 1–7, 9, 12–14, 19, 24–25, 27–29, 35–36, 41, 48–49, 54, 61–62, 69–70, 98, 109, 112, 114, 116, 118, 121–123, 127–138, 160, 178, 180–182
multiplicity, 4, 31, 33, 53, 70, 80, 88–89, 92, 158, 177

narrative construction of self, 180
negotiation, 77, 95
neuro-imagery, 114
neurogenerative model, 3
neuronal processes, 144

openness, 42, 54, 181
ought self, 49, 98–99, 112–113, 118, 133–134
ownership, 121, 149, 152, 156

perceived value, 12, 15–16
personality, 16, 43, 47–48, 53, 70, 80, 83, 111, 130, 158, 161, 165, 169–170, 172, 177
phenomenal self, 142–143, 145–147
phenomenological, 43, 45, 47–48, 146–147, 154–155, 158
possible self, 10, 36, 97–99, 109–123, 133–134
postmodernism, 75–76
power, 3, 46, 60–71, 75, 78–79, 88–89, 100, 110, 113, 123, 183
prevention focus, 134
private self, 93–98, 101–104
proficiency, 12–15, 17–18, 23, 25–29, 31, 33–34, 80, 99, 121, 133, 136, 166
promotion focus, 134
public self, 93–98, 101–104, 179, 182
purpose, 53–54, 81, 92, 137, 182

Quadripolar Model of Identity, 101
quality of contact, 25, 35

reading self-efficacy, 12
reality monitoring, 111
relatedness, 135–136, 157
relational context, 92, 101
resistance, 69–70

second language confidence (L2C) (see confidence, linguistic self-confidence), 3, 23–31, 33–36
security, 45, 52–54, 182
self
  self-concept, 2–3, 5, 9–12, 14–16, 41–54, 94, 96, 111–114, 116, 119–121, 127–128, 133–134, 162, 167, 178, 180
  self-concept certainty, 167
  self-confidence, 9–10, 15, 24, 49, 128, 166, 168, 170–173, 179
  self-congruency, 165
  self-determination theory (SDT), 6, 96, 118, 133–134, 136, 182
  self-discrepancy theory, 49, 97–98, 112
  self-efficacy, 2–3, 7–19, 42–43, 112, 127, 162, 179, 181–182
  self-efficacy for self-regulation, 11–13, 15
  self-efficacy measurement, 16
  writing self-efficacy, 15–17, 19
  self-enhancement, 165
  self-esteem, 2–3, 15, 41–54, 163, 178, 182
  self-evaluation, 26, 53, 165
  self-models, 144
  self-perception, 10, 24, 184
  self-presentation, 94–95, 97, 99–104
  self-protection, 165
  self-ratings of L2 proficiency, 25
  self-reference, 148–152, 157–158
  self-reference effect, 148, 158
  self-reflection, 7–8, 149, 157
  self-regulation, 4, 9, 11–13, 15, 112, 137–138, 182
  self-regulated learning, 11, 137

self-specific stimuli, 149–150, 152–153
self-worth, 10–11, 42–43, 128
sense of belonging, 46, 53, 75, 81–83, 135
site of struggle, 60–61, 95
social change, 3, 65, 71
social cognitive theory, 3, 6–8
social theory, 68
social-psychological (see Motivation), 100, 131
socio-contextual model, 25, 27, 36
sociocultural
  sociocultural adaptations, 27, 29
  sociocultural environment, 128–129, 132, 134
  sociocultural perspectives, 75, 77–78
  sociocultural theory, 77–78, 137
specificity, 15–17, 19, 42, 152–155, 181
stability, 42, 51, 163, 165, 173
strategies (see language learning strategies), 9, 11–15, 17–19, 36, 43, 102, 111, 114, 119, 128, 132, 136–137, 182
strategy use, 9, 12–13, 18, 137
symbolically mediated, 77

temporal self, 180
third-person perspective, 116, 123, 148, 154, 156
triadic reciprocality, 7

verbal persuasions, 8, 14, 19
vicarious experiences, 8, 14, 18

willingness to communicate, 25, 49
worthiness, 43–48, 52, 178

For Product Safety Concerns and Information please contact our EU Authorised Representative:

Easy Access System Europe

Mustamäe tee 50

10621 Tallinn

Estonia

gpsr.requests@easproject.com

www.ingramcontent.com/pod-product-compliance
Ingram Content Group UK Ltd.
Pitfield, Milton Keynes, MK11 3LW, UK
UKHW022218250326

4937IPUK00005B/47